EMPOWERING
Women
in Higher
Education

Gina Wisker

KOGAN
PAGE

First published in 1996

Apart from any fair dealing for the purposes of research or private study, or criticism or review, as permitted under the Copyright, Designs and Patents Act 1988, this publication may only be reproduced, stored or transmitted, in any form or by any means, with the prior permission in writing of the publishers, or in the case of reprographic reproduction in accordance with the terms of licences issued by the Copyright Licensing Agency. Enquiries concerning reproduction outside those terms should be sent to the publishers at the undermentioned address:

Kogan Page Limited
120 Pentonville Road
London N1 9JN

© Gina Wisker, 1996

British Library Cataloguing in Publication Data

A CIP record for this book is available from the British Library.

ISBN 0 7494 1618 1

Typeset by JS Typesetting, Wellingborough, Northants.
Printed and bound in Great Britain by Clays Ltd, St Ives plc.

Contents

Preface

This book focuses on enabling and empowering women in higher education, through change. It does not aim exclusively at a readership of women and intends to encourage all, men and women alike, to change the culture and practices of higher education in order to better enable women to study and work therein. It is reflective, grounded in experience, and practical, interested in sharing successful strategies for change. The book is based on a recognition that many of the discursive and grounded practices commonly developed by women have been ignored in higher education. We need to privilege them now, and change the ways in which higher education operates. The ways in which I shall use this set of driving beliefs is to look at how the structure, practices and discourses of conventional higher education can be changed to enable women students and staff to gain equality of opportunity and status. These changes will open up higher education more generally to be flexible, diverse, and more equal, using some of the best examples from feminist educational practices, women's studies and adult education as well as innovations in higher education itself. Higher education should be dynamic and put equality of opportunity into practice.

This book is aimed primarily at a readership of staff in higher education. It should appeal to women and men, both academic staff and support or administrative staff, at all stages in their careers. It is research- and experience-based. It draws on successful women-centred teaching and learning practices that aid the learning of women students, and equally successful practices in the professional development and training of women staff. The needs of two groups – staff and students – are seen as related but different. Each benefits from the kind of practical day-to-day and longer-term professional suggestions and strategies described and developed here.

Section A concentrates on women students in higher education, Section B on women staff. Section B has a staff development and training focus and tone, making practical suggestions about change and development based on both research and experience.

Chapter 1

Women Students and Mature Women Returners: Needs and Developments

As participation in higher education increases, women students are taking advantage of both undergraduate and postgraduate courses. They are succeeding in subject areas such as engineering and technology which have hitherto been seen as conventional male choices. The growing presence of women, particularly mature women students, has affected the climate of change in terms of curricula and course provision, teaching/learning and assessment practices. This chapter looks at who the women students are, where and what they study and how well they achieve in higher education. It argues that higher education has changed and must continue to change to better accommodate their diverse needs and learning styles, and to better enable their success.

Women students and participation rates

There has been a rise overall in the participation rates of women students in higher education (see Table 1.1, p.14). Women comprised 43.8% of the undergraduate and 37.9% of the postgraduate population in 1988/9 but rose to 48.7% of the undergraduate and 44.8% of the postgraduate population by 1993/4. Women undergraduates and postgraduates are increasing in number and proportion and women's participation rates are increasing (Table 1.2, p.14). Comparing figures for 1988/9 and 1993/4 (Table 1.3, p.15) it is clear that the proportion of women in mathematics, science and engineering, conventional male subject choices, is increasing.

In 1991 a total of 27,500 men gained science degrees against totals of 111,300 of all men and women in all subjects, while women gained 11,200 of all science degrees in 1991. By 1995, women students had not only grown in number – as had all student numbers – but more were taking science degrees. In 1995, 40,600 men gained science degrees, an increase of 51%

since 1991, and 23,200 women, an increase of 116% over 1991 (statistics supplied by the Higher Education Statistical Agency (HESA)). As numbers grow, women are participating at a higher rate than men, and mature women at a highest rate overall. There has been an increase in all women students, particularly mature women, since the early 1980s (see Table 1.4, p.16).

There has always been a high participation of mature women students in the adult education system including Workers Education Association (WEA), Extra-Mural board and Local Education Authority (LEA) classes. The numbers in continuing and higher education are now growing and there are lessons to be learned from models developed in adult education which could usefully transform continuing and higher education provision, ensuring that it better suits its client group.

Applications from mature students, particularly women, for places in higher education have been increasing since the 1970s. According to Bilham and Bell (1982), 'Between 1974 and 1980 applications to universities from mature students (men and women) increased by 39%, applications from mature women increased by 66%'.

The 1985 National Advisory Board (NAB) report recognized the value of increasing opportunities for women in general in higher education:

> We wish to encourage greater participation by women in higher education. We believe that it is important particularly in the scientific and technological areas, that the country should seek to use to the full all the talents of the whole population, and not merely the male half. (NAB, 1985)

The government White Paper of April 1987 urged that the increased participation of mature students, of women and of non-traditional learners be encouraged. They emphasized a commitment to the development of Access courses, which provide many non-traditional students with an alternative entry route into higher education. Particularly favoured were those targeted at disadvantaged students, mature women among them, and leading into science and technology subject areas. Clearly many of the aims of NAB and the 1987 White Paper have been realized and are continuing to come to fruition.

As Table 1.5 (p.16) shows, while men outnumber women in the 21–24 age range, there are more mature women over 25 taking undergraduate courses in 1993 than men (139,185 men to 153,198 women) but fewer are staying on for postgraduate study (overall figures of 197,295 men compared to 87,111 women) although, as we have already seen, the proportion of women staying on for postgraduate study is increasing.

Women are achieving good degrees in higher education, and the changes in pedagogical or andragogical teaching and learning strategies, as well as the presentation and curricula of courses, has no doubt played a part in this success. Many changes have been spurred on by the changing needs of mature women returners and initially often crystallized in demands and success in Access courses which lead into higher education, and in the Open University which has only recently been included in the statistics.

Provision for non-standard mature women entrants in pre-Access, Access and higher education courses

Mature women students are a heterogeneous group. They range from those who have no formal qualifications at all, who need basic education and training as well as confidence-building before they can enter higher education, to well-qualified women managing a career break and wishing to update or retrain before returning to work after, perhaps, bringing up a family. I have had experience of working with many groups. These include Afro-Caribbean TOPS (Training Opportunities) students in Hackney, refugee teachers needing to gain British qualifications in order to teach in England, women's studies majors in ex-polytechnics, women returning to study on Return to Study courses, Open University students, and mature women on pre-degree and degree courses at my own university. What unites this wide-ranging group is their gender and their age. While their study needs and abilities are varied, some of the course design elements, such as timing, funding and gender-related content, remain common areas of importance for course planners and managers to address.

For a number of reasons, many mature women students can be classed as educationally disadvantaged. Often they have left school early without adequate qualifications, perhaps because of the gender bias of subject choice available, or the bias of teachers who have been proved to favour the needs and responses of boys over those of girls (Stanworth, 1983), or the ethos of school itself, which demands concentration and study at a time when there are pressures to conform to peer norms and choose boyfriends over homework. There is much research into such issues (see, for example, Stanworth, 1983).

What can be learned from this negative information, however, is that any system seriously seeking to cater for the needs of mature women students must take into account all those issues of subject range, emphasis, gender bias in content, and teaching strategies. With the right blend of course design and content elements, mature women make extremely successful students, taking full and useful advantage of their 'second' or perhaps, more appropriately, 'first real' chance at continuing and higher education.

Special women-oriented courses have been set up to enable women students to return. Other women have come to higher education through Access courses, A-level courses designed primarily for mature returners, and through participation in local short courses for adults run by the WEA, and the universities' continuing education or extra mural provision. This last channel is currently flourishing with the advent of accredited and certificated courses, and is starting to provide a route in for some quite differently placed students: those in the more far-flung areas of regions. So, too, the spread of regional Access courses is similarly bringing in students in 'remote' and regional areas. The increasing development of franchises in many universities with a regional remit such as the University of Warwick, the whole LINCS scheme in the Manchester/Leeds area, Anglia Polytechnic University and the University of East Anglia among others are not only attracting mature mainly women students, to start their studies in a local college or school hall, but are then offering them the opportunity to move on at degree level in much the same place, within a franchise. The Access movement has been highly significant in returning mature women to education.

Quality assured courses satisfy admissions staff of the quality of the students' performance and act as indicators of future HE performance. They also provide a certain level of recognition to reassure the students, their family and partners that serious study which will lead somewhere is being undertaken. For many FE colleges the Access course development has transformed their own provision of courses for students more generally, and enabled staff to be motivated to work towards higher degrees. Often franchised first years or more local degree courses have followed. However, mature women students who start out on Access courses aiming to go into higher education have often found or find that there is no local university to attend. While they could fit in Access studies with their daily domestic and paid work, and still get home in time to pick up the children, suddenly transferring to study at degree level at the university 50-odd miles away on an extended day, and several days a week, is a major disruption and a severe test of relationships and the juggling of study and home. Franchising overcomes that difficulty.

Balancing home and study

We need to ask whether the educational offer in higher education has actually changed to accommodate the diverse needs of this different and growing student group, and to look at whether or not study in HE changes the patterns of women's lives and affects how they manage home and study.

Higher education has traditionally been aimed at young (18-year-old) white, middle-class males. The model of three year, full-time degree courses dependent upon a two A-level entry frequently does not meet the needs of mature women, depending, as it does, on mobility. The issue of educational opportunity for women has always been a political one in the very broadest sense. It is particularly so now when cuts bite deep into established higher education provision. In terms of sexual politics, access to and success in education are important measures of the increased awareness of women's equality of ability, and women's rights to social, financial and economic equality. Attitudes to study, the integration of home and university, and the economic context in which mature women study all need to be taken into consideration in course provision.

The OPCS survey (1989) looks at mature British students and finance. It noted that almost half the women surveyed aged between 26 and 35 were married or cohabiting and 37% of all these women had children. Pascal and Cox (1993) interviewed mature women returners who said they entered higher education to develop their abilities and also to escape domesticity, but often found that their partners only tolerated their studies when the domestic tasks were performed as before, and resented and disrupted studies which actually changed the patterns and provisions of 'normal' family life. Madeline Leonard's research (Leonard, 1994) notes the contributions male partners made to the household monies and how they responded to their partners studying. Some women who also worked in paid employment said that they felt less guilty about attending university because of this contribution; others played on the hope that a better job would result and thus a higher wage be contributed to the household. Some husbands controlled their wives through allowances or lack of them:

> This aspect of the data verified the proposition that money is the source of power that upholds male dominance in the family (Pahl, 1989).

> These males felt that because they were bringing in a wage to the household, they were entitled to domestic and childcare services from their wives. Wives were given money to be spent on household and not on their personal needs. University expenses were seen as personal needs. Often these men would use 'domestic sabotage'... to prevent their wives from achieving their objective, by making the wives feel guilty for not fulfilling their domestic roles. (Davies *et al.*, 1994, pp.170–71)

There are grim anecdotes. Students post-Access studying to be teachers have had essays ripped up or burned by irate partners who saw the study as a wedge between them. Other partners have used psychological as well as physical abuse as ways of showing how threatened they felt by the proof that their women folk were able to achieve academically. No doubt the patterns of resentment, abuse, rejection and hostility or just deliberate ignoring of the study undertaken, and its worth, could be charted over the UK and differentials in relation to class, age and race would be found. There have been many studies of mature women returners since I first undertook my own (Wisker, 1989) but even those looking directly at women's experiences, for example, Edwards (1993) have not focused on this often hidden area of women students' lives to any great extent.

Madeleine Leonard (1994) notes initial studies (Woodley *et al.* 1987) of mature students concentrated on questionnaire responses about their experiences, for example over attitudes to returning, study and intentions producing information about their backgrounds and successes but not their personal experiences. Smith (1993) comments that this actively silences women. Edwards (1993) has undertaken some powerful research involving self-disclosure which produced evidence of the lived experiences of a variety of women returners within a specific case study group.

Several arguments have developed out of feminist research recognizing that women's place and experience within the public world are conditioned and affected by their place within the family. Pascall (1986) and New and David (1985) argue that family life relates to the public and Sylvia Walby (1990) that it works the other way round:

> The public/private dichotomy thereby also casts the characteristics of the domestic sphere in opposition to the presumed characteristics of the public sphere: affective, altruistic and non-goal oriented as opposed to unemotional, competitive and mercenary. (Walby, 1990, p.19)

This can be seen as the basis of a patriarchal order which keeps women subordinated whether at home or in education and work. Edwards (1993) reports that mature women, particularly if they are Black and/or working class, can perceive themselves as 'deviant tokens' in a system largely organized for and devoted to the white middle-class 18-year-old male.

Apart from the middle classes, women have always had a split day and world between home and work, and overemphasizing the public/private dichotomy can operate against them to produce a rhetoric of inability as well as one of inequality. Sharistanian (1987) advocates looking for relationships between the variety of performances and demands expected in women's different spheres, noting not division, but 'complex multi-levelled, highly variable, and frequently shifting interdependence'.

Universities should be required to consider restructuring their provision to enable women students to combine family life with study. Qualities of learning traditionally felt to be more women-centred should be developed and rewarded within the education system. These suggestions parallel arguments for changing the demands on women academic and support staff to enable career breaks and the management of workloads in relation to domestic responsibilities.

Maggie Humm's women students who provide autobiographies as part of the selection process expressed their domestic/study connections in very different ways to men:

> Those written by women (which are often cultural products)... locate their multiplicity in the sites of childhood, family and relationships rather than in the practical and career skills privileged by male students. (Humm, 1987, p.16)

Considering women and work, the public and the private, Edwards (1993) cites several studies, for example Anna Pollert (1981), which indicate that women need to see links between the private and public. Sue Scott (1985), studying PhD students, found male students did not see domestic aspects of their lives as relevant, while women made these connections and discussed the strains between them. In working with mature women students I have found that their conversation as they are working necessarily moves between discussion of the work in hand and the demands of family life. Their working practices at university are more positive when there is space for such integration without letting the domestic strains take over.

Supportive admissions policies and counselling services, together with flexibility of the pace and mode of study, all helped mature women at Hatfield (Michaels, 1980). The findings of my own research into the careers of mature women at Anglia Polytechnic University at the Open University (Wisker, 1985), compare interestingly with those of Michaels. At Anglia in 1981 the two firsts in the Combined Sciences were achieved by women, one of whom was also a non-standard entrant. The greatest recruiter of non-standard entry students and mature women students was the Modern History degree with 33.79% of its students mature women. Taking all degree courses into consideration, nearly half of our students at Anglia are now mature and over half our students are women. This is comparable with similar proportions in most of the new universities.

During 1985 I conducted a small-scale research project asking 45 students on two Return to Study and one Open University Preparatory course I was running to complete a questionnaire focusing on their backgounds, views and experiences of returning to learning. I interviewed 12 of these students informally, in groups, about their learning experiences. Some expressed guilt. One said: 'I do feel pangs of guilt in that I am perhaps not contributing as much as I should to the running of the home, gardening and baking.' Another noted 'I have found guilt again for the self-indulgence of studying just for myself'.

Others felt they were shouldering an enormous burden of responsibilities which, not surprisingly, interfered with their study:

> The biggest problem that I foresee is that I am responsible for the house in general and if I don't do all the work I still have to arrange that it gets done by someone. This is the family woman's biggest disadvantage – washing, cooking, shopping, cleaning, general management.

Such comments about guilt and selfishness furnish examples of women's response to conditioning which leads them to view their study as a stolen pleasure, self-indulgence, an activity which should be sacrificed when other duties call. While some manage to balance both domestic and study responsibilities, for others it becomes a debilitating drain on their emotional and physical energies. Colleges providing higher education for such women need to ensure counselling facilities to support the student, nurseries to relieve some of the child care pressures, and part-time study routes so that some clashes of interest are more manageable.

Teaching/learning and curriculum changes can aid women

Integration between the personal and the public can take place in focusing on linking the two when studying and discussing, making links between experience and the academic world. Chapters 2 and 3 discuss this further in terms of pedagogy. Women science Access students whom I and a colleague researched during the course of their studies at Anglia were found to baffle their Physics lecturer who commented on their discussions about children's colds, food, heating and childcare, interwoven with discussions about the difficulties and achievements of homework as students settled into their classes and while they were performing practical tasks. He found this hard to relate to. Men students discussing football and politics seemed neither alien nor irrelevant (each kind of conversation was actually social rather than task-oriented, one being more familiar to the male lecturer but no more obviously relevant to practical Physics!).

Over the several years in which the Anglia Access course ran (1988–1993) Lynn Brennan, Alice Zeitlyn and I carried out a series of short research projects with the students, some of which was supported by NIACE funding through REPLAN and some through internal research funding, all of which contributed to publications, workshops at conferences, and internal monitoring as well as changes in practice (Wisker *et al.*, 1989). We used taped open discussions ranged around open-ended interview questions and fed the students who participated with tea and biscuits for their time. The research interview sessions added to the questionnaire information we had about students' decisions to return to study, support or otherwise of their family and friends, and the experiences they had as students in higher education. Students reported everything from wholehearted support from partners, friends and families who felt that they were at last working to achieve their potential, and shared chores and childcare, through to extreme hostility. In the latter cases the woman's study and achievement was seen as a threat to the self-image and self-worth of the male partner, and as some-thing which took away from the family the full-time service role of mother and wife. Women students reported on the extreme strategies they adopted to try to keep family and study from clashing, such as writing essays in the carpark or the middle of the night. Many of these students found deadlines during or just after half-term totally impossible, and some broke up with partners irretrievably (quite a common feature). These findings are confirmed by research, for example Clark and Haldane (1990) who found women experience tensions between the demands of paid work and family responsibilities, tensions which are similar to those of study:

> These will not only be pressures of time and physical energy; housework and cooking are also 'moral' categories which 'say something about' a woman's feelings for her husband and their marriage and which communicate to significant others such as parents, siblings and friends. (Clark and Haldane, 1990, p.27)

The status of being a student unsettles some friends and relatives but gives mature women an alternative identity. The demands of work might be excessive, the rewards inexplicit, but there is a gradual transition into the culture of achievement and self-recognition which could also end with a rewarding job. This begins with the first few pieces of work.

Women in Edwards' (1993) study and in our own questionnaires and interviews often reported feeling that study was self-indulgent, or that they would be 'found out' as not being able to achieve to the same level as their colleagues. Once the first few pieces of work were returned and marks scrutinized, a kind of objective measure of their abilities was fuel enough to keep them working and trying, although many never grow/grew out of worrying that their next piece of work would somehow prove the futility of all this study for someone like them! Many mature women hand their written work over apologetically, commenting that it could have been better. I have seen this on self-assessment sheets as an external examiner, received in written form as attached notes fom OU students; I have had it said to me quietly in asides by my own students. Men students very rarely seem to suffer this need to deprecate their own abilities and worry about potential failure – at least openly.

Lack of confidence, lack of support, confusion of roles and even hostility can all harm a mature woman's success as a student. But there are positive interactions between life experience, family and study which it is partly the job of the university to nurture and bring out so that students feel recognized, enabled and supported in their learning, and able to have their life experiences validated within the academic context.

Edwards (1993) concludes with a positive assertion about the potential for integration of women's family and study lives in a changed higher education system which recognizes and supports such integration, although she makes suggestions neither about teaching and learning nor curriculum changes:

> Women's caring within 'the family' can lead them to seek affiliations across the public/private divide.While higher education requires the separation of family life on the part of the women, it can also give them the confidence to want connections. (Edwards, 1993, p.157)

However, women students are, like women managers, in a male-dominated environment and society, experiencing:

> the expectations, values and requirement of both the masculinist institution of higher education and the individual men with whom women have relationships. While higher education policies and institutions concern themselves with inputs and outputs and privilege disciplines over students, and while the balance of male identity depends on a masculine/feminine demarcation that associates loss of power with loss of masculinity, combining education with family life (and relationships with men especially) will never be easy for women. The issues would appear to centre around not women's education but men's education. (Edwards, 1993, p.158)

Radical changes apart, attitudes and higher education practices can and should change to enable the mature women students who study and try to balance their domestic and their study obligations demands and potential.

It is in the design and redesign of HE degree courses to cater for the changing client group that providers can usefully look at the models of Access courses, other adult education and OU provision. One interesting popular development is the increase in part-time study, and the advantage mature students now take of the modular structures to achieve their degrees at a pace that suits other demands.

Birkbeck College, the only university college devoted to part-time study, partly led the way in this. As Malcolm Tight remarked:

> Access courses and part-time higher education have a fundamental aim in common – the opening up of opportunities for study and self-development to people who have not followed the conventional route from school to full-time further or higher education. Most of those who might go on to higher education from Access provision will probably not wish, or not be able, to study full-time. If their demand is to be satisfied, and their potential recognized, and expanded, a flexible system of part-time higher education will be required. (Tight, 1987)

Another way of increasing participation might be to increase the opportunities for open learning,, an enterprise which has been highly successful in the Open University. Ailsa Swarbrick comments on the usefulness and problems for women of open learning systems, from the perspective of the Women in Technology (WIT) programme in particular:

> For many women starting a family still means a clear break in paid employment. But the period at home can be used as an opportunity to develop new interests or to change direction vocationally. Open learning systems offer a way of overcoming such obstacles as lack of mobility and childcare, although open Access courses often fail to recognize the range of responsibilities, the continual distractions and the sense of isolation borne primarily by women. (Swarbrick, 1987)

Teaching and learning issues

As my own research (Wisker, 1985) and that of Alice Zeitlyn (1988) suggests, many mature women feel that the teaching/learning strategies and assessment procedures within traditional higher education do not truly fit their own learning styles and time-related stress factors.

Interviews and discussions held with women during my research in l985 and again in 1990 showed that courses often ignored or marginalized women's experiences. Many women felt that they had to 'read against the grain', ignoring elements of subject matter and responses valid in relation to their own frames of reference, and substituting readings provided by the (usually male) lecturer. Respect for the authority of the lecturer's position as holder of the knowledge, and the 'right' way to read, secured the uptake of the readings and valuations he encouraged, but a deep unease often remained, nonetheless. Disagreeing with his readings was felt to be a dangerously radical undermining of the established academic 'response'. Others commented on the authoritative and authoritarian teaching styles they felt prevented their involvement, and the validation and valuation of their responses. One woman student said: 'Our views on the books written by women aren't his – he ignores them if you do introduce them – says they're nothing really to do with the books.' In the case of a widely studied text, *Wuthering Heights*, students commented that the perspective taken ignored many of their responses. One commented of Heathcliff, the 'hero': 'He is a terrifying figure – not someone to meet in the dark. He [the lecturer] sees him as a Romantic, Byronic figure [but that he is to her a] 'wife beater and child torturer'.

Didactic, authoritarian and competitive styles, many felt, did not suit mature women students: 'Marks introduce competition and we should be helping each other'; 'The tutor's role should be to help everyone achieve within that structure'. And, on discussion of different viewpoints: 'He's got his idea and that's it.' Clearly they felt they had to fit in with a structure and practice alien to them. Others felt they moulded themselves easily to fit into the academic establishment's demands. The resilience and adaptability of women should not, however, be an indication of the worth of whatever they adapt to. Our malleability can mask important differences.

Competition militates against cooperative learning strategies. Aspects of assessment can also be problematic for mature women. Zeitlyn (1988) notes that some of the mature students in her Anglia research cohort 1984–87 found continuous assessment, that traditional substitute for the exams adults are thought to find so unfair, can itself provide enormous problems. One student I interviewed said the timing of continuous assessment essays was in constant conflict with her domestic responsibilities. Currently we set students major assessments for the first semester over the Christmas period, which can cause major family frictions.

These research findings suggest that many women students feel their interests and responses are considered unacademic and the established teaching/learning strategies of a male dominated higher education establishment give them little space to air their views, or learn how to value their own responses. Often even the assumed adult-oriented models of assessment, for example, do not enable them to produce their best work. Many might underachieve as a result of these difficulties. Others learn well how to 'play the system', producing the oral and written responses expected by their tutors, not commenting on what they feel about the texts but what they think the tutor expects.

Research into adult education models can provide positive lessons and models for change in the provision of higher education. The timing, pacing, costs and andragogical teaching/learning strategies of the best adult continuing education classes could act as models for developments in higher education. Some of these suggestions are further developed in Chapter 3. There are also pitfalls. One such is related to course designers and managers. While adult education has a client population of mainly mature women, and is largely taught by women, it is managed by men. This masculine control often affects the timing, development and classification of courses. Many courses which run at a level similar to that of higher education are classed as leisure pursuits, thus marginalizing interests and studies carried out by largely female groups, and leading to the Russell report's criticizing them as merely recreational 'leisure frills for middle-class women' as Nell Keddie (1983) puts it.

Jane Thompson notes: 'The organization and provision of courses takes very little account of the social, economic, cultural and political conditions of being female in our society' (Thompson, 1983, p.81). This shortsighted culpability is a result of an imbalance in gender and power between policy-makers, tutors and students:

> The career structure, the responsibility for organization and control, the arbiters of the curriculum, and the opinion leaders and policy makers who sit on bodies like the Russell committee are invariably men – men who operate firmly and squarely within the organizational structures, the cultural assumptions and the thinly disguised prejudices of patriarchal society. (Thompson, 1983, p.81)

The irony of the marginalization of women's education because of its common location within adult education is one addressed in the developing provision of Women's Studies courses, which began in an adult education context and will be explored further in Chapter 4.

As Jane Thompson notes:

> It is not merely a question of improving the chances of women to compete in a man's world – to supplement existing provision to that end – but to demand a radical change in the nature of what is being offered. This implies at least an

equal share in the determination of what counts as valuable knowledge within it, and at length an equal recognition that what is important about women's experience of the world is as valid as men's. Without such real equalities, notions of 'equality of opportunity' are essentially rhetorical. (Thompson, 1983, p.93)

Mature women students in particular have many skills gained either from everyday experience or from prior learning of a more formal kind. They need guidance in recognizing, for example, that the organizational, time-management and financial skills relevant in running a home can be transferred to managing their own learning. They learn that the information-gathering skills which helped them discover about cooking, gardening and childbirth can form the basis on which to develop research skills which will enable them to seek out academic subject-related information. Many of the students' established skills are relevant to study once reflection and guidance have encouraged them to usefully develop them. Such reflection and guidance will also enable the students to see in which precise areas they need more formal training in order that they can usefully progress in their chosen higher education studies.

The FEU (1985) notes of the recognition of prior learning at entry to higher education that:

There is now a growing awareness from the validating bodies that most women bring to education a variety of skills and competencies learned experientially outside the teaching institution, but colleges/polytechnics do not use the discretion allowed to the full.

Some higher education institutions, Anglia among them, have now developed schemes to recognize and credit rate prior learning, including appropriate prior experiential learning, where it can be demonstrated to relate to the course of study. In terms of the teaching and learning experiences of mature women students on degree courses, reference to, validation of and work which grows from their prior learning and their current experience will help them to integrate all elements of their lives and make the best of their lifelong learning skills.

While changes in the educational offer are suggested by research into mature women's education and by our own work with Access students, it is essential that students do not experience a watered down molly-coddling version of education which encourages sloppiness, leaves them without the opportunity to develop academic rigour, and reinforces the sense that they might be 'found out' at any moment. The ways in which we can teach, the timings of classes and the kinds of learning strategies and transferable skills recognized and encouraged, should all take account of the needs, abilities and demands of mature women students as well as the more traditional 18-year-olds. Green and Percey (1991, pp.155–6) warn that:

By adopting a highly flexible understanding and supportive posture to students, Access tutors may do a disservice to women in two respects: first, a flexible pedagogy may also be a non-demanding pedagogy... second, an understanding, kindly, hand-holding pedagogy fosters dependency, it suggests that students cannot cope and makes the transit into the tough world of higher education much more difficult.

Access courses have often developed a pedagogy or andragogy that genuinely relates to the needs and abilities of mature women students among other mature returners. This, along with the different shaped provision, at different times (sometimes open- and distance-based, sometimes evening-based), should be learned from by the university so that the most responsible teaching and learning is achieved. Relating experience and the personal with the analytical and the researched, organized into a variety of appropriate responses, is something from which everyone can benefit, even if it did probably originate in the classroom with the mature returners leading the way.

Table 1.1 *The proportion of undergratuate and postgraduate women in higher education in the UK*

	1988/9	1993/4
Postgraduates		
Total men + women	110,333	194,406
Women	41,856	87,111
% Women	37.9	44.8
Undergraduates		
Total men + women	647,039	996,181
Women	283,647	484,759
% Women	43.8	48.7

Source: DfEE

Table 1.2 *The participation rates of 18-year-old women in higher education*

	1988/9	1993/4
First degree	7.6%	15.7%
Sub degree	1.2%	2.4%

Source: DfEE

Table 1.3 *The proportion of women in maths, engineering and sciences*

	1988/9	**1993/4**
Postgraduates		
Mathematics		
Total men + women	5,672	9,909
% of women	23.2	24.0
Engineering/technology		
Total men + women	11,576	17,449
% of women	10.3	13.2
All sciences (including maths and engineering/technology)		
Total men + women	43,165	61,670
% of women	26.9	31.5
Total women, all subjects	41,856	87,111
Subject group with largest percentage of women	Education (28.2%)	Education (26.6%)
Undergraduates		
Mathematics		
Total men + women	38,183	61,362
% of women	25.3	26.7
Engineering/technology		
Total men + women	93,270	116,827
% of women	8.0	11.8
All sciences (including maths and engineering/technology)		
Total men + women	52,156	362,216
% of women	26.2	33.9
Total women, all subjects	41,856	87,111
Subject group with largest percentage of women	Education (12.3%)	Business/Finance (18.5%)

Source: DfEE

Table 1.4 *Mature women (21 and over) in relation to total undergraduate numbers 1979 and 1984*

	Total universities	Mature women	Total AFE	Mature women	Total OU	Mature women
1979	190,173	24,228	330,400	63,697	60,963	25,904
1984	186,197	28,141	407,200	88,600	77,992	33,095

AFE = Advanced Further Education
Figures provided on request from the Department of Education and Science (DES), the Open University (OU) statistics department, and the Universities Statistical Records.

Table 1.5 *Higher education students in England in 1993 (full time and part time)*

Level of study	Men	Women	Total
Postgraduates			
under 21	308	344	652
21–24	27,483	23,155	50,638
25+	79,504	63,612	143,116
Total	107,295	87,111	194,406
Undergraduates			
under 21	225,297	211,827	437,124
21–24	146,938	119,734	266,672
25+	139,185	153,198	292,383
Total	511,420	484,759	996,179
All levels			
under 21	225,605	212,171	437,776
21–24	174,421	142,889	317,310
25+	218,689	216,810	435,499
Total	618,715	571,870	1,190,585

Source: DfEE

Notes

(i)   Women were studying more in engineering and technology in 1995 than they were in 1991 with 1,300 women gaining degrees in these subjects in 1991 and 2,600 in 1995, an increase of 103%. In the same period, 11,300 men gained these degrees in 1991, and 15,100 in 1995 – an increase of only 36%. (Figures supplied by HESA.) There are comparable proportions of women to men students in medicine and related areas. Women's participation in humanities and social sciences has also increased.

(ii)   There was a significant rise in the numbers of mature women entering higher and advanced education in the early 1980s.

(iii) The numbers of male postgraduates rose from 15,784 in 1981 to 38,006 in 1993, but the figures for women were 7,883 to 36,238. The percentage of women postgraduates in 1981 was 33.3% and in 1993 rose sharply to 48.8%.

(iv)   In all undergraduate level studies a similar rise in the numbers and percentage of women is noted. In 1981, 22,1082 men and 12,637 women were involved in undergraduate studies of all kinds with women representing 35.9% of the overall student numbers. This number and percentage has risen: by 1993 there were 357,600 men studying at undergraduate level and a much more comparable figure of women at 349,479. From 35.9% of the undergraduate students in 1981, women grew to 46.5% of undergraduates in 1993. If the percentage of undergraduates and postgraduates were combined, we would see that women represented only 35.7% of the student numbers in 1981 in polytechnics and colleges but had grown to 49.4% in 1993.

Acknowledgement

The tables and statistics in this chapter were provided by the Higher Education Statistics Agency (HESA, 1996) and specifically for this book by the Department for Education and Employment (DfEE), Analytical Services, Darlington.

References

Bilham, G and Bell, G (1982) 'Supply and demand: Mature students in British universities', *Higher Education Review*, 15, 1, 29–45.

Brennan, L, Wisker, G and Zeitlyn, A (1989) *Adults Learning*, NIACE, Leicester.

Brennan, L, Wisker, G and Zeitlyn, A (1990) 'The interface: Access courses and higher education', *Journal of Access Studies*, 5, 2.

Clark, D and Haldane, D (1990) *Wedlocked?* Polity Press, Cambridge.

Davies, S, Lubelska, C and Quinn, J (eds) (1994) *Changing the Subject: Women in Higher Education*, Taylor & Francis, London.

Department of Education and Science (1987) *Higher Education: Meeting the Challenge*, White Paper, HMSO, London.

Edwards, R (1993) *Mature Women Students, Separating or Connecting Family and Education*, Taylor & Francis, London.

Further Education Unit (FEU) (1985) *Changing the Focus: Women and FE*, FEU, London.

FEU (1987) *Access to Further and Higher Education*, FEU, London.

Green, M and Percey, P (1991) 'Gender and Access' in *Post-16 Education: Studies in Access and Achievement*, C Chitty (ed.), Kogan Page, London.

Higher Education Statistics Agency (HESA) (1996) Press Release, January, HESA, Cheltenham.

Humm, M (1987) 'Autobiography and "Bell-piuns"', in *Writing Feminist Biography 2: Using Life Histories*, Grifiths, V, Humm, M, O'Rourke *et al.* (eds), Studies in Sexual Politics 19, University of Manchester Press, Manchester.

Keddie, N (1983) 'Adult education theory and practice', in *Learning Liberation: Women's Response to Men's Education*, J Thompson (ed.), Croom Helm, London, p.83.

Leonard, M (1994) 'Mature women and access to HE' in *Changing the Subject: Women in Higher Education*, S Davies, C Lubelska and J Quinn (eds), Taylor & Francis, London.

Lovell, A (1980) 'Fresh horizons: The aspirations and problems of intending mature students', *Feminist Review*, 6.

Michaels, R (1980) 'A custom-built degree for mature students', in *Equal Opportunities in Higher Education:* an EOC and SRHE conference report.

Michaels, R (1986) 'Entry routes for mature students: Variety and quality assessed', *Journal of Access Studies*, 1, 1.

National Advisory Body (NAB) Report (1985) *A Strategy for Higher Education in the Late 1980s and Beyond?* NAB, London.

New, C and David, M (1985) *For the Children's Sake: Making Childcare More Than Women's Business,* Penguin, Harmondsworth.

Office of Population, Census and Surveys (OPCS) (1989) *Mature Students, Incomings and Outgoings,* HMSO, London.

Pahl, J (1989) *Money and Marriage,* Macmillan, London.

Pascal, G and Cox, R (1993) *Women Returning to Higher Education,* SRHE and Open University Press, Buckingham.

Pascall, G (1986) *Social Policy, A Feminist Analysis,* Tavistock Publications, London.

Pollert, A (1981) *Girls, Wives and Factory Lives,* Macmillan, London.

Scott, S (1985) 'Feminist research and qualitative methodology: A discussion of some of the issues', in *Issues in Educational Research: Qualitative Methods,* R G Burgess (ed.), Falmer Press, London.

Sharistanian, J (1987) 'Conclusion: The public/domestic model and the study of contemporary women's lives', in *Beyond the Public/Domestic Dichotomy: Contemporary Perspectives on Women's Public Lives,* J Sharistinian (ed.), Greenwood Press, Westport.

Smith, S (1993) 'Uncovering key aspects of experience: The use of in-depth interviews in a study of women returners to education', paper presented at the British Sociological Association Annual Conference at the University of Essex.

Stanworth, M (1983) *Gender and Schooling,* Hutchinson, London.

Swarbrick, A (1987) 'Women in technology', in *Open Learning for Adults,* M Thorpe and D Grugeon (eds), Longman, London.

Thompson, J (1983) *Learning Liberation: Women's Response to Men's Education,* Croom Helm, London.

Tight, M (1987) 'Access and part-time undergraduate study' *Journal of Access Studies,* 2, 1, 23.

Walby, S (1990) *Theorising Patriarchy*, Basil Blackwell, Oxford.

Wisker, G (1985) 'Mature women students in higher education', unpublished dissertation for Diploma in Teaching and Course Development in Higher Education, London University Institute of Education.

Wisker, G (1989) 'Facilitating the learning of mature women students: A British perspective', *Studies in Continuing Education*, 10, 2, 66–85.

Wisker, G, Brennan, L and Zeitlyn, A (1989) 'Access students and higher education: The interface', *Journal of Access Studies*, 3, 2.

Woodley, A, Wagner, L, Slowey, M *et al.* (1987) *Choosing to Learn: Adults in Education,* Society for Research in Higher Education (SRHE) and Open University Press, London.

Zeitlyn, A (1988) 'Mature students in higher education', unpublished MPhil thesis, CNAA and Cambridge College of Arts and Technology.

Chapter 2
The Curriculum and Change

> The responsibility for organization and control, the arbiters of the curriculum, and the opinion leaders and policy-makers... are invariably men...

> The organization and provision of courses takes very little account of the social, economic, cultural and political conditions of being female in our society. (Thompson, 1983)

Issues to do with women's relationship to academic knowledge are central to any discussion of the curriculum and the institutional organization of curriculum delivery. The established curriculum, the one with which we are familiar in different contexts, has been produced and defined by those in power, which in Western society are usually white, middle-class men. More insidiously, what lies behind questions about the established curriculum is the recognition that definitions of knowledge and of the worth of varieties of knowledge are also produced by the same white, middle-class Western men. Within these relationships of power what tends to be either excluded, marginalized or evaluated as second-rate are the experiences of women and whatever might be descibed as women-centred or women-produced versions of knowledge. Feminist debate about women in higher education has focused on the patriarchal production and dissemination of knowledge which defines what is considered both legitimate for academic study and how to receive and deal with this information, the ideas (Culley *et al.*, 1985; Ramazanoglu, 1987; Klein, 1987; Gray, 1994). One important issue centres on the notion of what it means to be an academic, what academic subjects comprise and whether women-centred curriculum choices form alternatives wthin a patriarchally defined academic curriculum or are integrated within it. In the former instance we might see courses and modules which signal themselves as oriented towards and dealing with women-centred issues (for example, 'nineteenth-century women's writing', 'women, work and social stratification') while in the latter we might see modules that deliberately integrate ideas, information and knowledge production centred on women's lives and orientations into the mainstream curriculum ('gender, writing and sexuality', 'professional development and equal opportunities'). There are pros and cons with both these models, some of which will be dealt with later in the discussion on Women's Studies courses.

Women-centred perspectives

What do feminist perspectives or women-centred perspectives bring to the curriculum and the organization of knowledge which that reflects? What do they bring to the ways in which we can discuss, evaluate and articulate arguments about knowledge in different disciplines? Do any changes feminist perspectives bring only affect women's courses, women's studies, women's study?

It is more likely that approaches and assumptions, as well as the actual content of curricula, all change when a feminist or women-centred perspective enters the academy. One such effect is that on the syllabus and reading lists themselves in different subject areas.

Evelyn Torton Beck (1990) notes the positive and negative responses that accompanied changes in reading lists at Stanford University in the late 1980s when altered to reflect the different life experiences and perspectives of the variety of students and to therefore put into perspective the established, white, middle-class, male-centred lists:

> We are engaged in a contemporary 'battle of the books'. For the past 20 years there has been a major debate within higher education focusing on whether or not to expand (or in any way alter) the traditional curriculum. The recent decisions made by Stanford University faculty to change the readings in a required core course in Western civilization to include women, people of colour and non-Western classics, sent reverberations around the country – some of delight, others of dismay. (Torton Beck, 1990, p.212)

In my own work on teaching women's writing within the higher education curriculum (Wisker, 1984) it has become clear that in literature courses women authors were rare, their works unheard of, their inclusion on the syllabus so highly selective as to give students an extremely skewed version of the production of women and the kinds of issues on which women authors write. Their treatment was entirely silent about issues of gender. George Eliot, for example, was treated 'as an honorary man' in much the same way as James Joyce used to be treated as an honorary Englishman. The Euro-centred, male-centred focus and issues considered to be legitimate for critical debate ignored context, gender and race.

Works that concentrate on a feminist perspective within the academy (for example, Langland and Gove, 1981) consider the introduction and development of women-centred issues in different subject areas within the higher education curriculum. Other works (Richardson and Robinson, 1993) concentrate specifically on the women's studies courses which have fruited all round the UK.

There are several perspectives and arguments involved in a discussion of curriculum change:

- Set against silence and absence, women-centred issues and women's perspectives in traditional disciplines should be included in the curriculum.
- There should be a diversity of perspectives and issues which take into account the different issues with which women are engaged.
- Women are more likely to relate to, find themselves within and use material in higher education if they can identify with the demands of the subject and the contexts in which it deals with knowledge, conceptualization and experience.

There are issues too surrounding not just the curriculum but production and discussion of knowledge in academic practice which could militate against ways women might wish to relate to their work. Gillian Rose (1993) recognizes her sense of complicity with the controls and discourses of her subject area. She feels 'too complicit with my discipline's forms of and claims to knowledge to be able to map... new spaces' (p.72).

Interventions in established subject areas

In discussing interventions in conventional curricula, sociology, from which women's studies originally sprang, emerges as a radical subject area. Inclusions of women-oriented issues in the syllabi of sociology are taken for granted (Abbott, 1991). As a relatively 'new' and certainly challenging subject, sociology could be expected to have a broader perspective and more natural focus on the inclusion of women's issues and women-centred interpretations and constructions of knowledge. However, Oakley comments:

> Male orientation may so colour the organization of sociology as a discipline that the invisibility of women is a structured male view, rather than a superficial flaw. The male focus, incorporated into the definitions of subject areas, reduces women to a side issue. (Oakley, 1974, p.4)

Works concentrating on women in relation to sociology have been published in large numbers since Oakley's statement in 1974, and there has been a move for inclusion of gendered concerns: the quality and texture of some women's lives; women and education and so on. However, the established construction of knowledge and the main perspective in the teaching of sociology is still male-centred:

> Most sociological research still has a strong tendency to generalize from male examples to the whole population. Textbooks have 'women' as a chapter, rather than taking seriously the now substantial body of feminist work in all the traditional areas of sociology. While 'mainstream' sociology may now feel that

it cannot avoid the gender issue and still look plausible, it tends to deal with it as an addendum – a criticism of received wisdom, or an additional sub-area worth a lecture or two, or something for the women to teach as a third-year option. (Oakley, 1974 p.181)

Interestingly, this has also been my own experience. In 1986 and 1987 I was invited to contribute to sociology degree work at a polytechnic, delivering two lectures and one seminar on 'feminist social policy and practice' by student request. No doubt this is now mainstream work. Then someone had to be brought in from outside to cope with student demand (the lectures were very well-attended and students clustered in large numbers with questions afterwards). This was not an obvious part of the curriculum. Were issues about women and housing, tax, and benefits ignored elsewhere?

Arguments relating to curriculum change in sociology also apply to other subjects. They lead to three kinds of approach to the recognition of the value of women's issues and women-centredness.

- *Integration*: this involves research involving women, adding women's issues to the curriculum, but essentially leaves the basis of the discipline untouched.
- *Separatism*: an argument that in sociology (and in other subjects, in my view) there is a place for a version of the subject taught by women about women and probably mostly to women. In the sociological context it is interested in developing a sociological knowledge seen from women's perspectives and intended to change some women's lives. The problems of this is that it tends to lead to ghettoization and a rather skewed version of sociology because it ignores men (or could do) and does not concentrate on 'rational analysis'.
- *Reconceptualization*: this 'recognizes the need to locate women within social structures as a whole, and therefore to carry out research on boys and men as well as girls and women. However, at the level of theory it demands a recasting of sociology to make it compatible with the concerns, interests and experiences of women', which helps to explain gendered positions to each gender (Abbott, 1991, p.183).

The whole issue of 'adding women on' is problematic. The reconceptualization of established constructions of knowledge and approaches to recognize feminist or women-centred approaches and construction of knowledge is essential if women are to be accorded equality within higher education teaching and learning. However, assuming that all male academics have a conspiracy to prevent such a development is absurd. Many men also argue for the inclusion of a gendered perspective in the curriculum and feminist constructions of knowledge. The worldwide development of women's studies has helped both definitions and practices. Sociology was central to the early recognition of research and practice into women's lives.

Class and social mobility, work, medical practices, crime, the family in education and the issues of the conceptualization and construction of knowledge have sprung from sociologically based questions asked by Acker (1973, 1984) and Stanworth (1984) among others. Sue Wilkinson (1991) makes similar comments about the interventions of a feminist perspective and feminist practices in psychology, arguing its acceptance meets hostility and:

> Feminist intervention in psychology appears only to be acceptable insofar as it can be accommodated within the discipline's traditional empirical framework: for example, insofar as a feminist research orientation focuses attention on sex/gender bias, such bias can be removed, producing 'better science'... However, as soon as feminism begins to to challenge traditional epistemologies and modes of enquiry, and directs attention to hierarchies of power and status (and the institutional practices that maintain them), it is no longer welcome. (Wilkinson, 1991)

Victoria Robinson argues more generally:

> Gender, ethnicity and sexuality are still not established as ways of seeing the world in the way that class is within politics or history. More positively, though, if Women's Studies and feminist theory has only been in existence (in an institutionalized context) for twenty years, then even small shifts in mainstream thought can be seen as beginning to displace centuries of male academic bias and power. (Richardson and Robinson, 1993, p.6)

The construction, knowledge, articulation and organization of knowledge from a feminist perspective is variously acknowledged by and affects the academy. The existence of women's studies can change traditional mainstream courses when recognized as producing alternative approaches. Radical change is a long way off, Robinson argues:

> But even in areas such as cultural studies and sociology for instance, where feminist research is not only finding new answers but posing new questions about the invisibility and marginalization of women and their relationship to culture and the social world, a total intellectual revolution in the concepts, perspectives and methodologies of the subject area is far from being achieved. (Richardson and Robinson, 1993, p.6)

There are limited feminist interventions in the curriculum in the shape of labelled modules. More radical changes in theoretical perspectives and approaches, different constructions of knowledge and different discourses across whole subject areas, not just the women-labelled modules, can receive hostility. Rejection of feminist approaches is an insidious one which tends to be personalized: you are encouraging the students to write in a way that is too personal and so irrelevant; you are not writing well enough; you are writing too polemically/too emotionally/in a disorganized fashion with too much personal baggage to be published in this journal; you are always so shrill at meetings; what you seem to want included is marginal, trivial. This casts doubt on your own abilities to use the discourse and analytical apparatus, the research practices and the rigour of the demands of the subject. Your requests for change might be considered silly. As one colleague put it to me several years ago: 'Women in literature! We'll be talking about the dog or the boat next!'

These are attempts to control both by definition and by personal attack, demoting one's own scholarship while sidestepping a direct confrontation with feminist scholarship. Students receive the same kind of dismissal. Mature women students in particular have commented to me how their responses to social policy, literature, philosophy and art history have been rejected as irrelevant and too personal in seminars and tutorials. They are too polemical, too emotional, disorganized and focused on the wrong content and the wrong responses. Passing through the gates of the examination process, we all have to collude and sharpen our focus and expression. I would hope sharpening outweighs the collusion, and that once women academics have arrived as teachers in a university they dismiss the marginalization and rejection of women-centred forms of thinking, writing and interpretation.

Feminist theoretical approaches and expression in written or spoken assessed work and publications should not become a site for a wearing kind of battle: the slow drip of personalized disempowerment and humiliation. Some of these issues will be addressed in a positive manner when we consider women-centred pedagogy and assessment processes in Chapters 3 and 4.

A women-centred, student-oriented focus enables the validation support and refinement of feminist theoretical perspectives, approaches and expressions. For those of us still receiving the rejection slips and the odd broadside at planning meetings or assessment boards, however, the argument that the battle is won is laughable. On these points Kitzinger (1990) bravely notes of psychology:

> When I write as a feminist, I am defined out of the category of 'psychologist'. When I speak of social structure, of power and politics, when I use language and concepts rooted in my own understanding of oppression, I am told what I say does not qualify as 'psychology'. (Kitzinger, 1990, p.124)

and:

> Because those who control the definition of 'psychology' act as gate-keepers for the professional refereed journals, I cannot be published in them. Although I am constantly asked to contribute chapters to edited books and articles for the radical press, my work is generally rejected by the editors of refereed journals. (*ibid.*, pp.124–5)

> Central to these rejections, then, is the sense that my work is not 'balanced' or 'objective', that it is an attempt to 'persuade' the reader of a particular point of view, and that it is politically biased – 'polemical' or 'ideological'. Suggestions about my writing style are frequent: that it should be 'moderated' or 'toned down' – that it should be less 'journalistic' or 'emotion-laden'... 'The text is replete with value-laden words' commented one anonymous reviewer, 'a more scientific presentation is needed', wrote another. (*ibid.*, p.127)

Psychology is a science and, it is argued, a feminist approach to knowledge and its discourse is political, polemical, emotional – not science.

An approach through a feminist perspective and expression which recognizes oppression, context, the personal, is a legitimate one in all disciplines. Attempts to negate it as, for instance, 'not psychology' should be resisted. I could parallel this with dozens of examples from my own practice within literature and education and colleagues' reports from other subjects including geography, biology, medicine and history. Each of us carries around 'guilty secrets' of rejection and comments about inappropriateness and the 'wrong kind' of focus or discourse. We need to share positive experiences and build on the consolidation offered by women's studies. If women-centred approaches and expressions are constantly rejected in academic practice, it will be impossible to empower our students to recognize their validity and the prejudice and bias of those who demote and reject them. It is important to hone and refine theory, research practices and discourse to act as models for students.

Feminist theorists and practitioners within women's studies and mainstream courses have caused radical rethinking of the ways in which knowledge is constructed, how discourse helps us understand and articulate linked personal and analytical responses in all disciplines, as academics and as students. The difference made by feminist critical perspectives and practices affects everyone.

Discussing literature and feminist interventions Patricia Meyer Spacks notes:

> Feminist criticism, in other words, has provoked new debates: arguably the most important contribution any critical mode can make. Few literary commentators any longer believe – if indeed they ever did – that they have it in their power to proclaim definitive truth about a text. We believe now in the multiplicity of interpretation; most students of literature think that the richness, the multifariousness, the ambiguity of texts makes them compelling. (Meyer Spacks, 1981, p.8)

There are many feminist perspectives. One of the main, most widely enabling issues within feminist theory and practice is recognizing the multiplicity of views and versions, diversity of context, response and approach. This is essentially a *set* of approaches which refuses to just replace women-centredness or women orientation for the established critical orientation.

Instead it opens up diverse responses. It recognizes the issues and effects of class, culture and age without losing sight of the effects and affects of gender.

Feminist and women-centred critics define changes in curriculum, reading lists, approaches to disciplines and ways in which knowledge is constructed and debated. These recognize:

- the importance of experience in constructing approaches and conceptualization;
- how personal experience affects approach, reading, interests, arguments and expression;
- personal response especially as it helps analysis and reflection;
- a multiplicity of approaches and viewpoints critically arising out of different experiences and angles conditioned by class context, race and gender.

Women in science and engineering

Subject areas traditionally more related to experience and personal response, such as sociology and literary studies, are less resistant to feminist or women-centred approaches than those more traditionally considered 'men's studies': technology and science. Ann Bridgwood (1994) and Ailsa Swarbrick (1985) at the OU, among others, have carried out research into and put on programmes catering for women in science and technology. They take into account the negative image these subjects have as 'dirty', 'difficult' and rather mechanistic, which puts women off. They look at the curriculum content, examples and experiments which, while equally legitimate and taxing as conventional examples, relate and appeal more to women's experiences. They have also considered support systems and the discourse used in the classroom. Liz Bennett and Gill Kerr (1993) and Sylvia Gibbs (1993) describe confidence-building activities, pre-courses and support networks enabling women in science and technology degrees.

My own experience derives from team-teaching study skills on our science Access course (with the Geology professor). We worked closely to consider women-oriented examples: the Chemistry met in gardening and cooking, the Physics met in the operating of appliances in the home, the car and at work, all of which provide examples and opportunities to experiment and discover laws in operation. One issue that is essential in providing a curriculum that enables women is to ensure that the quality of the science is not in any way watered down. Women are very vociferous about not being 'palmed off' with second-rate scientific experiences, and it is our duty to avoid that kind of patronizing, limiting behaviour.

Ann Bridgwood's work at the University of North London is a good example of women-centred science and technology provision. Her project built on the proactive approach to recruiting and teaching women of all ages and backgrounds taken by the faculty of science, computing and engineering and the success of one Access to science and four foundation courses in collaboration with local FE colleges.

Women entering traditional 'male subjects' expressed lack of confidence in both mathematical skills and practical skills and were often noted in classroom situations to be taking the notes while the male students performed the scientific manipulations. Some felt patronized, some sexually harassed, Bridgwood notes, and others, going to staff for further explanations, 'had their work done for them, with little explanation of what was going on or of underlying principles' (Bridgwood, 1994, p.50). Women's domestic experiences were drawn on in a food and consumer studies class. The commitment and social learning skills of women students contributed to energy and success in all classes.

Ailsa Swarbrick's WIT (1985) research concentrated largely on the T101 Introduction to Technology course at the OU, which was designed partly to increase women students' participation. To that end a support system was set up to help students develop appropriate study skills and manipulative skills for experimental and technical work. The examples on which students worked included domestic ones both familiar in context to women and testing knowledge and skill in technology, thus avoiding potential alienation when all examples derive from less familiar industrial contexts. During the course all the women students were supported with self-help and study-support groups which aided confidence-building and provided a safe environment to discuss concerns about skills and practice. As the course continued it recruited proportionally higher numbers of women students than its predecessor, T100. Sadly it was replaced by T102 which, in its demands that each student use a computer at home, actually excluded many women from its activities.

The good and successful practices developed in courses which clearly enable women should be built on rather than jettisoned as if that token gesture had liberated every following generation of women into the world of science and technology. Taking away diversity and support disadvantaged potential women students. Women's participation in science and technology is on the increase (see Chapter 1) and there should be changes in the curriculum and support to reflect and encourage this.

Leslie A Barber (1995) asks fascinating questions about the changing numbers and percentages of US women achieving bachelors and doctoral degrees in science and engineering and discovered a massive increase in women achieving first and doctoral degrees matched by UK figures.

> There is no question that the number of women in science and engineering
> has increased over the last three decades. In 1960 women received 19,362
> bachelors degrees and 381 doctorates in these disciplines; by 1990 the numbers
> had risen to 123,793 bachelors degrees and 6,274 doctorates. (Barber, 1995)

This took place as college participation rates rose, but nonetheless showed
a significant increase when compared with data on men's involvement in
degrees. Over the 30-year period studied, it reveals a greater than threefold
increase in the percentage of women high-school graduates who went on to
obtain college degrees in science or engineering, while for men 'no clear
change is apparent' (p.219). As with the UK, there is a fixed gender-gap
difference in doctoral degrees between men and women which did not
narrow any further after 1976. Equity is still a long way off. Asking why,
Barber goes on to look at some of the behaviours valued within science which
clash with those encouraged in or considered natural for women.

> Many scholars have noted that as a culture, science values independence,
> emotional toughness, objectivity and the capacity for 'purely' rational thought.
> These are also qualities that Western culture identifies as masculine. Inter-
> vention efforts that fail to note this reality do a disservice to those they are
> intended to support. (Barber, 1995)

Boys are socialized to develop these capabilities and behaviours, girls less
so; and so in approaching professional science they are disadvantaged. Equity
is not an impossible goal, Barber concludes, but the structure of presentation
of science courses and of professional science needs to be more flexible and
to change to recognize women's skills and abilities. The essay does not go
quite far enough in suggesting ways of doing this but it does argue for
cultural change over and above curriculum and support developments:

> The cultural worlds of science and engineering must change if they are to
> integrate a wider variety of people: women's support of each other is one
> favoured move, while mere assimilation into existing culture is not favoured
> alone. (Barber, 1995)

Discussions about curriculum and change involve a myriad of elements. The
underlying construction of knowledge, critical perspectives on and
approaches to knowledge and the discourse of articulating it are major areas
in which women-centred or feminist positions must be taken into account.
Selective tinkering and marginalized courses are no substitute for genuine
long-term change. Enabling course presentation, structure, content,
examples, facilities and support systems also need to be in place.

A recipe for curriculum and other changes

- Women need to be consulted, involved, and in control of decisions which affect students.
- Institutional and curriculum changes that enable women students as well as men should be encouraged.
- The advertising and marketing of courses needs to be aimed at women too. Advertising could be put in women's groups, local health centres, local radio, libraries, major shops, playgroups as well as newspapers. A variety of examples of women students studying a variety of courses should appear in prospectuses and the tone and image of advertisements should be checked to ensure that courses appeal to and are genuinely available to women as well as men.
- Courses should be put on to enable women and men to become familiar with and develop skills in mathematics and science areas early on in their first semester, and as support during the whole course if necessary.
- Subjects which women have 'traditionally' studied, such as domestic science, are frequently devalued and deskilled because they *have* been studied by women. Nell Keddie (1983) has frequently argued that such subjects should be revalued and upgraded and also that ghettoization should not be a result of this upgrading: women should not be pushed towards these subjects if they do *not* wish to take them.
- Course content in all subjects needs vetting for the inclusion of women-oriented examples and practice, and for the recognition of women's interests. This can be at the level of ensuring that women authors appear on a literature syllabus, women in history on a history syllabus, women artists and the representation of women on an art syllabus, each signalled through the name of the course and as a matter of course.
- With subjects more 'traditionally' studied by men, examples from the domestic sphere or gender-free examples can be chosen to illustrate rules and points. The adult education/Access experience is helpful here: assessing and recognizing the transferability of prior learning by women in a science context leads to many hitherto 'non-scientifically oriented' women being able to undertake and succeed in subjects like Physics and Chemistry.
- We should consider how we can develop course content which reflects and causes reflection upon women's lives. We should ensure that *all* subjects are welcoming to women, in terms of course content, examples, structure and modes of presentation.

In addition, for mature women in particular:

- The institution needs to provide a customer friendly reception and information area where women with small children will not feel out of place if attending interviews or coming in for information.
- Crèche and nursery facilities need to be provided, with times that span the college day (nurseries that close earlier than lecture schedules cause immense problems), and with a special extra provision of care during school half-terms.
- Interviewing and admissions procedures should be flexible so that times suit women with children. During interview, women with domestic responsibilities should be made aware of the possible ways in which they can combine these responsibilities with study: the flexibility of modes of study, the availability of concessions (which could enable them to take part in courses for which they have to pay fees, without feeling they were taking the money out of the family food allowance) need to be explained.
- Taster days and open days could be put on for all to see what courses were available, and to discuss these issues informally before a formal interview.
- Accessible returner courses should exist to ease the move from home and/or work into study, for women who have been in paid or unpaid work, inside or outside the home, and for whom the institution might seem threatening, the courses 'not for them' because of low self-perception.
- Courses should be available in part-time, associate and CATS modes so that women can take them alongside child-rearing and part-time work, and can move courses if their partners move jobs and regions.
- The times at which courses are put on are important: these should also be accessible to women with families. Open learning could enable some women to work at their own pace at home.

Curricula, pacing, modes of study, and course context and content are all necessary and important practicalities involved in ensuring the appropriateness to and accessibility of women of higher education and ACE courses. Crucial also is a concern with women-centred or feminist methodology as they are involved in the selection, management, analysis and reproduction of knowledge and students' study practices. A profound contribution of feminist methodolgy and epistemology to higher education has been the recognition that in all discipline areas there is really no such thing as objectivity in terms of the selection and management of knowledge. Critics who reject feminist methodologies as too subjective and too related to personal experience are ignoring the same sorts of influences governing what has been conventionally acceptable to teach and discuss, even in the physical sciences.

Women-centred methodologies open up debate and avoid essentialism (of which they have often been wrongly accused as if they were looking to find and describe truths about the 'essential woman') by highlighting the contextualization and multiplicity of perspectives on knowledge, theories, concepts, practices, skills and attitudes in higher education, in all subject areas. Liz Stanley explains:

> a distinct feminist methodology not only exists but is harnessed by most feminist researchers and indeed is a defining feature of 'feminist' in academic terms. Here 'feminist methodology' is defined as a long-standing set of research practices in which feminist theory is derived from experience: the feminist researcher locates herself as on the same critical plane as the experiencing, researching and theorizing people she deals with; and in which feminist academics reject the subjective/objective dichotomy, recognizing instead that 'objectivity' is a set of practices designed to deny the actual 'subjective' location of all intellectual work. What these premises signify is actually better described as a feminist *epistemology* than a methodology. (Stanley, 1991, p.208)

The ways in which knowledge is generated and disseminated all need attention. Recognition of subjectivity, of the link between experience, reflection and understanding, between the personal and the theoretical, need to inform the writing of texts published and studied, and the content and forms of teaching/learning strategies. Changes to curricula and course delivery alone are not enough. The ways that knowledge is produced, selected and transmitted need changing too.

References

Aaron, J and Walby, S (eds) (1991) *Out of the Margins,* Falmer Press, London.

Abbott, P S (1991) 'Feminist perspectives in sociology: The challenge to mainstream orthodoxy', in Aaron and Walby, *op cit.*

Acker, J (1973) 'Women and social stratification', *American Journal of Sociology,* 78, 2–48.

Acker, S (1984) 'Women in higher education. What is the problem?' in *Is Higher Education Fair to Women?* S Acker and D Warren Piper (eds) SRHE and NFER Nelson, London.

Barber, L A (1995) 'US women in science and engineering, 1960–1990: Progress toward equity?' *Journal of Higher Education,* 66, 2, March, 213–23.

Bennett, L and Kerr, G (1993) 'Is maths a barrier for women to the study of engineering?' paper delivered at the WHEN conference, Lancaster University.

Bridgwood, A (1994) 'Teaching science and technology to women', in *What's So Special about Women in Higher Education? Vol 2,* G Wisker (ed.), SEDA, Birmingham.

Cocks, J (1985) 'Suspicious pleasures: On teaching feminist theory', in *Gendered Subjects: The Dynamics of Feminist Teaching,* M Culley and C Portuges (eds), RKP, London.

Culley, M and Portuges, C (eds) (1985) *Gendered Subjects: The Dynamics of Feminist Teaching*, RKP, London.

Gibbs, G, Jenkins, A, Baume, D *et al.* (1991) *Problems and Strategies with More Students; Lecturing to More Students*; and *Discussion with More Students*, Oxford Brookes University, Oxford.

Gibbs, G, Wisker, G and Bochner, D (1995) *Supporting More Students*, Oxford Brookes University, Oxford.

Gibbs, S (1993) 'Developing student confidence and the creation of a learning community', paper delivered at the WHEN conference, Lancaster University.

Gray, B (1994) 'Women in higher education: What are we doing to ourselves?' in *Changing the Subject*, S Davies, C Lubelska and J Quinn (eds), Taylor & Francis, London.

Hughes, M and Kennedy, M (eds) (1985) *New Futures: Changing Women's Education*, RKP, London.

Keddie, N (1981) 'Adult education: A woman's service', unpublished paper, quoted in Hughes and Kennedy, *op cit.*

Keddie, N (1983) 'Adult education theory and practice', in *Learning Liberation: Women's Response to Men's Education*, J Thompson (ed), Croom Helm, London.

Kitzinger, C (1990) 'Resisting the discipline', in *Feminists and Psychological Practice*, E Burman (ed), Sage, London, pp.119–36.

Klein, R D (1987) 'The dynamics of the women's studies classroom: A review essay of the teaching practice of women's studies in higher education', *Women's Studies International Forum*, 10, 2, 187–206.

Langland, E and Gove, W (1981) *A Feminist Perspective in the Academy*, Chicago Press, London.

Maher, F (1985) 'Classroom pedagogy and the new scholarship on women', in Culley and Portuges, *op cit.*

Meyer Spacks, P (1981) 'The difference it makes', in Langland and Gove, *op cit*, p.8.

Oakley, A (1974) *The Sociology of Housework*, Martin Robertson, London.

Ramazanoglu, C (1987) *Feminism and the Contradictions of Oppression*, Routledge, London.

Rich, A (1985) 'Taking women students seriously', in Culley and Portuges, *op cit.*

Richardson, D and Robinson, V (1993) *Introducing Women's Studies*, Macmillan, London.

Rose, G (1993) 'Some notes towards thinking about the spaces of the future', in *Mapping the Future: Local Cultures, Global Change*, J Bird *et al.* (eds), London, Routledge, p.72.

Russell, M (1985) 'Black-eyed blues connections', in Culley and Portuges, *op cit.*

Stanley, L (1991) 'Feminist autobiography and feminist epistemology', in Aaron and Walby, *op cit.*

Stanworth, M (1984) 'Women and social class analysis: A reply to Goldthorpe', *Sociology*, 18, 159–70.

Swarbrick, A (1985) 'Report on women into technology', Internal research, Open University, Milton Keynes.

Thompson, J (1983) *Learning Liberation: Women's Response to Men's Education*, Croom Helm, London.

Torton Beck, E (1990) 'To make of our lives a study: Feminist education as empowerment for women', debate documented in 1988 in *The Chronicle of*

Higher Education, which continues in *Storming the Tower* (1990) S Stiver Lie and
V O'Leary (eds), Kogan Page, London, p.212.

Wilkinson, S (1991) 'Why psychology (badly) needs feminism', in Aaron and
Walby, *op cit.*, pp.192–3.

Wisker, G (1984) 'Teaching the magic toyshop', in *Literature Teaching Politics*,
Cambridge University Press, Cambridge.

Wisker, G (1989) 'Facilitating the learning of mature women students: A British
perspective', *Studies in Continuing Education*, 11, 1.

Chapter 3

Women-centred Teaching, Learning and Assessment Strategies

Women are silenced, objectified and made passive through both the course content and the pedagogical style of most college classrooms. (Maher, 1985)

Reason and emotion are not antagonistic opposites. (Cocks, 1985)

Women-centred teaching, learning and assessment strategies should go hand-in-hand with curriculum and institutional change to reflect the needs of women in higher education.

In thinking about women-centred teaching methods it is useful to look at women's studies as a model because it is here, in a subject overtly underpinned by feminist theory and practice, that much pedagogical experimentation has initially taken place. More mainstream developments often spring from and are transferred across from women's studies successes and it is here perhaps that the greatest challenges lie.

We know that to bring women fully into the curriculum means nothing less than to reorganize all knowledge, and that changing *what* we teach means changing *how* we teach. (Culley and Portuges, 1985, p.2)

Many books and research papers concentrating on feminist or women-centred pedagogy talk about the 'fervour', the energy, vitality and radical upheaval which the women's movement and its development in educational terms, the flourishing of women's studies courses, has brought to higher education for women. Much of the most enabling teaching and learning takes its models from adult education.

Some suggested changes in institutional provision, course structure and content might initially seem to benefit only mature women students. One argument is that younger women students can study the same things, the same way, at the same time as the young men. Ironically, perhaps, I have found that it is my 18-year-olds who are often most vociferous about the exclusion of women's texts from literary lists, and about the *way* they are taught, usually by men (because with a few exceptions most higher education teachers are men). Mature women often find their experiences at odds with study experiences. Equally often they believe it is they who must change to fit into something they desire to enter, and which seems fixed in stone in terms of academic subject content, discourse and knowledge.

There are also important links to be made between our own experiences as women academics and managers, and those of our students in their learning. What kind of model are we as academic women presenting to our students in the ways in which we work and write? We need to look at the language we use and the continued commitment to recognizing personal context, reflexivity, variety of response, diversity and flexibility. A destructive model would be one in which the woman academic embraced the relationship of the personal and the analytical, encouraged these responses in students but herself jettisoned them in favour of writing, publishing, talking and achieving professionally along very different lines, colluding in fact once she had 'made it' herself. The culture of academic life is not necessarily one which adapts favourably to nurture women students and women academics.

Breda Gray (1994) defines the problem as one of ambivalence for women staff who desire the rewards that accompany conformity to male-determined norms of articulation and behaviour, but wish to develop their own and their students' women-centred practices. In our work on the MA in women's studies at Anglia, we constantly deal with issues of tensions and ambivalence. Women might want to study and discuss in their discipline and also express themselves at a recognizable level, in this case 'masters' level. They feel torn between the reflection, personal connectedness and community-oriented approaches which they often wish to move towards and the demands of the academic nature of a higher degree which expects and rewards logic, analysis, and balanced decision-making. Gray (1994), Rose (1993, p.72) and Kristeva (1981) acknowledge honest ambivalence. Rose warns: 'I... feel too complicit with my discipline's forms of and claims to knowledge to be able to map... new spaces' and 'It matters that I'm a woman advocating ambivalence, able only to say with Julia Kristeva, "that's not it, that's still not it" and having nothing more certain, more prescriptive to add' (Rose, 1993).

Gray's awareness of ambivalence centres around keeping her distance from some of the demands and decisions to be made within the academy:

> To participate more fully in the academy would involve the following options: to accept the rules and procedures; to resist these; or to engage in constant personal and professional negotiation, making some compromises along the way. (Gray, 1994, p.79)

Continued lively debate between the demands of discourses and behaviours of more conventional and conformist academic practices and the experimentation and new horizons of women-centred developments can be immensely creative. From the tensions can spring a positive 'ambivalence', both honest and empowering:

it allows for reflexivity, negotiation, movement and communication. Either complete acceptance or rejection of the academic involves the dangers of reinforcing positions and a closing down of possibilities. (Gray, 1994, p.79)

Multiple, diverse approaches have creative potential. Understanding the ways in which knowledge is created from a relationship between personal, social and academic context and experience can feed into flexible, responsive and enabling teaching/learning practices. Women-centred teaching and learning strategies can highlight the changing relationship between conventional and experientially based, creative construction of knowledge and discourse. These strategies and assumptions can enable all students:

- by changing the nature of the kind of authority and power of the classroom and developing practices which enable cooperation and integration of academic study with experience;
- by ensuring the development of abilities and appproaches which enable students to focus, reason, argue, analyse and articulate their understanding.

Margo Culley notes of feminist education that it:

- is interdisciplinary;
- legitimates life experience as an appropriate subject of analysis;
- concerns itself with process as well as product;
- is multicultural and explores interlocking sytems of oppression based on sex, race and class. (Culley and Portuges 1985, p.214)

Any discussion of changing teaching and learning strategies will beg the question whether these will merely refocus the recognition and reward system. Will they train, recognize and reward the learning strategies of women students and particularly mature women returners above those of white, middle-class 18-year-old males? Diversifying teaching/learning strategies is the issue rather than wholescale change. A repertoire of strategies will enable a larger variety of students to succeed and will, if appropriately focused, also enable and empower the marginalized, women and those with learning styles unrewarded in conventional educational practices. One benefit in this plethora of suggested change is that the kinds of teaching and learning strategies suggested as a vital part of the developing repertoire encourage lifelong learning and transferable skills which all students now strive to attain. In many cases these derive from group work, social skills, related study practices, cooperative, collaborative, communicative, sharing, learning situations and focused, analytically processed integration of personal experience and the academic, theoretical and conceptual (Bunch and Pollock, 1983; Culley and Portuges, 1985).

'Is a feminist pedagogy possible?' asks Penny Welch (1994, p.149), arguing that since the political nature of teaching and scholarship exists, women and particularly feminists should engage in changing conventional and discipline-based teaching/learning approaches. The challenge to established pedagogy takes place both in conventional discipline areas and in the very nature of the interventions women's studies make.

Discussing feminist pedagogy and women-centred teaching and learning strategies raises issues about the politics of the production and management of knowledge. Knowledge appears to be a given, handed down as authority by those in authority. It is difficult both to challenge this exclusivity of content and approach and to enable engagement with the production and management of knowledge involving students' experiences before, during and after study. It is important for both staff and students to provide space and a repertoire of strategies to engage in debates arising from and inter-relating disciplines, and linking these disciplines with our lives. Issues of production, ownership and use of knowledge are raised by questioning conventional pedagogy and by moving towards adopting andragogical approaches based on the adult learner, as a person, in the world as well as in the classroom (Knowles, 1984 and Lewin 1948).

The women's movement in the 1970s both in the USA and the UK greatly affected our awareness of the need for teaching and learning to change in these ways. Setting up women's studies courses was an early form of feminist activism for women in the women's movement, wishing to impact on teaching and learning strategies. The First National Women's Liberation Conference in Britain in February 1970 was established by women dissatisfied with the male-dominated structure and content and format of the Ruskin College History Workshop. Since then, changing teaching and learning has been on the agenda of many women academic staff, whether women's studies teachers or not.

The women's movement established and nourished the ground for change in terms of courses and teaching/learning strategies. Study groups developed, pamphlets and newsletters flourished, networks grew and *Spare Rib* fuelled this (established 1972). Virago opened up a variety of texts by women which greatly enabled the change of the curriculum (established 1973) and women's studies seminars and courses started running in adult and higher education establishments from 1973 onwards (Dix, 1973). Women's studies courses intended to make available debates around women's position and their activism within a study context to a wide number of people (Bird, 1980). But a set of developments which hinged on the women's movement felt its overt waning quite poignantly. It has sometimes been difficult to maintain the existence of women's studies courses, and to spread the teaching/learning strategies that evolved from women's studies and adult courses into the mainstream curriculum and our main practice. However, where these courses have continued, or where courses have been run by women involved in women's studies and aware of the power of transferring strategies into the mainstream, some genuine change in classroom practice has occurred and become the norm.

That successful practices should spread to change teaching/learning strategies in all courses is essential if women are to be empowered in subjects *other* than women's studies, and if their empowerment is then to be engaged with actual practice in the world of families, work, relationships and society in general. Rowbotham problematizes the isolationist developments of women's studies:

> The women's studies courses which emerged out of argument and struggle have now begun to grow into a little knowledge industry of their own. At the risk of biting the hand that feeds, it is not sufficient to produce for an academic milieu, for this does not engage with the power relations involved in the ranking of certain forms of knowledge and understanding. (Rowbotham, 1989, p.xiv)

Research into women's socialization provides background information as to how and why women might often be seen to have different approaches to learning and to articulating that learning. There are illuminating implications for classroom strategies from research into psychology and nurturing as well as educational development:

> The equation of male psychological development with the 'norm'; particularly for Freud and his followers, left women inherently inferior (and silenced), because of their lack of assertiveness, individualism, rationality, and 'objective' standard of moral judgement. The recent work of Chodorow (1978), Gilligan (1982) and others, however, has given us a picture of 'normal' female development as differently staged, toward different ends, than that of males. In these models, the interpersonal and responsible qualities of females are conceptualized not as 'inferior' and failed strategies for a (masculine) autonomy, but as particular strengths. (Maher, 1985, p.37)

Recognition, reward and encouragement of specifically female behavioural traits are essential in the classroom. Some elements of these involve encouraging different strategies for knowledge construction and for the integration of experience and academic disciplines. Others include setting up interactive teaching/learning situations which enable students to test ideas out in discussion, and which reduce classroom authority to enable exploration and shared understanding.

Authority and Relations

Reducing the distance between staff and students and the consequent sense that authority defines knowledge and right answers has been an important element in women-centred teaching/learning developments. In adult education settings, in women's studies courses and courses specifically for women in the adult sector, it has been the norm to lessen the distance physically and academically between staff and student and to encourage negotiation of curriculum and practice within the classroom. Obviously there are constraints of the curriculum, especially on courses which have learning outcomes and curriculum defined and monitored by professional bodies. Even professional bodies are aware of the need to change and the specific need for lifelong learning, updating and flexibility. Empowering students to become involved in negotiating elements of their own study, however constrained by an outside curriculum, can foster those lifelong experience-related flexible skills that employers desire and that are so useful for students. Such practices also return power to students. Learning contracts can be negotiated to help students determine their learning outcomes and the ways in which they will achieve them. Independent study project modules at Anglia, independent studies at UEL and learning contracts for adult independent studies at the University of Technology in Sydney, among others, are examples (Anderson *et al.*, 1996). A largescale and even a small, single assessment-related learning contract encourages students to internalize the learning outcomes, recognize the importance of the activities engaged in and the information to be acquired, managed and organized, and the ways in which they can solve various assessment and learning problems. Involvement fosters a sense of ownership and the internalization of the learning. Learning contracts also reduce the sense of authoritarianism, the disempowerment of the classroom. For women and men, they enable a fruitful dialogue between staff and students, students and discipline in their construction and their fulfilment.

Paulo Freire's work (1972) underlies many teaching and learning strategies empowering the learner. His 'pedagogy of the oppressed' explains that the current education model is a banking system in which the teacher controls the knowledge and the students have none. Teaching deposits knowledge in students. Freire advocates a problem-posing and problem-solving version of education in which both teachers and students are subjects:

> This pedagogy makes oppression and its causes objects of reflection by the oppressed, and from that reflection will come their necessary engagement in the struggle for their liberation. And in the struggle this pedagogy will be made and remade. (Freire, 1972, p.25)

While Freire argues that this teaching/learning model will only operate outside the formal education system until such time as the oppressed seize power, hooks (1989), among others, believes there is much to be developed inside mainstream education. I would argue that the underlying notion of empowering students by enabling them to focus with staff in exploratory talk, problem-solving, integration of their experience with learning, movement towards articulation and of making learning their own, all empower. It certainly is not worth waiting for the Utopian revolution to change the ways in which we teach and recognize learning: in fact it is almost impossible to collude with an oppressive educational practice when you have experienced empowering alternatives.

Encouraging shared constructions and interpretations of contemporary poetry in secondary classrooms and small group work with OU students revealed to me the ways in which the reduction of authority in the classroom could empower students alongside structures and practices based on negotiation. A totally experimental or sharing humanist event is not being advocated. It is essential to enable and empower students and to do this they need to have access to the structures and discourse of the discipline and interdisciplinary issues; to be given the opportunity to frame questions, investigate shared ideas and discuss; to construct knowledge, test it out and measure it against established versions. This takes place in a negotiated but structured classroom. There are social spaces for other dialogues: the classroom is a space for dialogues and experiences related to learning the disciplines and integrating them with our lives.

Chodorow (1978) and Gilligan (1982) highlight the caring networks of female relationships and a shared production of knowledge. This has implications for our recognition of women's interventions in classroom discussion. Women's hesitancy in speaking might come from a sense of powerlessness, but it could also be a wish not to close down discussion, a regard for others' points of view, and to form a shared response. Pedagogy or andragogy should be developed which encourage interaction between staff and students and between students themselves in a non-authoritarian climate.

bell hooks speaks from an Afro–American perspective and experience of subordination in an education system which ignored whole swathes of history, literature and experience and silenced Black women and men. She sees the women-centred, feminist classroom as very much a site for struggle and construction. It is an active place where everybody is engaged:

> Feminist education – the feminist classroom – is and should be a place where there is a sense of struggle, where there is visible acknowledgment of the union of theory and practice, where we work together as teachers and students to overcome the estrangement and alienation that have become so much the norm in the contemporary university. (hooks, 1989, p.51)

For the feminist or women-centred teacher it is often difficult to know when to let go of the overall authority and to pass decisions and the development of discussions to the students.

Laundering our language of specifically male-oriented adjectives, nouns and examples helps to include women students. One specifically useful enabling strategy is to share discourse, construct a common vocabulary with the students with which the discipline issues will be discussed, encouraging a shared understanding and building of understanding of the meaning and use of key terms. As Rich argues:

> Sexist grammar burns into the brains of little girls and young women a message that the male is the norm, the standard, the central figure beside which we are the deviants, the marginal, the dependent variable. It lays the foundation for androcentric thinking and leaves men safe in their solipsistic tunnel vision. (Rich, 1985)

Bringing in experience and using it

Some of the strategies which have developed involve sharing experiences and ideas, and engaging these with the new knowledge, in discussion, shaping understanding through exploratory talk and through engagement with life experiences. The influence of Carl Rogers' (1951) humanist approaches have encouraged an awareness that students bring personal agendas to the classroom, which both affect their ability to learn and the ways in which they learn. Strategies which enable the airing of these agendas and their engagement help learning. Space to mention 'what's on top', air concerns about what is under discussion, help students to focus and relate, while the act of negotiating content and activities encourages ownership and empowerment. Engagement with the personal experience of students also helps them share and own knowledge and ideas. It also recognizes that all knowledge is actually produced by an interplay between the subjective and the elected elements of the world. Westcott encourages such an interplay with women students so that it is recognized there is, 'intersubjectivity of meaning of subject and object. The questions that the investigator asks of the object of knowledge grow out of her own concerns and experiences' (Westcott, 1979, p.426). Students become the investigators and experimentors. Their subjectivity is a vital part of the process, as is their learning experience during it.

Group Discussion and Group Work

Similarly, a learner-centred classroom will involve students in discussing issues, debating set questions and coming up with their own questions, managing disparate items of information, cases and concerns, through discussion, sharing tasks and the production of shared assessments. Many areas of women's lives revolve around the ability to work cooperatively, in the domestic sphere, in the world of shops and piecework, in girls' and women's groups. Structured group work helps to build on these tendencies and skills. It encourages women to see knowledge and arguments as not rigidly fixed, but part of a changeable dialectic.

Encouraging group work, networking and sharing ideas and tasks prevents study from being competitive. It builds on the networking and community-oriented skills women develop. It also gives a sense of solidarity, enables discussion and encourages a variety of viewpoints. It fosters interaction and the involvement of women who might be silenced, unconfident, unsure of the value of their contributions, unused to contributing and thinking out loud on an analytical, theoretical issue.

Women's experiences should be built on. Women should be encouraged to relate experience to the subjects studied, and to move on intellectually after that accessible base has been established. For adult returners this is essential. For women students studying subjects traditionally taken by men, such as technology and science, the inclusion of examples from their experience helps the uptake of knowledge and encourage a relatedness which secures understanding. Empowerment does not mean merely recognizing the experiences women students bring to their classrooms and enabling them to reflect on them. It actually means helping them to integrate the experience with the academic learning and go on to change and to practise.

Talking of Black mature women returners in downtown Detroit, Michelle Russell notes:

> They have come to you for help in getting pulled together. The loose ends of their experience jangle discordantly like bracelets from their arms. You must be able to do with subject matter what they want to do with their lives. Get it under control in ways which thrive on complication. (Russell, 1985)

The knitting of experience and academic disciplines and the knitting of life and study are essential in many women students' lives. The cohesion and coherence of the two helps produce a framework for learning and development.

Some of the concerns which have been expressed about the effectiveness of women-centred strategies and situations have been aired by some of our own students on the MA course in Women's Studies at Anglia. They have argued that the work we do is too cerebral and does not provide opportunities for intervention in the world from which they come and from which others come. There is clearly a difficulty for academics who would wish to be involved in feminist political activism actually spreading out from the classroom. Teaching and learning might become subsumed in that activism and the projects which result, however useful, would be a different product. I think it is important to encourage women students to make the links themselves and for us all to transfer our theory to practice and, where appropriate, to activism but not to blur the classroom experience – which integrates theory and experience – and the out-of-classroom experience – which puts change into practice. Many students will be involved in both.

Articulating and Organizing

One issue which has dogged discussions in our own MA Women's Studies is that of academic discourse and the forms of expression and structure in which we choose to write. Many women perceive academic subjects and their discourses as chosen and developed by men to reflect their experiences and ways of commenting on and forming them. It can be argued that some women at least want to express themselves in ways which would not fit the rigor of a male-defined, established academic discourse, and suddenly insisting on this fixed mode of response seems at odds with the flexibility of content, of approach, of study modes, of group work. I think there are two answers to this. Many women do not write or speak naturally in that rather artifical mode, the academic essay. Neither do many men, of course! We all have to learn to conform to the shape of academically valid modes of expression for assessment. It is possible, though, that the shape need not be so permanently and rigidly defined, and that different forms and means of expression could be found other than the academic essay itself. This is not to advocate inchoate expression. Adrienne Rich warns against embracing disorder in the name of feminine discourse *per se*: 'A romantic sloppiness, an inspired lack of rigor, a self-indulgent incoherence, are symptoms of female self-depreciation' (Rich, 1985).

There is no point in being disordered to the point of incomprehensibility, and there is no growth or development involved in merely putting down the confusion of initial ideas, on the page, in a disordered fashion. This is just poor expression. Ideas are not articulated and communicated. Why sell women short by accepting this kind of work? We all need to develop ways of managing our ideas so we understand what we experience and what we study. Analytical study and writing, structured and grammatical writing are not antipathetic *per se* to the expression of women's perceptions, attitudes and understandings. 'Reason and emotion are not antagonistic opposites' (Cocks, 1985) and women can learn to do formally what they do naturally: integrate the two. It is important, then, to set up working situations in which creative thinking and expression are released, in which women and men students can approach the issues and ideas in a number of ways, some imaginative, and then work to incorporate them into an organized, analytical answer whether written or spoken. Harnessing the diversity of thoughts, experiences and responses and helping to shape them is an enabling process. Some strategies which help this to take place include:

- brainstorming and negative brainstorming;
- mind-mapping;
- pair or buzz-group work;
- role play;
- fishbowl work with observers;

- triads with one acting as an observer;
- using synectics and metaphors to solve problems.

Brainstorming

Students call out words and phrases, without expansion, in response to a question, word, idea or problem. These are collected on the board. The flow is allowed to run its course and no comments are made until the end by the teacher/facilitator. At the end the teacher/facilitator or a student look for common ground, collections of concepts and arguments, and groups them. This starts the forming of blocks of response and argument. Discussion follows, building up and developing further ideas, looking at pros and cons, shaping them into aspects of an argument. The discussion can be with the whole group, tutor-led, or in small groups. Once the ideas have been shaped, they can be logically ordered and grouped by individuals or pairs into the basis for an oral presentation along ordered grounds or for an individual piece of writing. A variety of intuitive, experiential and thoughtful responses have been gathered, the reflection and shaping has taken place, and the piece of work can then be an ordered one which has harnessed that creative experiential response.

Negative brainstorming

Students call out all the worst things that could happen in a scenario, all the rotten aspects of an issue or idea. The shaping process starts to build up arguments for and against, or ways of controlling, managing and answering problems, having recognized their full potential horror.

Pairs or buzz-groups

Pairs or buzz groups are so called partly because of the interested 'buzz' heard when students are involved in discussion. At the start or end of a lecture or seminar, or when a very brief stimulus to thought on an issue is needed, students are asked to discuss in pairs or buzz groups (buzz groups *can* contain more than two). They might be asked for responses, or the involvement in discussion might be thought to be active enough in itself. Such discussion causes thought and articulation. It is quick, informal and stimulates focus and concentration.

Mind-mapping

This strategy can be used in essay development. It involves students working visually together or alone, considering a problem, questions or issues, brainstorming ideas and responses on a page, then finding the central issue/concept/problem/question, placing it centrally visually, elaborating on and then linking main points, sub-points, residual questions and problems. Various links between this problem area and previous experience can also be collected as students start to visualize how they come to understand the issues and relate them to previous learning and scenarios. This planning and exploration process enables a structured argument to be visualized and produces a list of issues and areas which the student needs to explore selectively for information, note-taking and problem-solving. When the presentation, report, essay, project or dissertation starts to be written, the mind-map is returned to for direct clues on how to link the developing and related points and contrary points together into a logical ordered whole, where to fit information, where to make the links.

These several strategies help to form ideas into a shape for an essay in well-established ways. Others contribute towards that process too eventually but aim more to develop deep understanding through the use of experience, linking situations, information and ideas with previous experience and learning, modelling situations, reflection then building upon reflection and experiential process.

Role play and games or simulations

These can enable students to work on problem issues, to put themselves in the place of, for example, social workers working on a case, lawyers trying to solve a legal problem, architects considering a project or problem, business people considering the specifications, constructing, putting forward and assessing/having assessed their solutions to business problems, and so on. In a role play or simulation, students need briefing about playing roles; they need to feel safe because of some disclosure which could take place and perhaps because of excess identification with the roles. They also need ground rules and advice on how to take the role play or simulation seriously. When the role play is over they need to debrief and remove themselves from their roles but also have plenty of time to reflect on exactly what was learned within the role in the scenario. Using observers helps this feedback. If students simulate a role play or case study, they are enabled to internalize the processes, think strategically and logically within the problem situation, and so move beyond either a collection of facts or an emotional response towards a response based on experience and action. Making the best of this and shaping it into a response takes place with and after the debrief when what has happened, what has been decided, how the ideas and information can be ordered to be expressed are all discussed. The students then need to build on this and decide how to transfer what they have discovered from the role play or simulation, to their real-life scenarios.

Fishbowl

This situation enables half the group to play out a role play or discuss a problem, observed by the other half, although in a large group one small group might carry out the activity observed by the rest. The experiential process is similar to a role play, and the debrief is essential. In a fishbowl, those not playing literally sit and watch like looking at fish in a bowl. If the groups have been evenly divided or if another round of experiential role play is useful, others/the other half go into the fishbowl and the activity is repeated.

Triads

Students are encouraged to work together in threes. A threesome enables discussion which is more flexible and varied than a pair and the third member can also take a different role as chair of discussion, as observer etc, so changing dynamics.

Synectics

Students frequently find it difficult to engage with problems, cases or issues which require creative thinking when they are in classroom situations. Synectics involve the use of creative metaphors with which students can engage. They might be asked, for example, to compare a particular problem position to a fruit, flower, supermarket – and the elements of the comparison free up their thoughts. Similarities and differences can be collected and problems or issues addressed. Other synectic tactics involve separating approaches and issues by listing them under different headings on a flipchart and asking for different kinds of comment, information and contributions under each heading. Students can be asked to give information, and suggest areas in which they need help, under separate headings on the flipchart. They are then enabled to offer information or help out of the main group, and their offers or points are collected on the flipchart. By dividing up elements of interest and information it acts as an enabling device.

I am not arguing that these are only women-centred ways of working. They work well with most students when appropriately structured in an appro-priate activity because they free up the thought process and enable linking with experience – either previous and/or current – as produced through the role play. They enable organized reflection which can then be led into problem-solving and short and long written tasks of a structured nature. These scenarios and strategies recognize the importance of discussion, using experience and reflection, and using emotion, ways women work, often ignored in more conventional teaching siutations. Forming the responses from a well-structured scenario into a structured piece of written or oral presentation work follows, and must be supported. These strategies encourage deep learning, and originated with adult students and women's studies classrooms. They enable the linking of the social, the cooperative, the experiential and emotion and reason with which women students thrive, and which a wide variety of learners of either gender and of many different cultures also thrive. These sorts of strategies actually help to utilize the difference rather than marginalizing it, and to value and utilize experience rather than rejecting it as irrelevant in an academic situation.

Women students in particular work well when there is a collaborative, social orientation to their tasks within the class and outside it. This is also true of many men students, and not true for all women, but group work and task-oriented groups recognize the importance of working together, sharing, forming responses, building upon the experience in the group, and enabling each other to contribute from group security, on behalf of others, even when speaking out does not come naturally to quieter, or less confident students. We are all familiar with research into classroom responses where, under the conventional scenario, the teacher in the primary, secondary and adult classroom is seen to reward the interventions of the male students more frequently than those of the women partly because they are more frequent and demanding of attention and partly as a cultural response (Stanworth, 1981). Group work whether in pairs in small discussion exercises, threes with an observer, fives and sixes involved in problem-solving, completion of tasks or exploratory talk around a set of questions, encourages students to take an active part in the exploratory talk and to take it in turns to report back (Jaques, 1984). The potentially unformed, personal, tentative, inchoate response is thus shaped to be heard, but the experience is not over-awing. The vociferous (often mature) student can also be controlled, because roles can be assigned and reporting back rotated.

Women's classroom participation is often more cooperative and con-structive than conventional male-determined and reinforced patterns which tend to be competitive:

> Common patterns of competition and argument in discussion came not only from 'masculine' modes of speech, but from traditional notions of learning, wherein we search for objective truth and the single 'right answer' rather than for shared and comparative conclusions about multiple experiences. (Hale and Sandler, 1982, p.32)

Women students' interventions are more likely to end with questions than closed responses, as if asking for more discussion, for agreement and debate, conducive to the discussion as 'a cooperative development of ideas' rather than 'competition from the floor'. Findings show more interaction takes place with women students as well as men when women are teaching classes.

Nelson (1981), for example, looks at a sociology course which encourages students to integrate their experience and lives with their studies and so encourages fuller participation and fruitful interaction between academic work and personal experience. Group work recognizes that problem-solving and responses can be shaped cooperatively from multiple perspectives and that knowledge is not a single reductive truth, but fluid and many-sided. These groups can often be based as OU groups, in self-help, or tutorless and self-managed.

On the Women's Studies MA at Anglia, for example, in an early session on the representations of girls and women, the ways text, image and other media devices represent and tend to form women's versions of themselves and options as roles, we ask questions, present images, read textual extracts analytically, and use reflective group discussion exploring personal experience, pulling the whole together and relating the items in an informal presentation from each group at the end. In sessions where cultural difference is a key issue, a cultural self-identification 'round' starts the session. Everyone briefly introduces their cultural context saying where they and their families come from, the countries they have connections with and so on. This reflection and sharing form the basis for the open discussion of cultural difference issues and effects. This strategy is also essential as an initial ice-breaker when working in mixed cultural groups and using personal experience and other material: it focuses positively and interactively on the different cultural contexts from which students and some of their expect-ations and responses come.

Relating the personal, the problem-solving, the academic and the analytical opens up responsive, affective ways of working and sharing and encourages deep learning. The students really relate to the issues and engage with them personally as well as academically.

These strategies involve personal and experiential learning and encourage approaching ideas and arguments cooperatively from a multiplicity of viewpoints. This disempowers the established powerful beliefs that know-ledge and truth are givens to be discovered and correctly passed on, that there are single right answers sought and that those who can produce and reproduce these single right answers have all the power. Group and interactive strategies involve everyone; they do not exclude the different thinking processes and the different experiences of students who approach ideas unconventionally, and those who approach them from the different learning bases springing from cultural difference. They use these approaches, and encourage imaginative, creative responses which reward flexibility and respect difference.

Students need to be empowered, not just allowed to speak, to learn the discourse of the subject, the thought processes which go into deliberating issues within the subject and within different subjects. They need to be able to form arguments not just explore issues. In our radical and necessary assertion that the feminist teacher must validate the personal and the emotional, we have sometimes ignored the equally necessary validation of the intellect. In our sensitivity to the psychology of oppression in our students' lives, we have often denied ourselves the authority we seek to nurture in our students (Culley and Portuges, 1985, pp.2–7).

To enable others, we have to grant ourselves the authority to be more than facilitators, but guides and midwives, bringing ideas and expressions to birth. We have to ensure we give students the models and opportunities to see a variety of ways of articulating their analyses and syntheses, putting together their presentations, projects, reports, essays and dissertations, or whatever alternative forms of assessment we have helped devise, so that there is the personal subject, experiential and multiple shared perspective, in a form which can be communicated, with authority, to others. As Margo Culley notes, authority is actually important:

> It is only in accepting her authority – by this I mean the authority of her intellect, imagination, passion – that the students can accept the authority of their own like capacities. The authority the feminist teacher seeks is authority with, not authority over, and part of that picture is the authority of our anger. (Culley and Portuges, 1985, p.215)

Assessment is the most politically difficult area and potentially a very creative and liberating one.

Assessment

Assessment, that ultimate form of authority, the gatekeeping and stamp of approval, can also be facilitating, recognize experience, enable the creative and personal to be integrated with the newly discovered learning of an academic disciplinary or interdisciplinary nature. Assessment forms which enable the use of and development of group work, sharing and knowledge development can lead to flexibility in the shape of forms of expression offered for assessment: orals, group work, variously structured individual or paired essays, group performance, presentation or project. In both women's studies and English courses as well as sociology and social work modules, group work towards the solution of case studies, or the gathering of project materials for presentation in relation to issues, for example, of popular culture, all encourage the sharing of ideas and experiences, the gradual forming of arguments and collection and the management of material and information. This is then shaped into a collaborative, analytical and structured presentation in answer to certain questions ranged around appropriate issues in the subject area.

In a CertEd module on equal opportunities, staged experiential hands-on sessions run by students help us to experience what it is like to be suffering from certain disabilities. We can briefly experience partial vision or impaired hearing, discrimination for one reason or another, and hear about the specific equal opportunities issues in operation in college and subject area contexts and how they might be managed. A group presentation assessment format helps the group form and present ideas; discussion helps shape versions of arguments; and experience gives us insights to match with the researched and experiential information. Together a response is produced.

Interdisciplinarity is also important, as is the recognition of multiple points of view and a movement towards some answers rather than a search for and expression of a single answer. In terms of the academic essay, the established form of argument presenting ideas, there could be a welcoming use of a variety of ideas. Women's Studies is a model for this interdisciplinary flexibility. It refuses the rigidity of academic subject boundaries and knows that history spills into art, technology into history, and so on. Ideas, too, are not rigidly separated from each other. A fluid but structured expression of a variety of ideas and related arguments builds on the recognizably female desire to perceive links and related alternatives, rather than making rational, strict, rigid choices and developing a hierarchy of arguments.

Assessment exercises can encourage personal experiential knowledge to integrate with that of the discipline, highlighting multiple perspectives and enabling different responses. On some courses related to health and education within Anglia we use a module which is assessed by reflective writing. This encourages the development and use of reflection, personal experience and forms of articulation charting development, hesitancies and decision-making processes, as well as showing how the attitudes of the students are changing. Through the use of logs and diaries, students can chart their developing responses to teaching, to nursing, to subject areas and issues which specifically demand self-awareness and change, and a development of attitudes as part of their learning outcomes. In using portfolio and log responses on the Black and Asian women's writing module at Anglia, students can chart their responses to the material studied, the contexts, the challenges to their assumptions and their silences, and can integrate their previous and current experience with their studies. The changes these studies start to encourage spill over into their lives and are discussed in the log, charted and reflected in the portfolio (Wisker, 1996).

Other assessment practices imported from adult learning contexts and the best practice in higher education also enable women students and all students. These include the use of self- and peer-assessment. Self- and peer-assessment both reduce the authority of the teacher and the sense that there is an absolute mark which by rights accurately belongs to a piece of work. With the development of self-assessment strategies, students can learn to internalize the meanings on the ground in practice of the actual criteria perhaps, initially, negotiated with the staff member. They can also learn to internalize the ways in which their various responses are variously rewarded in the discipline in practice. This should encourage an awarenes of a multiplicity of acceptable expressions and approaches in relation to stated and agreed learning outcomes and criteria, rather than the kind of 'secret society' activity of offering up work and awaiting the final stamp. Students learn autonomy. They share in the learning practice, recognizing assessment to be not the final point but part of the learning process. Peer-assessment formats also encourage such sharing and building of knowledge and approaches. How responses are shaped by those involved and measured against outcomes and criteria can be part of a discursive process. This should encourage the internalization of negotiated understanding of the learning outcomes and achievements possible in the discipline area. Group assessments which similarly involve peer- and self-assessment elements will also help to share the learning experience, show how there is no one single right answer, and enable students to internalize the forms learning outcomes can take in practice.

Skills need developing, ideas transforming, rigid boundaries dissolving. Women need to be enabled to study in higher education as it currently exists and to articulate and urge for change in the provision, the definitions of subjects and how they are taught and assessed. It is only with these sorts of changes in how and what we teach that we will fully be able to facilitate the learning of women students of different ages, backgrounds and interests. And as staff we can ourselves learn from these student-oriented models, networking, arguing for the validity of our own experiences and responses, urging the transformation of the curriculum, the institution, and the forms in which understanding and argument are legitimately managed and expressed. Building on the experiences of our other colleagues working with women students will enable fruitful networking, cooperation, challenge and change in our teaching work.

References

Anderson, G, Boud, D and Sampson, J (1996) *Learning Contracts: A Practical Guide*, Kogan Page, London.

Bird, L (1980) 'Setting up women's studies courses', *Spare Rib*, 93, 52–3.

Bunch, C and Pollock, S (1983) *Learning our Way: Essays in Feminist Education*, Crossing Press, London.

Chodorow, N (1978) *The Reproduction of Mothering*, California University Press, Berkeley, CA.

Cocks, J (1985) 'Suspicious pleasures: On teaching feminist theory', in Culley and Portuges, *op cit*.

Culley, M and Portuges, C (eds) (1985) *Gendered Subjects: The Dynamics of Feminist Teaching*, RKP, London.

Dix, C (1973) 'Where to study women's studies', *Spare Rib*, 18, 3–36.

Freire, P (1972) *Pedagogy of the Oppressed*, Penguin, London.

Gilligan, C (1982) *In a Different Voice: Psychological Theory and Women's Development,* Harvard University Press, Cambridge, MA.

Gray, B (1994) 'What are we doing to ourselves?' in *Changing the Subject,* S Davies, C Lubelska and J Quinn (eds) Taylor & Francis, London.

Hale, R and Sandler, B (1982) 'The classroom climate: A chilly one for women?' Project on the status and education of women, Washington DC, American Association of Colleges essay.

hooks, b (1989) *Talking Back: Thinking Feminist, Thinking Black,* South End Press, Boston MA, p.51.

Jaques, D (1984) *Learning in Groups,* Kogan Page, London.

Knowles, M (1984) *Andragogy in Action,* McGraw Hill, London.

Kristeva, J (1981) 'Women can never be defined', in *New French Feminisms,* E Marks and Ide Courtivron (eds), Harvester, Brighton.

Lewin, K (1948) *Resolving Social Conflicts,* Harper & Row, New York.

Maher, F (1985) 'Classroom pedagogy and the new scholarship on women', in Culley and Portuges, *op cit.*

Rich, A (1985) 'Taking women students seriously', in Culley and Portuges, *op cit.*

Rogers, C (1951) 'Student-centred teaching', in *Client-centred Therapy,* C Rogers (ed.), Constable, London.

Rose, G (1993) 'Some notes towards thinking about the spaces of the future', in *Mapping the Future: Local Cultures, Global Changes,* J Bird *et al.* (eds), Routledge, London.

Rowbotham, S (1989) *The Past is Before Us: Feminism in Action Since the 1960s,* Penguin, Harmondsworth.

Russell, M (1985) 'Black-eyed blues connections', in Culley and Portuges, *op cit.*

Stanworth, M (1981) *Gender and Schooling,* Hutchinson, London.

Welch, P (1994) 'Is a feminist pedagogy possible?' in *Changing the Subject,* S Davies, C Lubelska and J Quinn (eds), Taylor & Francis, London, p.149.

Westcott, G (1979) 'Feminist criticism of the social sciences', *Harvard Educational Review,* 49, 4, November, 422–30.

Wisker, G (1996) 'Assessment for learning: Encouraging personal development and critical response on a writing module by student-centred assessment and teaching/learning strategies', *Innovations in Education and Training International,* 33, 1.

Chapter 4

Women's Studies Courses

> Women's studies shares neither the assumptions of the dominant cultures, nor do we find the present compartmentalization of knowledge adequate to pursue our questions. To introduce feminist insights means to challenge radically the generation and distribution of knowledge; it means changing the whole shape of the course, or the problem – or the discipline. Such a concept of women's studies demands more than having a course 'on women'. (Bowles and Duelli Klein, 1983, p.3)

A major development of the women's movement has been the proliferation of Women's Studies courses. Women's Studies courses are now running at every level, ranging from short adult sessions which are consciousness-raising oriented, to return-to-work classes, undergraduate courses/fields, whole degrees and postgraduate courses. As an opportunity for experimentation in practice of the feminist principles underlying the women's movement, Women's Studies courses have been rich and fertile. Many of the experiments in interdisciplinarity, interactive teaching and learning, cooperative non-authoritarian strategies and integration of the personal and experiential with the more academic, have fruitfully developed within Women's Studies courses.

Of course, there are difficulties associated with the very separatism which women's studies suggests. It has been argued (see Chapter 1) that all conventional courses have been in some way men's studies since women have been silenced and excluded, and usually just left out by accident, based on a conception of knowledge as value-free and objective in relation to tradition and gender. It could be suggested that hiving off studies of women in the various disciplines, or identifying a gendered perspective, marginalizes and ghettoizes the study of women in relation to these subjects, highlighting the difference of approach and study. With such marginalization it is possible for those in charge of mainstream courses to insist that there is no need to include women's perspectives or to be at all experimental because that is being done elsewhere in women's studies. There is an argument, too, that women's studies becomes quite vulnerable in ages of cuts, because it is clearly out on a limb when all other subject areas are recognizable and established. Students might question: 'Women's studies, what is that? Is it real study? Is it just a study of "women in"? Why are we not studying the real subjects?' They might feel they were being advised to study something second-rate, not a real subject area. Women in particular, given the chance at last to study for themselves, to put their own development first, might well baulk at the idea of taking this specialized, seemingly marginalized course. Women's studies, however, could benefit by its relative marginal status and remain on a radical, self-critical edge. This would help prevent it from atrophying, becoming dull and out of touch. Opportunities have been seized and are still being seized. Any stigma retires into the background as students go on to use their degrees.

Interdisciplinarity is essential to Women's Studies courses, and in itself this undermines the traditional departmentalization and compartmentalization of knowledge, the established hierarchies of disciplines with their rigid boundaries. Victoria Robinson notes:

> The organization of knowledge into separate and distinct disciplines meant that the new questions and methods of feminist enquiry that emerged from putting women at the centre of theoretical discourses were not adequately answered or dealt with. The crossing of theoretical boundaries – multidisciplinary, inter-disciplinary or transdisciplinary (going beyond the disciplines) – allows an issue or an area to be examined from a variety of intellectual standpoints and has been seen as most appropriate to women's studies. (Robinson, 1993, p.6)

Another issue is whether women's studies is genuinely heterogeneous, whether it serves the needs and reflects the experiences of a diversity of women. The original developments in women's studies grew out of a reaction to patriarchal culture and produced courses which had their 'own problems with heterosexism, classism and racism in (its) predominantly white programs' (Bowles and Duelli Klein, 1983, p.5). It could be too exclusive in its own approaches, although those working within women's studies as early as 1983 recognized and started dealing with this. Gerda Lerner's work in women's history highlights some of the other concerns about women-centredness: that it challenges more than just the construction of knowledge within the academy, considering the ways in which we see the world and conform to its essentially patriarchal controls:

> the move of women from marginality to the center shattters the system. That is too dangerous a thought for most women to contemplate. We abort our thought in order not to lose the spiritual safety provided for us within the patriarchy. Without our cooperation it could not exist. (Lerner, 1980, pp.21–2)

It is a huge undertaking to move out from a (subordinated) position within patriarchy and go it alone with women's studies. However, trying to transform the whole curriculum from within is an enormous task, and Bowles and Duelli Klein (1983) emphasize the ways in which attempting this as individuals drains the energies of both women staff and students. Continued striving after change, continuous challenge actually needs the basis of a Women's Studies programme and group from which to work. We need autonomous and independent Women's Studies programmes or departments within universities so that feminists from a variety of backgrounds and interests can engage in active dialogue among themselves in order to build feminist scholarship and to bring it to the classroom. There need to be Women's Studies groups and Women's Studies programmes to enable focus on research, debating practices and change, working in an interdisciplinary manner, and taking some experimental risks with practice so that our individual energies are not dissipated and lost in the struggle for major change in itself.

This is not an isolationist argument but one for a nurturing space and a focus from which to develop critiques, visions and strategies united in the focus on equality and the establishment of new ways of working and thinking, springing from collaboration and vision. There is a similarly strong argument for the development of women-oriented and women-only staff development and training. Here women can work together to integrate theory and practice, experience and analysis, looking at issues of professional and self-development unsilenced, validating each other's approaches and practices, questioning and critiquing without being shot down and undermined by some of the different assumptions and practices possible in mixed staff development and training groups.

The presence of women's studies on a campus suggests a centre, maybe physical, more likely to be located in a network of people, for women who wish to share and develop ideas and practices together. There are some fundamental issues which will probably always be on the agenda such as finding the voice to challenge established oppressive practices and suggest, develop and build on more cooperative practices. There will be new concerns and needs as higher education itself and its demands change. Women's studies as an area of study cannot remain ossified but needs to be developing to recognize new issues, approaches, needs and interests.

Mary Ruth Warner, who teaches Black studies and women's studies at the University of Massachussetts at Amherst, expresses the desire to mainstream women's studies and subjects related to Black women and racism:

> while one of the goals of the program is to foster the mainstreaming of women's studies into the university curriculum, our primary focus had been the development of women's studies as a discipline. (Dinnerstein, quoted in Bowles and Duelli Klein, 1983, p.5)

This tackles the problem of potential ghettoization by enabling women's studies to be developed in its own right. Its practices and reformations should permeate the whole curriculum. Women's studies constantly develops and changes to recognize the importance of difference. Warner, Dinnerstein, Duelli Klein and Bowles argue for a recognition of class, sexuality and race in terms of curriculum examples. The recognition of different learning styles as they show themselves in practice is also essential. The huge strides made in developing non-authoritarian classrooms, encouraging feminist praxis, enabling a diversity of students to have their experience validated, recognized, shared and forming the basis of their studies, should not remain an isolated successful experiment, but should also permeate the curriculum and pedagogical practices as a whole (and not instead of).

In my experience the opportunities and the models of women's studies have been immensely fruitful. Experiments I have tried with Women's Studies courses and students have richly informed everything else I do. Learning strategies which students have been encouraged to recognize and develop on their Women's Studies courses have spilled over most fruitfully into all their work. Students I have observed and worked with over ten years, taking joint courses, find they transfer the approaches of women's studies to their other subjects and include personal experience, work collaboratively and reflectively, integrate life and academia, produce innovative assessment responses, are willing to share, grow and discuss exploratorily in creative ways.

Women's studies challenges the deficit model of women as lesser beings than men. It redraws subject and discipline relations and re-empowers women through study enabling women to create knowledge, use it and integrate it with their experiences, together, cooperatively. Women's Studies courses have:

> reordered subject disciplines in an interdisciplinary way and from a different perspective which has evolved into new academic disciplines. Women's studies draws upon, as well as reinterpreting, academically respected research. (Hughes and Kennedy, 1985, p.26)

Women's studies works in several ways which ensure cooperation and experiential links; interdisciplinarity which breaks down the authority of subject boundaries; the establishment of teaching and learning strategies which refuse the authority of the classroom; the undermining of divisions between staff and students and the refusal of single reductive readings of issues and subjects. As women's studies staff, we need to model these practices and encourage their development in our students. In terms of interdisciplinarity:

> too often it is left to the students to attempt to synthesize the separate disciplinary elements with which they are fed. We can actively demonstrate how this can be done, as well as the problems encountered, through our approaches to teaching. (Aaron and Walby, 1991)

Methods of teaching and learning should encourage students to reflect on and integrate the person with the subjects and issues studied, in groupwork, in discussion and in peer-group work as well as in individual explorations leading to creative and reflective projects.

Central issues in the women's studies classroom are:

- the relationship of experience to academic study;
- the interdisciplinarity of women's studies. How to integrate the different disciplines to enable the student to integrate them in their studies;
- the importance of providing a recognized and valued space for women's studies;
- the necessity of avoiding marginalization and ghettoization. Avoiding hiving-off all study from a feminist or women-centred perspective into the Women's Studies courses;
- provisions of women's studies at all levels, some more accessible to those without the power of academic qualifications and fees;
- refusal of authoritarian behaviours in teaching and learning and development of cooperative behaviours such as group work, negotiated contacts, sharing of learning outcomes and criteria;
- integration of the personal into the academic through involving and ecouraging the building on personal response and personal experience;
- accessibility of theory and its development into a rigour which enables analysis, clear expression and clear argument about the mostly ostensibly woolly, subjective issues such as motherhood and power;
- the encouragement of assessment processes which enable students to show their development, capture their personal responses, give a glimpse in the development of their learning.

Authority

Issues of power are crucial in any discussion of women's studies. As women academics we need to ensure that we can cope with the contradictory nature of our position. The subject area and the pedagogy/andragogy in women's studies are meant to empower those involved, particularly the students. How can we as staff genuinely cope with our potential disempowerment? How can we hand over the control from the classroom, the shaping of knowledge and understanding to the group, help the students to flourish in their own ways, without compromising this spirit of equality with the intrusiveness of our own positions as academics, in control of the course? Alternatively we might simply let the sessions run on their own accord, which is often tantamount to insisting on no structure and no aims. Treading the course between enabling structures and authority which actually disempowers is difficult. With the establishment of the MA in Women's Studies at Anglia, we fought many battles over these issues. The feminist classroom remains a site for such debates. Each time the team teaching the class make decisions about what happens next or guide a set of responses, the sense of authority returns, affecting the developing personal responses. Letting the class deteriorate into personal conversation threatens our dedicated time slot. This we know would unfairly jeopardize our students' chances of making intellectual leaps. They have sacrificed and committed much to a 'Masters' course (the irony of the title never fails to lose its frisson!).

Language

The expression possible in the women's studies classroom will take all forms. Maggie Humm points out that a crucial element is the refusal to conform to specifically codified language – the language of the academy which would translate experiences into something else and shape responses merely into a form suitable for assessment. Again, the problem at issue here is that women's studies students want to achieve the qualifications and growth these assessments seem to measure, just as do students of biology, history and law. Flexibility can lead to a licence which sells the students short and, given the personal and social as well as monetary commitments many have to make to attend a women's studies course, this would hardly be fair. It is important to develop feminist discourse and empower students in their expression. Maggie Humm argues for specific discourses of women's studies:

> Fundamental to feminism is the premise that women are not represented in codified knowledge, and the description and analysis of women's experience is the most significant contribution made by second-wave feminism. The specific issue in this is an attack on the polarized categories of subjective/objective as feminist writers refuse to accept these as discrete categories and make a fresh and feminist encoding of the experience. (Humm, 1991, p.53)

The blending of the subjective personal experiential response with the object of study so the two are fused demands a new kind of discursive practice. In the women's studies classroom practices of disclosure and identification, whether personal or cultural, enable a sharing and articulation of difference, which is a basis of understanding and the forming of shared knowledge. A very empowering set of experiences for women's studies students derives directly from the articulate performance of women from various ethnic groups, from Black and Asian women who refuse any simplistic unitary insistence that women essentially are either this or that, feel and want this or that, can be legislated for in certain manners. Their assertion of difference opens up a multiplicity of perspectives. As the poet Audre Lorde says, 'difference is not a reason for destruction but for celebration' (Lorde, 1984).

Recognizing cultural differences leads to recognizing differences in approach and in framing our versions of ourselves and the world. In women's studies groups you can hear the way students from different cultural groups share and shape their expressions into a group response, translate responses into each other's understanding without losing the personal.

The future of women's studies

Politically women's studies has some issues to face. Mary Evans notes:

> Now that women have, in a sense, arrived as part of the academic consciousness of the male academy, the problem arises of where women's studies might go next, and in particular what might happen to that once subversive and radical category of 'women'

especially because:

> in the academy, as much as in the politics of feminism, questions have been asked about the validity of studying a single sex, when every theoretically sophisticated person knows that we are all constructed out of a number of situations/discourses/circumstances. (Evans, 1991, p.67)

Perhaps all women's studies should now be gender studies and cultural studies? Or is there still an issue to be brought into the open which specifically concerns women and the difference that makes? Mary Evans insists on retaining women's studies. It allows a space in the academy at all levels for the specific study of women and for feminist theory and practice. This avoids dissipation into differences or relativity which could then so easily lose momentum and disappear back into a consensus of conventional approaches to a conventional curriculum, where the 'norm' rules. Those of us who have been teaching in women's studies for several years will testify to the quicksand into which women-oriented courses are sucked once we release them, their worth 'obvious', back into the single discipline home. Similarly, if we just allow them to be described as cultural or adult studies, how soon anything to do with recognizing feminist theory, practice and pedagogy and women's studies approaches and content is subsumed under the heavy weight of all that curriculum content which is somehow 'necessary' before anything to do with gender as it is described can enter. 'We have done that', 'We did that last year'. Even the most convincingly espoused feminist male sometimes switches to next year's critical approach with a kind of glee, shelving the women's studies oriented modules as last year's clothes. Evans goes on to suggest that far from feeling there is no longer anything to argue about, so much ground has been won:

> there is a lot to be said for the expansions of further missionary activity into the academic curriculum. It is not as if sexism and/or sexist understanding had disappeared from the world of learning. (Evans, 1991, p.70)

Maintaining the interdisciplinary study area of women's studies enables a permanent and changing forum for the study of women and women's interventions in and different formations of the disciplines. Evans defines three stages of response to women's studies:

(i)   a remedial activity;
(ii)   favouring integration into mainstream courses;
(iii) advocating separatism.

Some of us are torn between these positions, seeing each as useful in different times and places.

It is important that there should be a feminist or women-centred intervention in the mainstream discipline-oriented curriculum. This enables women to study any subject with the breadth of focus in and integration of theory and practice which are the hallmarks of women's studies. Crucial also is the theoretical, political and practice base of a Women's Studies course or department which provides a home, structure and security to the development of the courses.

The students

If approaches to women's studies differ, so too do the staff and students who come to the course for a variety of reasons. Some believe that because it has a personal focus, women's studies will change their lives. Others choose it because it will help them to tackle sexism. Still others see it as a course among other courses but do not want to become too involved in the feminism. For some students the notion of structured courses and assessment rules is anathema to their hopes of women's studies as a channel and forum for personal reflections and feelings as nascent or developed feminists in the world. How far these students will conform and shape their expressons to the developed norms differs from student to student. Negotiating with them is a challenge but something is certainly lost in the collusion.

Women's studies classrooms are sites of change, not just critique. Marcia Westkott argues:

> By engaging in 'negations that yield transcendence' our women's studies classes are 'educational strategies' for change. First, by articulating that which we oppose and by envisioning alternative futures, we identify the goals and strategies for action; that is we clarify what it is we want to move *away from* as well as what it is we want to move *toward*. Change is thus informed by purpose and goal. (Westkott, 1983, p.213)

The dialogues and developments in the classroom are between the students and staff, the personal and the intellectual, oppression and its critique, and suggestions for change. And then 'we not only produce models for other contexts, but also learn about processes for creating feminist change', it is a 'criticism-vision dialectic' (Westkott, 1983, p.214). Women's studies programmes and departments are crucial centres for developing feminist thought. This is the place in the university where our ideas are taken seriously. Here we can build and test our theories, confident that critiques will be substantive and engaged. This is, by the way, how the disciplines function for scholars in other fields (Bowles and Duelli Klein, 1983, p.14).

Women's studies is an academic discipline which integrates experience and theory, and engages with the personal as well as the analytical. It also has the power to transform other disciplines and affect change in everything from thoeretical base to methodology to pedagogy. In September 1994, in considering the future for the humanities, Middlesex University enabled several of us to get together and discuss 'Is feminism the future for the humanities?' and decide that yes, its effects would enable a diversity of experiences to be recognized. Feminism underpins a transformation of the curriculum, discourse and formation of knowledge, practices and behaviours within higher education and pedagogical/androgogical practices.

Ultimately what women's studies provides for the university and women and men within it is an informed critique of established practices, ways of constructing and working with knowledge, ways of teaching and learning, ways of making sense of the world and enabling others to make sense and articulate that changing sense. It provides a home base for theory and practice and for experimentation which leads to change throughout the university. As with the need for staff development and training in women-only groups, women's studies, which is not exclusively either studied or taught by women, provides a women-focused safe place from which to air critiques and visions and to develop new enabling and empowering practices.

References

Aaron, J and Walby, S (eds) (1991) *Out of the Margins,* Falmer Press, London.

Bowles, G and Duelli Klein, R (1983) *Theories of Women's Studies*, RKP, London.

Evans, M (1991) 'The problem of gender for womens studies', in Aaron and Walby, *op cit.*, p.67.

Hughes, M and Kennedy, M (1985) *New Futures – Changing Women's Education*, RKP, London, p.26.

Humm, M (1991) 'Theory experience in womens studies', in Aaron and Walby, *op cit.*, p.53.

Lerner, G (1980) 'Placing women in history: A theoretical approach', paper delivered at the Organization of American Historians, San Francisco, CA, pp.21–2.

Lorde, A (1984) *Sister Outsider*, Crossing Press, Trumansberg, NY.

Lubelska, C (1991) 'Teaching methods in women's studies: Challenging the mainstream', in Aaron and Walby, *op cit.*, pp.41–9.

Robinson, V (1993) *Introducing Women's Studies*, Macmillan, London.

Warner, M R (1981) quoted in *How to Integrate Women's Studies into the Traditional Curriculum*, a report of the Southwest Institute for Research on Women (SIROW), Women's Studies, University of Arizona.

Watkins, B (1983) 'Feminism: A last chance for the humanities?', in Bowles and Duelli Klein, *op cit.*, p.79.

Westkott, M (1983) 'Women's studies as a strategy for change: between criticism and vision', in Bowles and Duelli Klein, *op cit.*, p.213.

Chapter 5

Women's Studies: Specific Case Studies

Women's Studies short course

In 1985 I reflected on the short Women's Studies course I had been running for several years (Wisker, 1985) and found much support and several correspondents as a result of the publication. It seems there were and are many of us working to develop, put on and maintain the kind of short Women's Studies course which not only raises consciousness but introduces women students to a women-oriented approach to established disciplines, to interdisciplinary approaches to issues in women's lives, and to cooperative, non-authoritarian approaches to study. The course I ran began in the early 1980s, and lasted for just over ten years, running once a year, for a 10-week term, 1–3 pm on Mondays. Because of its home in an academic institution, initially a college of arts and technology, subsequently a university, the course involved safe entry into the demands of study more than consciousness-raising.

The students were diverse, with a wide variety of educational backgrounds. A woman lorry-driver who delivered beer to pubs sat next to a PhD student from Cambridge University who ran the women's graduate society; housewives dropped their children at playcentres, nurseries and schools and came along for the two hours; retired and single women of all ages (the eldest, in her seventies, came because her grandaughter was studying A-levels and she felt she was being left behind!) joined in with some of our own undergraduates who wanted an entrance into the subject and a place to talk from a women's studies set of approaches. A major achievement was to use 'the system' to enable needy students to pay concessionary fees. This was subsidized by Head of Department support and my giving my labour free (it did not appear on my timetable, and anyone who joined in with the teaching also did not have this credited to their timetable). The department did not have to openly account for use of room space. For some of the time two of the team taught the course, for the elements on text and image (Penelope and I) or reflecting on being a woman student (Ros and I). Interestingly, some of the students were escapees from the pressure cooker of Cambridge University, as undergraduates, struggling there, resisting its controls, sometimes having already dropped out.

We looked at women and education, women and history, women and religion, how social policy and practice affects women, women and literature, but around these women and study focuses we discussed subjects and issues which integrated the disciplines, such as women's economic positions, women's work, social policy, education and related issues. It was a unique melting pot because of the diversity of students, some of whom were making a first step into studying. In order to ensure that students did have a non-authoritarian experience, classes were as far as possible based around a negotiated agenda of issues, and constituted some input led by me and others, and group discussion work. This was augmented by students working in ones, twos or threes on their one piece of assessment, a short project. While I should have preferred to further encourage the cooperative approach by suggesting that all work in pairs and threes, for some women with domestic responsibilities, living at a distance, this would not have been feasible and would have excluded them from the pulling together of ideas, reading and experience into an assessable item. I wanted to retain that activity because it seemed to give a valuable opportunity for shaping and articulating ideas, which the student could then see as a product. Because there was no credit for this course, there was no need for summative assessment based on fixed grades and norms. Instead all students were given feedback midway in their work, and formative assessment comments at the end. This also helped to foster an enabling atmosphere because it was ostensibly non-judgemental.

Students chose to work on a number of different topics. These ranged from looking at Virginia Woolf's comments on women's lives and opportunities, relating these to their own experiences of coming into study, and starting to write, through to a paired study of the aims and achievements of a menopause support group. A threesome interviewed women about the operation of the local women's refuge; another pair visited and found out about the women's resource centre. Surveys on women and work, and surveys and interviews on attitudes to returning to study among mature women were other popular studies. Others looked at more conventional issues to do with women, gaining their information from a variety of sources, questionnaires, interviews, reading, the media and their own personal experiences. They were encouraged to integrate reading with experience and to include comments on the personal with the reflective and analytical. They were also encouraged to partially run some of the later sessions disseminating their work, if they so wished. This led to some exciting sessions involving shared experiences and even the modelling of relaxation techniques and assertiveneness practices (a topic).

For some, this was probably a unique experience, and certainly I did not see them again 'in the system' of educational courses. This first step into or back into education led the majority of these women into further study. Most returned to Anglia or joined the Open University. One or two of them have sailed through women's studies, returned to study, the Access course, a degree course, the MA in Women's Studies and are now teaching part-time for us at Anglia (or elsewhere). Others have moved into other courses or have taken jobs.

The course provided a focal point for the further development of Women's Studies courses in the university, and initially helped to ease returners entering the MA into the issues of Women's Studies. Sadly, due to financial constraints, the course folded just as the undergraduate Women's Studies course was being written and validated. Although the time was not being 'counted', the space cost money; trying to put the course on at full fee to cover this excluded the majority of its participants. There is still a need for it, however, in a subsidized version.

Women are often economically straightened. Course fees can exclude them from education. Some participants, for example, in WEA courses, have savings or a reasonable income. Others studying on conventional degree courses have grants, partner's financial support or their own income. But costs effectively exclude a whole swathe of lively, able, interested women who live on income support, raise their children, cannot even afford to work, and certainly could never square the costs of a course fee and travel with their conscience when money is needed for food and heating. Cambridge is hardly an area of extreme poverty, but some students did not have the money for the fees and found the concessions enabled them to 'do something for themselves', as they put it, and 'get started'. The course raised confidence by proving in action that these women could engage with issues in an analytical as well as a personal way, and it provided a supportive environment and group which could never be costed. I miss it.

Issues of the climate and practices of Women's Studies

However, the fact that my own labour and that of contributing colleagues was never properly costed raises all sorts of issues for Women's Studies generally. So often Women's Studies courses actually operate on the generosity and goodwill of the women staff involved who would rather use the opportunity to make the kinds of interventions that a Women's Studies course enables, without recognition in terms of hours and money, than not be involved. No doubt the university benefits from this. As the courses become an increasing part of the advertised repertoire of the university, they attract funding and produce the usual proliferation of paperwork and committee meetings. So the issue of donating one's time, were it one's own to donate (and many of us have line managers who would not smile on this) becomes an awkward one. It seems to emphasize the marginality of the subject, as well as, yet again, to reinforce the economic subordination of women, in which we are seen here to actively collude. This debate has raged furiously around the Anglia MA in Women's Studies which itself started out based very much on fringe activites and goodwill, actually on determination to develop it and make it work, but it has run into administrative, financial and perhaps personal space trouble over the years. This is partly to do with our decision to team-teach when funding only caters for one teacher at a time.

Oddly enough, the most recent addition to the small group of women's studies courses at Anglia, the full-time undergraduate course, has not produced these same tensions. As an undergraduate course it has been firmly rooted in the systems and administrative practices from the start, so it has to conform.

MA in Women's Studies

The genesis of the MA in Women's Studies is an example of cooperative planning. As articulate academic women we came together to survey our positions and the provision of women-oriented courses and then to move into the development of women's studies as an MA. Initially we met to consider our marginalization and to carry out a survey of the existence or non-existence of women-centred topics and courses in the curriculum as a whole, and to what extent the college actually recognized the needs of its own women students in its curriculum offer and facilities. From a discussion group we grew into something of a pressure group. It became obvious that developing a specific course would help to focus the interest we had in feminist theory and pedagogy in relation to our discipline areas. Planning was a growing, sharing and often sparring experience much helped by long discussions in the evenings and an away-day with friends and advisers from other insitutions who had variously experienced similar concerns and achievements.

In order to challenge the traditional hierarchical power relations of the structure of courses and their management within the university, we decided that there would be a triumvirate (but that is the wrong word!) taking it in turns to manage the two years and the course committee. This caused amusing internal confusion. No one was quite sure to whom to address the memos from other departments. It did mean that we all felt we owned decisions. It was a shared responsibility to write parts of course documents, and contribute to the growth and development of the course through various validations, reviews and revalidations. In six years this energy has not dissipated, aided by the shared structure. There is a clear vision underlying the MA in Women's Studies, and one we developed and share – and share, we hope, with our students. It depends on and emphasizes the importance of interdisciplinary study, a focus on representations of, cultural constructions of and constraints upon women. Feminist critical theories and practices lend cohesion to our approaches. Team-teaching, group work, negotiated essays and dissertations, and the integration of the personal with the academic represent teaching/learning pedagogical/andragogical approaches aimed at empowering the students.

However, the downside of our management structures and team-teaching practices are that our Women's Studies MA has no home base and no full-time members of staff. It is assisted by a half-time secretary, and by the commitment of the diverse women who teach on aspects of the MA and share responsibilities. When political power means identifying individuals and articulating a specific image, Women's Studies finds it hard to hold on to its own, and it is relatively recently that most of us have had the hours we teach on the MA 'counted' against our overall hours and actually accounted for by transfer of monies into our home departments. For some the stress of this and the lack of recognition, together with the tension of demands from the home department, have meant involvement has had to be in smaller measure than they would ideologically like. For others it respresents a commitment to which 'counting hours' is unrelated to Women's Studies commitment, often operates on the generosity of the staff, and the import-ance that the ideas and practices of Women's Studies have for all concerned. If the subject is to be properly resourced we need to redress this imbalance.

The MA Women's Studies provides an interesting andragogical model. We have developed an interdisciplinary approach largely by ensuring that each session is team-taught by staff with different discipline specialisms and a growing specialism in Women's Studies itself. The curriculum itself is interdisciplinary and ranged around a number of themes to do with recognizing oneself as a woman, representation, mothering, childhood, adolescence, becoming female, and issues to do with being a woman in the world. The curriculum does not take enough notice of lesbian experience, Black and Asian experience, or the experience of women with disabilities. We are constantly scrutinizing our examples, focus and practices in order to enable the curriculum and practices to relate more fully to the diversity of women's experience in the world. This is helped by our own work in these areas, our own development and increasing confidence and repertoire. It has been important to ensure there is a specific session, for example, on issues in Black and Asian women's writing, and that Black and Asian women's writing and experiences consequently appear as examples throughout.

Students experience a diversity of teaching styles and have the opportunity to reflect on and evaluate them. Evaluation and log comments are noted in a special 'green book'. We know that some of us tend to teach more from our own discipline base while others now feel much more integrated with their team-teaching partner's approaches. They could reverse the respons-ibility for discipline areas easily, because they have become seamless/interdisciplinary.

Sessions in which Penelope (the Art historian) and I (women's literature) are involved tend to be composed of several parts. Issues are raised with initial reading and a short introductory video. This is followed by group work to discuss these issues, encouraging the integration of personal and analytical responses, then more formal input pulling together ideas, issues and adding information and arguments. There is often a student presentation based on the topic and we encourage students to present interactively, involving other students. More input and more group discussion and group work follow, for example, on stimulus questions or comparing texts and images. In most of our sessions we intermix video, slides, handouts, text, group discussion and tutor talk, trying both to highlight issues and stances taken by various feminist theorists and practitioners, and asking students to engage with these and test them out against their own personal, shared and contextualized experiences. The classroom becomes an experiential place where issues are aired, reflection is encouraged and a shared set of responses are built up. This contributes to a learning cycle for students who test new theories and discourse against experience, reflect and move on.

Some assessment issues emerging from the MA in Women's Studies help focus on the integration of analysis and the experiential/personal, provide examples of the relationship between theory and practice and raise questions about authority. They query acceptable practices and expressions, testing the theories and commitments upon which Women's Studies are based. They have also, incidentally, provided some marvellous models of innovative practice which have fed usefully into our practices, the BA Women's Studies and our home base disciplines. What has worked for me with Women's Studies students on the MA I have translated, as far as the system will allow, into practices within my English teaching.

Student body

Much of the innovative development has been spurred on by the diverse students who join the MA group. The recruitment policy recognizes and accredits prior learning, including experiential learning. Many who join us come from work, domestic responsibilities and a variety of learning backgrounds. The police force paid for one student, who gained an Equal Opportunities award from the force during her time with us. She wrote her dissertation on representations of, and attitudes towards, women in the police force. Others pay for themselves. Hardship has been an issue for the younger students who take poorly paid jobs to enable them to study and in some cases have had to intermit.

Some of our students come from backgrounds of practice rather than theory. One student who certainly tested our assessment beliefs and strategies was a practising local artist dealing in photographic work and installations. For her first piece of work she reflected on the forms her and other women's shadows cast, producing cut-outs of these. The piece was about the representation of ourselves. She built up some of what she wanted to say by bringing the pieces in and sharing them, asking us to comment. There was no analytical or contextual write-up accompanying the work. This caused immense problems. We were positioned as stuffy academics in a course which presented itself as *avant garde* and enabling. But perhaps that was not the case. A viva produced analytical and critical responses which proved feminist theories and practices informed the artwork. These could be articulated and communicated. From discussion, taped for the record and the external examiner, emerged case history. We could see more now why analysis, reflection, articulation and communication were necessary parts of a submitted piece of work. Creative work in itself might be response and critique. When submitted for the MA assessment it needed to be shared with others. Encouraging the development of a critical discourse helped articulate and share the work's critique. This was enabling all round.

The second piece of work was similarly experiential and creative but, accompanied by analytical explanation, it engaged with theory in practice in its own form. It was an apron produced for the student/artist by her mother. She worked with it to show her engagement with issues and explorations around motherhood, relations, mother as artist/artist as mother, women's communication and creativity. This grew out of personal reflection integrated with, and stimulated by, reading and thinking about the work of Hélène Cixous and Julia Kristeva, two French feminist theorists. The response to these theorists and the apron was written around the stitching. The whole was shared with the rest of the group who produced their own responses, building a cooperative group set of responses. It was accompanied by an analytical explanation of how the piece united and articulated theory, experience and the personal in practice. Staff development sessions and validations which debate assessment are likely to hear about the Women's Studies apron from me. It always provokes extreme responses!

Our working together to understand and assess this piece of work has helped change practice elsewhere. It has been much easier for us to recognize what sort of shape an analytical but personal and reflective piece on issues to do with women in history, a portfolio or log response to literature and culture, or a sociological set of concerns might consist of, and how they might also be expressed in our home base disciplines.

Women's Studies has transformed our practices in all spheres. The students have excitingly put into concrete form and articulated the responses enabled by our shared study group experiences. We have all benefited. Students in other discipline areas also now produce reflective and creative work accompanied by analytical response exploring and making conscious contributory debate and processes.

Undergraduate Women's Studies course: BA half field in Women's Studies

The undergraduate Women's Studies course at Anglia provides a paradigm for Women's Studies courses at this level. It has equal recognition with other programmes of study, has been through the same validation and recent revalidation procedures, been subject to the same scrutiny, forced to express itself on paper in the same kind of way addressing issues of student experience, appropriateness of teaching, learning and assessment modes. It is still only a half field at Anglia, however, combined with another subject area for the students. This is both a marvellous opportunity to take a Women's Studies approach into their other subjects and problematic if it increases the fragmentation some students feel when involved in an inter-disciplinary course. The main driving force and theoretical underpinning relates to issues and practices around women's experience and feminist theory and perspectives. It is also interdisciplinary. Students come to us mostly straight from school or after a short break, although there are several ex-Access students and other mature returners. Interdisciplinary study initially somewhat confuses students trained in a more conventional system, who need to develop the practices and carve their own way. While this is enabling, it can also be rather daunting, so much time is spent in initial modules setting out what interdisciplinary Women's Studies is, what kinds of discourse it uses and how to integrate and articulate the personal and the academic.

In our teaching/learning strategies we encourage students to explore their own personal experiences and to integrate these with and inform them by theory and debate deriving fom Women's Studies and feminist critical practices. Students are encouraged to move beyond merely talking about motherhood, growing up, pornography, women and wage earning, medicine and women, for example, from their own experience, reading or media experiences and to scrutinize these experiences and reflections using techniques and discourses offered by feminist critical practices. They are encouraged to build up ideas through exploratory talk in group work, and to be involved in group-based projects and presentations, as well as to be involved as small groups in the processing, analysis and presentation of their understanding of theoretical pieces. These students are not just left with experience; they are enabled to articulate analytically and theoretically within a framework, so that a sharp but flexible set of critical perspectives operate in their work. It is essential that they do not just view work on different modules as thematic, but recognize the feminist critical approaches they can take. Both group and individual work encourage this, as do using buzz groups, role play, rounds and andragogical practices involving everyone in articulating, trying out their thoughts and ideas, and sharing and building on them (see Chapter 6).

In one first year, first semester module which I team-teach with a colleague, we ensure that students develop the skills they need to make presentations, which form the main assessment mode for the module. Students discuss group work and group dynamics, and then form groups to work on themes. They are shown and try out models of presentation formats, introduced to the video technician who can help them make videoclips, enabled to practise on the overhead projector (OHP) and given the opportunity to share group ideas with the rest of the class, centre stage, well before they formally present. To date, the resulting group presentations have been stunning. Students put up posters, bring in artefacts, make displays, and present, each member joining in, using OHPs, videos, texts, images, handouts or slides, as appropriate. They take the rest of the group through an organized, analytical and experientially based presentation about, for example, the different definitions and arguments on pornography; the forms and underlying beliefs of romantic fiction and the romance industry; women and body image; the representation and construction of versions of women at different stages in their lives. We team-assess the presentations and the students peer- and self-evaluate using evaluation sheets. Each teacher then separately produces marks. We read through the evaluations and use them to help us decide on a joint mark and feedback.

Bari Watkins (1983, p.86) sees feminist scholars like ourselves on the BA and MA in Women's Studies as outsiders who have challenged and changed the university, to everyone's benefit:

> In the past decade, therefore, feminist scholars have mounted an open instit-utional challenge to ordinary life within the university, demanding changes making it a better place for everyone. They see undergraduate education as a central part of their duties, share research efforts and results, resist authorit-arianism in their own classrooms and programs, and generally try to resist the bureacratization of intellectual life. Because they are outsiders, they feel strongly that the university should be open to a diversity of personal styles and priorities.

Many of us would argue with the definition of 'outsiders'. With increased student numbers, increasing bureaucratization and increasingly pressing time demands, it is essential to keep the Women's Studies space, the women's forums, the women-only development groups so that we can continue to build on and share theories, practices and experiences. However, we also need to ensure that these spread to our other work within the university. It is increasingly frustrating to find that innovations based on a Women's Studies cooperative, flexible model are ground down and out of the curricula of our home base subjects as larger numbers make more responsive assessment practices harder to insist upon and accomplish, and as paperwork demands tend to separate us further from individual students.

We need to work towards enabling the developed, self-managed, student-led groups to provide some support and opportunity to try out ideas and share experiences, when we can no longer be as involved in those activities ourselves (Wisker *et al.*, 1995). Empowerment and cooperation are achievable outcomes. It is essential that there be a space for Women's Studies as a discipline in itself. Here academic staff and students engage with ideas and practices, and move towards change and vision.

References

Watkins, B (1983) 'Feminism: A last chance for the humanities?' in *Theories of Women's Studies*, G Bowles and R Duelli Klein (eds), RKP, London.

Wisker, G (1985) 'From kitchen to classroom', *AUT Women* (Association of University Teachers), 1, 3, 1.

Wisker, G, Gibbs, G and Bochner, D (1995) *Supporting More Students*, Oxford Brookes University, Oxford.

SECTION B:
What's So Special About Women in Higher Education?

Chapter 6

Pyramids and Glass Ceilings: Women's Positions in Higher Education and the Management House

Figures from the Association of University Teachers (AUT, 1993) assert that less than one in 20 of the UK's top academics are women. Even though women make up nearly half the student population and over one-fifth of the total academic workforce, only 4% of them are promoted to the rank of professor, a slight increase in 1991 figures (3%), but once professors, women are paid on average £1500 less than their male peers. However, the current campaigns waged by the AUT and other professional associations for women in higher education have tended to focus on white, middle-class women. (Henry, 1994, p.49)

The leadership and management structure of higher education is still dominated by men despite the inspiring numbers of women higher education vice-chancellors and other leaders (six VCs in all).

Recent figures published by the *Times Higher* (Ince *et al.*, 1996) focus sharply on the dearth of women academic leaders in higher education. The statistics show that:

- Only 7.3% of professors are women, although women make up 30% of academics.
- New universities top the league-tables for women professors.
- One university (UMIST) has no women professors.
- In engineering and technology the proportion of women professors is under 1%.
- There are no women professors in either agriculture or science.

The article further emphasizes the skewed and prejudiced nature of recognized grounds for promotion, and promotion procedures. Coupled with conservative practices, these effectively exclude able women, even those who have achieved high status in their representation on external bodies, Royal societies and commissions, and internationally in terms of their reputations.

Table 6.1 *Proportion of female professors by subject*

Medicine and dentistry	5.9%
Subjects allied to medicine	14.0%
Biological sciences	7.7%
Veterinary science	0.0%
Agriculture and related subjects	0.0%
Physical sciences	1.6%
Mathematical sciences	4.9%
Engineering and technology	0.9%
Architecture, building and planning	5.4%
Social, economic and political studies	11.9%
Law	9.8%
Business and administrative studies	5.9%
Librarianship and information studies	29.4%
Language studies	12.5%
Humanities	8.7%
Creative arts and design	13.8%
Education	16.1%

Source: Ince *et al.* (1996) 'Chipping away at the glass ceiling', *Times Higher*, July 26, p.17

According to figures published in 1993, the proportion of women in the new universities and HE colleges in relation to grades in academic and management positions is comparable to the figures for the old (UFC) universities. Women in the new universities and HE colleges are clustered in the lecturer and senior lecturer grades, but there are only two women principals/directors in each sector. On management scales there are 99 women in the new universities and 60 in other HE colleges, 541 women in the new universities and 120 on principal lecturer scales in HE. Comparable figures for men are 11 new university principals/directors, 14 in HE colleges, 781 men in new university management, 371 in HE, 2752 male principal lecturers in the new universities and 501 in HE.

At the lecturer point in the scale there are almost identical numbers of male and female staff, but the pyramid structure is marked as we consider principal lecturers, readers and senior university staff. (Figures for APT and C 'support' staff from the DfEE confirm this.) Some women are attaining posts in senior management, but they are still too few and as Millsom Henry (1994) points out, those women who do succeed are white and middle-class. It is far too early, therefore, to become complacent about women's success in higher education. Perhaps the women who are rewarded with promotion are those closest in background, origins and style to successful men. Some others, though, are models of the kind of entrepreneurial cooperative flexibility which women-oriented management research has come to associate with successful high-flying women.

Table 6.2 *Full-time lecturers in new universities and higher education colleges,*
31 March 1993

	Men		Women		Total	
	New universities	*HE*	*New universities*	*HE*	*New universities*	*HE*
Principals	11	14	2	2	13	16
Management scales	781	371	99	60	880	431
Principal lecturers	2,752	501	541	120	3,293	621
Senior lecturers	6,514	2,289	2,289	1,054	8,803	3,343
Lecturer scales	1,485	1,088	954	657	2,439	1,745
Other scales	136	188	108	109	244	297
Total	*11,679*	*4,451*	*3,993*	*2,002*	*15,672*	*6,453*

There is an urgent need to develop and maintain positive action, embed good practice, produce guidelines, and work to promote not only women but the diversity of women and the working styles of women. These are often flexible, cooperative, responsive and generally more suited to the demands of rapid changes in higher education.

Much of the work which has been done to define the ways in which women can carry out professional and self-development which fits them for success in higher education focuses on the individual alone. A familiar criticism is that while a few women make it to the top or thereabouts, they provide neither viable role models nor do they give other women a helping hand upwards, in their own way. Communicating and sharing information about women's successes and ways in which we might all benefit and change higher education is important. We need to recognize that cooperative working practices and shared models are the products of networking across and despite hierarchies.

Crucial to women's empowerment in higher education is women-only training. This allows women to focus on specific needs and development strategies. The timing, content and tone of conventional management training programmes tends to be aimed more obviously at men. Men are more likely to attend because of current positions. Women often report feeling silenced in groups dominated by men. Women's training, however, can be limiting if it is only geared to their current positions.

> In terms of training and development women often appear to be at a disadvantage. They tend to receive less training than men of comparable ability and in general their training tends to be narrower and more job specific. This may be due, in part, to initial job choice. (MSC, 1980)

Running her finger down the list of course members on a (mixed gender) first-line management course, a manager of my acquaintance remarked that she could not see why *those* women were attending since they did not have appropriate responsibilities. Maybe not. Perhaps they would like them, though, and one way to start reflecting on and developing the appropriate skills is through training. As the successful, enabling strategies of women's studies classrooms flow into our practices in other discipline areas, so too do practices developed in women-only staff development sessions flow into our other sessions. With them flow the women, empowered by beginning their training in the nurturing, initially safely challenging environment of women-only sessions.

> Women's development training aims to help all women gain an opportunity to win or succeed at what they want in life. It is not about taking a group of women who have a 'problem' and patronizingly giving them a women's development course to make them feel better. (Willis and Daisley, 1992, p.3)

Much training or staff development writing focuses on the individual and advises 'analysing personal and professional goals, competencies and potential' (Somers Hill and Cragland, 1995). Much of my own work in staff and educational development has this focus, but many of the strengths of women's training and development practices derive from strategies involving sharing and cooperation not only in the sessions themselves, but outside, in our working practices. Some of the most powerful and useful sessions with which I have been involved have been with groups of women sharing experiences, building confidence and developing strategies. Other empowering practices include mentoring schemes (Fullerton, 1996). These are growing in number and involve men and women in more senior positions mentoring younger or less senior colleagues. Mentors negotiate and discuss job opportunities, skills audits and future potential, offer some job shadowing and a model even if it is not one which totally accords with the mentee's own self-image. At Anglia we are developing a mentoring scheme for women to work with senior colleagues.

Considering the success rate of women who seek and achieve top jobs does not help to redress the imbalances in lower-paid scales nor necessarily encourage a change in the philosophy, practices and culture of the university. Work carried out on the status and success rates of Black and Asian women academics shows an even greater imbalance in the power structure. There is evidence that Black women staff, often used to show how anti-racist a university is, are actually on sensitive ground in terms of their contracts or positions. One staff member canvassed for her experiences notes:

> As a black woman, nothing surprises me any more. I am on a temporary, part-time contract in a poly with a clearly stated equal opportunities policy... we attract a lot of black students, and I am used as a selling point. But if a fall in recruitment threatens, I am told by my head of department, who is a white woman, that my contract might not be renewed. (Morley, 1993, p.16)

Another says:

> The 'glass ceiling' debate... essentially addresses the problems of the already privileged. (Weston, 1993)

Ethnicity must not be overlooked as we strive to empower all women in higher education. Women-only management training helps women to focus together on concerns they have with their positions in the universities, and with organizational cultures which often seem exclusive, valuing skills and behaviours traditionally more often seen in men than women. Together, women can build confidence in their abilities, work towards further professional roles and develop the kind of networking and supportive relationships which could underpin organizational culture change. Successful women need to change the perception of 'norms' and articulate and value different ways of managing jobs and interactions. This recognition of difference includes cultural and sexual difference and should both integrate with and fuel further equal opportunities work. Initiatives such as 'Opportunity 2000' which aim to audit and improve women's positions and experiences and opportunities within universities can build upon the networks established through management training/staff development.

Equal opportunities in the management house

In 1990 I was asked by the Equal Opportunities Committee at Anglia to put on a series of staff development workshops for women on the theme of women and management. Pehaps it was the very fact of the existence of the committee, along with specific questions asked about the proportion of women in key roles, on key committees, at accreditation, that sparked off the request. Perhaps it was time that an institution, new to merger, felt settled enough in its own structures to scrutinize who took part in those structures, at what levels, and to ask questions about women in management roles. I suspect it was a combination of all these that set the series going. There are some general issues which have been features of the series and which could be of interest to those intending to run women-only educational management and development sessions.

Women as Managers, Staff Development Series: Distribution

Distribution of information about the series of workshops was carried out through heads of department and heads of schools. At first there seemed to be a strange selection process going on for the receipt of fliers. Aimed initially at a management-related training level, the workshops deliberately invited applications from all women, administrative and teaching staff, on the assumption that we all might aspire to or develop our roles in the direction of leadership and management, although none of us was yet a senior manager. Some heads targeted a couple of colleagues, others all the women. For the second workshop they were asked to target all women staff, although, in the event this still left many out. As the series continued, networks grew up to pass on information, and women came from the far-flung mid-West and South Essex hospitals, even to distant sessions. (Anglia University has campuses in Essex and at Cambridge.) Distribution, several years on, is to all women in the university on all sites, including franchises and hospital sites. The intention is that they themselves choose whether this stage of development activity will be useful.

The series designed contains a variety of workshops. Some are appropriate for every woman in the university, others are more obviously directed at women already in leadership and management roles. They include:

- introduction to management;
- women managing meetings;
- women managing time;
- women managing stress;
- women and assertiveness;
- leadership issues and practices;
- supervision;
- teamwork;
- making the most of those you work with;
- giving bad news;
- dealing with difficult clients;
- women chairing meetings;
- conflict resolution; and
- appraisal.

After the first couple of workshops, one on one campus, the second on the other campus 50-odd miles away, it was recommended that each should be run twice. Many women staff are not at the levels which afford them their own cars, nor are they 'masters' of their own time, so they cannot take additional time travelling.

Numbers at the meetings have ranged between 16 and 32, some women attending all sessions and others selecting those that appealed to them. Women attending come from all levels of staff, too, including secretarial staff, finance clerks, middle managers in the registry, lecturers, senior and principal lecturers and several heads of department, or the equivalent. From general discussions, several issues emerged about their feelings and positions.

Reasons for coming

In discussion and evaluations of the workshops, women have reported that a series of women-only sessions felt like a supportive endeavour. It seemed possible to speak although silence for some might have been their normal response in meetings and workshops. Some came for the solidarity, meeting with and sharing with women in similar roles across different hierarchical levels, administrative and teaching staff, across campuses. Some emphasized that they wanted to 'do something for themselves' for a change. Others acknowledged a sense of guilt. Perhaps they should be still working (this training was not seen as working), doing something for someone else, for the system, rather than for themselves. Some said that although they knew they did not have the time, they still needed to come and think for a change about their own development. Holding sessions on Wednesday and Friday afternoons helped relieve guilt.

Some responses and experiences

Not everything went perfectly and events varied in quality because of the combination of presenters (this was and is usually me, but I daresay I vary in quality too), group, circumstances, timing and the usual ingredients. But the overwhelming evaluation responses have been very positive. Formal and informal networking has been a major result. We now all have contacts in key places: finance, registry, secretarial, the library, teaching staff in other subject areas at our own level and middle managers we can contact for support and information. Some alternative organizational behaviours have resulted, as have cooperative course development and other initiatives.

Networking relieves stress, reassuring you there are others suffering and coping, managing with the changes in HE, doing a good job and sharing tips on how to do it. Networking actually contributes to visible developments, course team unity, cross-site activities and agreements. Men network too, but differently, and many men in HE work together as a function of their regular high-level meetings.

Format and structure of sessions

Room layout and the kinds of activities in sessions help or hinder involvement in the same way as they do in teaching sessions (see Chapter 3 on women-centred teaching strategies). We usually use a horseshoe style of room layout and break into small groups for discussion, pairs and task-oriented group work. We use brainstorming, negative brainstorming and mind-mapping to help the emotional and creative opening up of thoughts and attitudes, and pairs, triads or syndicate groups for longer tasks such as modelling teambuilding activities or problem-solving. These strategies and the climate for learning derive both from women's studies classroom practice and adult learning. They also derive from Schön's (1990) work on the reflective practitioner because of their integration of experience and reflection. Brookfield defines such a climate of learning as one in which adults can feel free to challenge one another and can feel comfortable with being challenged... the honest expression of differences in an atmosphere where challenge and dissension are accepted as part of the educational process (Brookfield, 1986, p.13)

Liz Stanley (1990) and Patti Lather's (1991) descriptions of feminist praxis coincide with Brookfield's own in relation to working with adult learners. With women-only staff development, it is important to be involved in exploration, discussion, action, reflection and the movement towards new thoughts and practices, through connection with experience and through modelling.

> The notion of praxis as alternating and continuous engagements by teachers and learners in exploration, action, and reflection is central to adult learning. It means that explorations of new ideas, skills, or bodies of knowledge do not take place in a vacuum but are set within the context of learner's past, current and future experiences. (Brookfield, 1986, p.15)

Kolb's (1984) learning cycle lies at the heart of the processes used. This involves relating experience and knowledge to the learning process and the problems posed, experimenting, reflecting and moving on to further experience and reflection (see Figure 6.1).

On the staff development programmes I provide stimulus questions, encourage discussion and reflection on experience and use creative and experiential processes involving metaphors and comparisons. I try to keep a balance between letting exciting experiential activities and discussions take off, and ensuring that there are focal points, approaches to answers to questions, and some action planning for change or consolidation of existing practice. Women often report that these sessions give them confidence, that they reassure them their practices are working, that they can see, through trying out interactions and activities, how they might use them. These are similar responses to those noted by others involved both in adult learning and in women-oriented educational management training (eg Willis and Daisley, 1992; Gold, 1993).

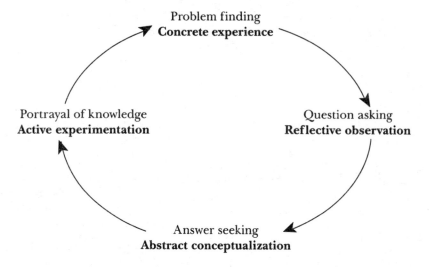

Figure 6.1 *Kolb cycle of experiential learning*

Progress of women-only staff development and training

Since those early days there have been a number of developments. A new woman staff developer, Janet, now runs a series of workshops aimed specifically at support staff (mainly women). I have run a series of six first-line management training sesssions, for men and women, and the Women as Managers series has continued, operating at both levels. It has also been possible to liaise with women elsewhere involved in women's training. Janet has been trained to run the women-only 'springboard' sessions, while I have been in touch and worked with women managers in the Higher Education, Research and Development Staff of Australasia (HERDSA) and women at Sydney University in 1994 and 1996 respectively with Women as Managers issues, followed by two-day workshops in 1996 and (forthcoming) 1997.

Women as Managers sessions – defining problems

One focal point in our Women as Managers sessions has been experience and reflection on the different behaviours of men and women in educational management roles. We work on ways to clarify, develop and put in practice positive women-oriented strategies. Looking at male organizational behaviours which exclude women, Di Parkin (1993) notes that there are several negative, exclusive, gender-based forms.

Barrack Yard/Authoritarian Culture: A bullying, hostile culture which undermines the value of women's nurturing pastoral work and secretarial support and validates conflict and hostility.

The Locker Room: Male bonding excludes women and sexual harassment can follow.

The Gender-Blind: Men ignore gender differences and refuse to recognize women's domestic responsibilities in relation to work (they have wives – women do not).

The Feminist Pretender: Espousing the values of feminism and ostensibly supportive of women's culture and practices, this kind of male can suddenly switch tack and turn into the bully with his women colleagues, while sounding a convincing feminist to the students. He also deteriorates into someone cynically critical of 'political correctness' and sees it as merely temporary.

The Smart Macho: Higher education currently emphasizes performance targets, measurable outcomes from Investors in People and league table points for teaching and research. This business-oriented cultural product often excludes and ignores women's valuing of diversity, pastoral care, and refusal of competitive spirit.

The Gentleman's Club: Old fashioned and paternalistic. Men in this culture support women if they do not criticize or change things and remain in traditional areas of women's work, not aspiring to high professional roles.

(Adapted and developed from Di Parkin's examples.)

Women clearly need to be able to spot such destructive strategies, develop explicit alternatives and insist on their validity. Behavioural change is supported by confidence and networking. Less isolation, shared knowledge and interests and a sense of solidarity all contribute to self-worth and motivation and can encourage organizational change.

Women in the management house

One early workshop on women and management roles highlighted the range of issues, concerns and developments which have been a feature of the series. As a training experience and catalyst, this particular workshop epitomizes the kind of dynamic permeating the whole series.

One powerful activity was the use of synectics or metaphors to open up feelings and experiences. This helped us define how we might relate to the established structures and practices of university management. 'Women in the management house' was an exercise arising from reflections and discussions about women working in organizations, and our feelings about organizational roles and positions. My own example, which initiated the exercise, was an organization to which I was seconded. I related this experience to the feelings that I and other women colleagues have shared about the physical, emotional and hierarchical structures of higher education management. There is something homely and domesticated about the idea of a house which somewhat contrasts with the power and communication structures we found in largely male-dominated universities. We used synectics – creative metaphors that enable the exploration of ideas and help solve problems through the recognition of parallels and visualization. This synectics exercise used the energies, experiences and imaginations of the whole group. It proved creative, revelatory and productive.

I drew a picture of a terraced house and together we explained the levels, functions and assumptions about it. The different floors and communication channels within the house reflected the different work roles and positions of those within it, the men and the women who worked there. On top were the researchers, beavering away in the attic, surrounded by paper, out of touch with whoever came in and out of the building. On the next level were the managers, not in the attic, but removed from the daily goings on, only two staircases away from the secretaries and the researchers who worked for them, bypassed by any lift which could go straight up to the top, ignoring the managers and leaving them free to work in their corridors of power. On the next floor were the teaching rooms with students working with lecturers, some managers and some researchers. On the ground floor by the entrance were the secretaries ready to deal with anyone entering the building. They were the first port of call, aware of all going on and asked to do most of it. If there was a basement it would probably contain a few other managers who wished to escape the hurly-burly and felt safe there, or it might be more productive as an escape place for making toast and tea.

The shape of the house was hierarchical, the networks of communication set up within it were and would be top–down, with information and jobs then going back upwards. The whole management floor could continue undisturbed. Having decided that we all had a shared understanding of the hierarchical positioning in this old terraced house, I then invited everyone to think about it and to add graffiti to the poster, which they did. The graffiti were added increasingly quickly as we considered what we wanted to contribute and reflected on the contributions of others. Responses varied from those condemning the current structure and reactions, to those suggesting alternatives, from comments of personal isolation and alienation to those about overwork and too much one-way communication. They revealed a great deal about the way we, as women, felt we worked and were treated in largely male-defined management structures. Some of the responses were:

- We all have to maintain the fabric.
- I am building a bungalow next door (I don't think this is the right structure for my style of working). It is a masculine hierarchy house. They do the timetabling. The senior management team floor is the most peaceful.
- Fire doors on the senior management floor are shut – people are kept out – importance of personal space and time. Who built the stairs?
- The women are networking up and down the stairs and the men have to communicate hierarchically.
- I am a bee building a cell. The woman runs up and down the stairs pollinating (causing action). I should like to do a bit of stinging.
- Is there a bolt hole? Is it in the garden? Out of the structure, out back?
- Where are the ladies' loos?
- I am next door and told to build another structure, like this one, but I don't have enough materials to do it. I want to build another structure and I have encouragement.
- Is part of bowing to this structure our own fault?

These responses testified to our rejection of the current structure but recognition that we collude in its perpetuation. Some questions were whether, if we could build another structure, it would be that different, what our roles would be and whether we would get the backing for this alternative management structure.

Working on our responses to the poster of the management house enabled us to articulate frustrations and annoyances at the constriction we felt we were being trained to work within in the current male-dominated management structures. It helped us to air some ideas we had about the specific nature of our different working patterns and ideas. We wanted the support and strength to continue to develop differently, successfully. We went on to define what we felt these differences might be, with the aid of brainstorming, and collected ideas visually. We identified our strengths as women and managers, and also our fears and weaknesses.

We agreed we did not want to be vindictive, dictatorial, intimidating, condescending, incompetent, to sit on a fence, to divide and rule, to avoid taking responsibility, to not delegate, to take credit where it was not due, to operate by paperwork alone or to devalue others' skills. We had experienced too many of these negative characteristics of management in relation to gender already, but we were often dangerously close to mimicking them ourselves. On the more positive side, we identified ways in which we wanted to behave as managers and developed a very thorough list of 'female' traits of negotiation and cooperation.

We want to be considerate, cooperative, valuing, able to listen, able to delegate, able to make decisions, consult, prioritize, organize, manage our time and that of others, to be communicative and supportive, open in our dealing, flexible, creative. With these positive goals in mind we came up with some general tenets. We wanted to stick by what we believed in, put forward the importance of our skills, highlight and close the gap between our skills and the kinds of roles in which we found ourselves in the current masculine dominated hierarchical structures in higher education.

One exercise involved describing a woman manager who was behaving exactly as a male manager might, and deciding which of her characteristics and behaviours we might adopt. We moved beyond rhetoric, thinking carefully how and how far we could operate alternative communication channels, networks, different relationships of power which yet ensured that as managers we rightfully took responsibility. We collated models and guidelines. Recognizing the mismatch between our needs and skills and current hierarchical structures, we decided to define valuable alternative, women-centred styles. Considering how as women we could change working practices and develop different, less hierarchical behavioural models was refreshing and thought-provoking without being either unduly idealistic or carping and pessimistic.

Considering the training of women in management roles always leaves some sense of irritation. However, because so few of us get the chance to play these roles, 'employers frequently assume women to want little more than a routine job to perform, but do not assume the same about men' (Collinson, 1987). In his survey of insurance companies and banks, Collinson discovered discrimination in four different British banks. He predicted that women would only secure career progress by ensuring that they gained management training places. This was seen as something of a contradiction for those employers who deliberately employed women in the expectation that they would want to stay at the level at which they were employed and not train and rise within the organization. Vaughan and Lasky (1991) use human capital theory to suggest that it is a waste of resources keeping women down and away from management positions if they are able to perform them. Training opportunities, sex role conditioning, disadvantaging because of career breaks and lower expectations by women employers all contribute to a low participation of women in leadership and management positions. Promotion is a gender-related move:

> An individual's placement within the organization has been shown to influence promotion outcomes as well as the route of promotion of women related to men. Women tend to be clustered in entry-level positions in higher education organizations; thus, their placement may influence their ability to achieve outcomes to promotion. At the same time, men are predominant at high levels. Prior location may serve men as a resource, whereas it acts as a vulnerability for women. (Johnson, 1992)

Policies actively played out would negate the discriminatory practices undermining women's opportunities for management roles. We decided in the workshops that we needed to tackle those organizational myths that (a) good women do not apply for positions of power, and (b) women in positions of power are frightening, negative models. In so doing we worked on our sense of not fitting in with established management cultures and models, our need to overcome negative versions of women in power. We developed positive models, guidelines and practices.

Universities need to move to a position where they afford equal management opportunities to qualified and able women as to equally qualified and able men. There is a large gap between the awareness of discrimination, the resultant policy changes and the actual action or practice changes. Lip service is paid to equality issues. However, it is our role as women aiming at leadership and management positions to ensure that we have a developed idea of the range of roles we can play. These neither have to be an exact copy of the male managers we see around us, nor Margaret Thatcher!

References

Atchison, H (1993) 'Women and management training in the 1990s', in *Women in Education Management,* J Ouston (ed.), Longman, Harlow.

Brookfield, S D (1986) *Understanding and Facilitating Adult Learning,* Open University Press, Milton Keynes.

Collinson, David (1987) 'A question of equal opportunities – a survey of staff in a large insurance company', *Personnel Review,* 16, 1.

Gold, A (1993) 'Women-friendly management', in *Women in Education Management,* J Ouston (ed.), Longman, Harlow.

Fullerton, H (ed.) (1996) *Mentoring,* Staff and Educational Development Association, Birmingham.

Henry, Millsom (1994) 'Black women in higher education', in *Changing the Subject,* S Davies, C Lubelska and J Quinn (eds), Taylor & Francis, London, p.49.

Ince, M, Griffiths, S and Morriss-Kay, J (1996) 'Chipping away at the glass ceiling', *Times Higher,* July 26, p.17.

Johnson, L K (1992) 'Administrative promotion: The power of gender', *Journal of Higher Education,* 62, 2, March/April.

Kolb, D A (1984) *Experiential Learning,* Prentice-Hall, New Jersey.

Lather, P (1991) *Getting Smart: Feminist Research and Pedagogy within the Postmodern,* Routledge, New York.

Manpower Services Commission (MSC) (1980) *No Barriers Here,* MSC, London.

Morley, L (1993) 'Glass ceiling or iron cage? Women in UK academia', paper presented at the 1993 Women's Network Conference, Nene College, Northampton.

Ousten, J (ed) (1993) *Women in Education Management,* Longman, Harlow.

Parkin, Di (1993) 'Cultural barriers to women in academia', conference paper for Women in Higher Education Network Conference, Lancaster.

Schön, DA (1990) *Educating the Reflective Practitioner,* Jossey-Bass, San Francisco.

Somers Hill, M and Cragland, J (1995) 'Professional and self-development', in
Women as Educational Leaders: Opening Windows, Pushing Ceilings, Corwin Press,
Sage Publications, London.

Stanley, L (ed.) (1990) *Feminist Praxis: Research Theory and Epistemology in Feminist
Sociology,* Routledge, London.

Vaughan, E and Lasky, B (1991) 'How will women manage? A speculation of the
effects of equal opportunities', *Management Training Journal of General
Management,* 16, 4, Summer.

Weston, C (1993) 'Women, discrimination and work', *Association of University
Teachers (AUT) Bulletin,* 195, October.

Willis, L and Daisley, J (1992) *Developing Women Through Training,* McGraw Hill,
London.

Statistics in this chapter are courtesy of the Universities and Colleges Employees'
Association (UCEA) (University and College Staff Statistics, 1994), The Universities'
and Colleges' Staff Development Agency (UCoSDA), HESA (Press Release, 1996),
the DfEE Database of Teacher Records (produced for this book 1996) and (histor-
ically for 1984 figures) the DES (produced for research carried out in 1984).

Chapter 7

Women as Managers

If the process of promotion and development were working properly, about 44% of senior management would be women. (Nicholson and West, 1988)

The present scenario of turbulence and change depicted in much current general management literature has resulted in enthusiasm for 'changing the culture' of organizations, and an advocacy of different management behaviour which is closer to behaviours typically associated with 'feminine' behaviours, notably collaborative and cooperative behaviours and humanistic values. (Al-Khalifa, 1989, p.93)

Women are underrepresented in higher and middle management positions in higher education, even in the current post-feminist climate when many people claim there is no need to assert that equality must continue to be striven for. Perhaps it can be argued that women are not cut out for management responsibilities and management roles, or that they do not seek such appointments and promotions. Certainly many who interview and recruit would insist that women do not come forward for such jobs in the first place. Once the few who do get there are in post, there are often rather negative responses to them. The organizational myth is that women, when they do become managers, tend to become shrill and assertive, or more like the traditionally stereotypical male managers than the men themselves. In many cases both men and women say they would rather not work for a woman boss.

All the literature and much of my own direct and indirect experience suggests that some women can make very good leaders and managers. Perhaps the advertisement, or the job specification, the role as it is currently presented, the person (usually male) in post all signal to a potential woman manager that she would be out of place. Perhaps the models of women leaders and managers we do have around us are extreme, often negative. The women who have made it to near the top have had to adopt what they interpret as male manager modes of behaviour. Some of these modes probably work for both genders. Others clash with many of the qualities women are often promoted or recognized for, and the woman turning away from her own successful characteristics will be neither a happy person, nor a successful manager. I do not mean to imply anything essentialist here: I cannot subscribe to the image of women as naturally and universally anything, as nurturing, naturally caring, always good at being cooperative, sensitive to pastoral issues, illogical, passive, quiet, hysterical and all the negative images which go along with those rather underrated more positive images of 'woman'. We are all different. There is no essential 'woman' and it is important to recognize cultural, sexual and other differences which all affect women and how they respond. There are, however, some characteristics probably more frequently observed in women, which can be strengthened in a woman manager rather than downgraded, even if, to some extent, some of them have appeared previously to keep her in her non-managerial place.

Models

One of the best bits of advice from books I have read suggests we consider models of ideal or good managers we have known and define the varied characteristics they display. Even flawed managers have some good characteristics which can be spotted; and bad, unsupportive managers can be scrutinized for what they lack or confuse which makes working for them so awful. Insights into these characteristics inform the developmental decisions a woman who is aiming to be a good academic leader or manager can make. Understanding the kinds of role demands, stresses, potential problems and pleasures of being a manager contributes to the picture we build up of what we feel we can do well, can move towards doing well, and how we feel we would like to do it. There is a repertoire of behaviours associated with managers which as women we might find alien and unacceptable. When we meet such conflicts and contradictions we need to consider how the job can be done, how the role can be maintained, while doing it 'our way'. One of the strongest messages which chimes with my own feelings and experience is that if we attempt to totally restructure ourselves to fit a range of male-determined and imaged models of managers we see around us, we will end up confused, unable to realize our own potential, and unlikely to be able to work towards that important leadership/managerial aim, helping others to realize their potential.

Learning to be a Manager

Ellen Van Velsor and Martha Hughes from the Center for Creative Leadership, North Carolina (1990) used various research data of face-to-face interviews and questionnaires to analyse what kinds of events and activities provided the recognized learning opportunities for women who become managers. They set these findings against data of the opportunities most commonly recognized by men. Their sample of executives contained 78 women and 189 men. The women in the sample:

> represented the first non-traditional group with whom organizations have worked – those few, primarily white, women who had reached and maintained a top-level job in about two dozen major American corporations by 1985. As such, they provided, for most of these companies, the first experience with adjusting to and assimilating women managers at higher levels. (Van Velsor and Hughes, 1990)

Men and women were asked to report key events in their learning which led to their becoming (better) managers. The main differences were that:

> The women were focused on discovering who they were as individuals in these organizations, on finding their niche, and on integrating self with environment. The men appear focused on the mastery of more specific business skills. (Van Velsor and Hughes, 1990, p.9)

Van Velsor and Hughes speculated as to why this was. They deduced that the women probably had less organizational experience (fewer women in organizational management roles, so less experience to build on) and many of the men had actually had such experience in business, or in the armed forces. Another key factor was that characteristics describing effective *men* are usually almost identical to those describing effective *managers* but effective women, less often seen in a managerial role, are less likely to be so described. It is difficult (but important) for women to identify with a gender-related set of alternatives and behaviours (Schein, 1975; Massergill and di Marco, 1979).

> So female managers probably spend more time engaged in a process of self-analysis; learning what a female manager is by identifying the traits of a male manager she does not possess. (Van Velsor and Hughes, 1990, p.10)

They argue that the process of cognitive adjustment may never end for women. Operating within a more limited repertoire of behaviours, women may be constantly adjusting a combination of seemingly contradictory behaviour 'such as being tough but not macho or being ambitious but not expecting equal treatment' (Morrison *et al.*, 1987). Women also feel isolated, from peers not at the same level, from managers and superiors who are likely to be men. Morrison *et al.* reported that all the executive women they researched 'had been in situations where they felt people were uncomfortable with them because they were women' (1987, p.86). The working environment is more complex for women because they are in a minority. They need to define their roles and to fit in – and this leads to a concentration on their own self-development. They were often reported as asking: 'Am I really cut out for this? Is this me? Is it worth it? Could I be more successful somewhere else?'

In terms of their learning, women reported that reflective self-assessment, challenge backed up with support, good bosses, sponsors and mentors all helped their development. As Gisele Asplund (1988) also reports, in becoming managers women often have different ends in mind from those aimed at by men, and different descriptions of their roles. Looking at her survey of women in management roles she says: 'Women are not so ready to talk about careers in terms of status and power. They are more likely to be motivated by psychological factors and self-realization (Asplund, 1988, p.28).

In the minds of the women she surveyed, what stops them from succeeding is more to do with being unable to get the right kind of training, beginning in jobs which did not lead to promotion, and being taken less notice of by their bosses. The men surveyed argued that women did not succeed because of family pressures and a lack both of risk-taking and of desire for promotion. There is clearly a disjunction here! It is all too easy for someone already in power to use the excuse that the one seeking power, status and self-realization is hampered by a split family role and responsibilities, or does not really want that kind of stress. This is a set of arguments familiar to anyone who has worked with equal opportunities issues. It certainly relieves the speakers from having any sense of responsibility towards the aspiring woman manager.

Van Velsor and Hughes considered particular learning events or scenarios which helped women become successful managers. Women learned from turning a business around, from other people, and from 'values playing out': scenarios where women observed or joined in situations where one or more people did something to someone else. They recognized the importance of certain behaviours and values in this scenario. Morrison *et al.* (1987) reported that every successful woman manager had *sponsorship* from above – mentoring, advice, feedback. Good bosses were a key factor: their visible demonstration of faith in the woman's abilities boosted credibility and their encouragement nudged her into accepting challenges and responsibility and developing her potential.

Carol Gilligan (1982), Nancy Chodorow (1978) and Jean Baker Miller (1976), feminist theorists attempting to understand the gender differences in human development, argue that women see themselves in the context of human relationships. Men consider themselves as individuals, separate. Creative and positive human relationships can be used by women and by helpful male bosses to nurture women at work. If women build on their skills in such relationships rather than downgrading or rejecting them once achieving management roles, they will find their insights and experiences in social relationships immensely helpful in the community in which they work. Women managers in touch with themselves and the needs and potential of others in the work community can change the management culture for the better all round. If they reject these recognitions and qualities, and try to turn into surrogate men, the culture will stay the same. They will also be edging into ill-fitting roles.

Miller reinforces these views about women's qualities: 'women stay with, build on, and develop in a context of attachment and affiliation with others' (1976, p.169). Van Velsor and Hughes considered some activities affecting women on the way to becoming top managers. They found three categories of events which affected them most of all. Assignments, hardships, other people and personal traumas all affected women's learning. Positive events *and* negative events, properly understood and used, all contributed to learning. For example, in a specifically business or managerial context, being aware of their own and other people's business mistakes, analysed and *discussed*, helped women to develop.

Women in the Van Velsor and Hughes study were clear that gender affected their treatment, setbacks and promotion. On career setbacks, 43% reported gender discrimination as a factor. Successful they might be, but they were aware of times when they had been ignored, put down, patronized, sidestepped, silenced, overlooked, criticized, denied because of their gender. Sometimes the negative responses were covert, sometimes overt, but they were spotted. In some reported cases it took a long time before the women concerned could recover and try another strategy, regain confidence, keep working well.

Geraldine Bown and Katharine Brady (1991), focusing on the ways in which women achieve management status and roles through a training perspective, ask some specific questions about management style in relation to past performance:

> If a woman had been successful so far in her career by adopting a more cooperative method of working, should she change because she has been promoted? To do so may jeopardize her chances of success, particularly if she was promoted *because* of her cooperative style, not in spite of it. (Bown and Brady, 1991, p.12)

They make useful conclusions about self-realization and remaining true to one's own characteristics in a different, management role context, while developing other suitable behaviours *compatible* with personal style. They also add insights as to how to get into management positions. Their main arguments concern being visible and being heard, speaking up, taking on roles of responsibility and working energetically and hard at them to make them successful, being firm not shrill, and coping with pressure. Women finding it difficult to see themselves in the male role of manager say:

- I couldn't possibly;
- I don't really like being an authority figure;
- I don't want to be seen as 'pushy';
- I want to be liked;

- I want to get this right first;
- I'm only seen as a daughter/mother/wife;
- But I'm only a... ;
- I'm not the type;
- I'll see what the company has in mind for me;
- Things change slowly;
- I'm not very ambitious;
- I'm frightened of power/success.

(Bown and Brady, 1991, p.21)

Some of these responses image women as sensitive, not pushy, and emphasize the clash of images of women and traditional managers. Others relate directly to women's beliefs that someone else will spot their potential and find them a niche if they work very hard indeed and have got 'it', the management potential. Like Van Velsor and Hughes' insistence on the importance of self-awareness, self-realization, learning and developing your self from reflections on experience and models, Bown and Brady point out that we have to spot our *own* initiative, seek positive mentors to help *us* develop it and be given the opportunities to show *our* abilities. We have to push *ourselves* forward rather than waiting to be discovered. They point out that it is important to think ahead to the next role you want to be in rather than just perfecting the current one; to be seen to be ambitious and capable; to take opportunities and to work hard on them; to be visible, straight in dealings; to work on recognizing good managerial characterstics and to practise them. These do not have to be at odds with one's own personal style, but a development from it. Capitalizing on one's strengths as a woman is essential:

> Women can provide the flexible, innovative and creative approach which organizations seek. Indeed, women have an opportunity to draw upon the qualities of care, concern and intuition which have often been undervalued in the past. Make sure that you recognize and promote the strengths that you have. They are an invaluable asset to your career. (Van Velsor and Hughes, 1990, pp.53–4)

I would add as a rider to this that nurturant abilities and strengths deserve a new profile. There is parallelism between these qualities often identified as commonly found in women, and the qualities of a good manager, who is a people person as well as an organizer and achiever. If the parallel goes unrecognized, these women-centred behaviours will continue to be relegated second to the more cut-throat thrusting qualities one associates with managers. Nurturing and success can be aligned, but it takes some necessary changing of representations and perspectives to achieve this. We need to avoid negative stereotypes and change our practices. Women often try to avoid confrontation because they do not want to be disliked. They are therefore considered passive, lacking in leadership potential. In other cases, however, they can be seen to be bitchy, pushy, shrill and power-mad in their competitiveness. I am not arguing that women are completely misunderstood and actually rather perfect. Perfection is not human! There are too many Great Mother myths of female goodness around which can lull us into a false sense of our own (misunderstood, unrecognized) superiority. Inaction and lack of development perpetuate marginal status. We are all very cooperative (ideally) – but we can all remember the female playground bullies.

Jane McLoughlin points out:

> There are grounds for hope that ambitious women in competitive situations are gradually becoming self-confident enough to refuse to see each other as enemies. Ironically, once the competitiveness goes out of enmity, they are free to dislike each other heartily without the guilty feelings associated with competition – there was always the suspicion that dislike came from sour grapes after losing, and was therefore something to be ashamed of. Or they can continue to like each other, because competition no longer involves the end of a personal relationship with the women they compete with. (McLoughlin, 1992, p.127)

Growing out of comfortable responses born of a passive secondary role, learning to lose, learning from this and moving on, without agonizing, are all most important. Also important is learning not to depend on clearly undependable others and to create an effective team and be there for others when problems arise.

Some Learning Development Strategies

A variety of factors influence women's attainment of and development within management roles. Some strategies for this development can be deduced from definitions of necessary skills and abilities and attitudes, activities associated with attaining a management position and then being a successful manager. Argyris is very clear about the importance of self-realization for both the manager and those who work for her, and feels that once this is achieved, the 'seven dilemmas of power' can be solved by the manager. They are:

1. How to be strong while also acknowledging the dilemmas that surround us.
2. How to assert our opinions without becoming dominant.
3. How to fight for our ideas while encouraging others to question them.
4. How to deal constructively with our subordinates' fears when we are also afraid.
5. How to live with our own fears while asking other people to overcome theirs and act more openly.
6. How to exploit fear as a way of achieving greater understanding.

7. How to get people to believe that we genuinely want to change our leadership style when we ourselves are still uncomfortable with the 'new' one. (Argyris in Asplund, 1988, p.96)

As Asplund (1988) notes, overcoming these fears and managing well calls for self-respect, confidence and awareness of one's own integrity. People who continually have to assert their power are actually rather fearful and unsure, while those who have achieved self-realization can enable others to question them, and to achieve their own self-realization and success. These are generous and positive behaviours, and they also recognize the place of emotion – not as explosion and indulgence, but as a necessary part of human interactions. Ultimately such positive moves will generate good teamwork, which is what successful, sound organization is all about.

> A good organizational culture embracing a healthy team spirit combined with respect for the competence and needs of every member will favour individual growth and development as well as effectiveness and the achievement of organizational goals. To generate a good organizational culture is the foremost responsibility of the leader. (Asplund, 1988, p.98)

Development questions and strategies

The following questions and suggestions are based on ideas and practices of being a good manager and have been used successfully in women-only training and staff development sessions:

- Identify good managers you have known and list their skills and behaviours. Think of specific instances when they handled poeple well, perhaps in difficult circumstances; when they managed an awkward situation such as introducing an unpalatable change; when they put people right and when they pointed the way forward for a plan. Identify their characteristics, what they did and the order in which they did it.

- Ask yourself how you fit in with the variety of behaviours and characteristics noted in good managers and leaders. Which of these are not in alignment with being a woman, in your mode, and which could be?

- Ask yourself if you can motivate other people, how you can do it over time and in times of slump and crisis.

- Can you think widely both of the context of the institution and changes and developments, and the needs and potential of those working with and to you?

- Can you liaise with people above you in the hierarchy, find out plans, mediate with them, get the message of those with whom you work across to the hierarchy, and to those who are on a parallel with you? How can you do this without being unnecessarily forceful and irritating?

- You need to find ways of working with others so that they feel valued, recognized, their needs thought of, their potential understood, and so that you have a clear vision both of what should go right and what could go wrong and of how to deal with it.

- In your dealings with the hierarchy, those of similar status, or your 'subordinates', do you feel you need to emphasize hierarchical positions? Or only if it came to a particularly awkward moment would you 'pull rank'? Does this matter?

- You need to decide how you could liaise, negotiate, communicate with others at all levels, particularly over good ideas you or a subordinate have.

- You need to work out strategies to deal with problems and breaking bad news to subordinates.

- It is important that you supervise the work of others without intruding, delegating but retaining responsibility, ensuring that the work is appropriately planned and managed. When work is completed, commend the success, point out faults in a constructive way tempered with positive comments where appropriate to maintain motivation.

- You need to cope with pressure and stress, harnessing it to make you work well, or avoiding it by taking planning and communication precautions.

- You need to be able to handle being misunderstood, disliked and misquoted.

- Can you maintain energy and work levels to plan, develop, manage and see projects through to the end, while balancing everyday work *and* looking ahead to longer-term planning and activities?

- Can you utilize the skills of others and their contributions, summarizing what they have said, developing and building on what they do, showing empathy about their feelings and things they say, understanding non-verbal as well as verbal communication?

- Can you present information and ideas persuasively and cope with criticism for them? Are your presentational skills good?

- Can you ensure that the meetings you hold are needed, well-planned, well-communicated, well-chaired, get through a timed, well-organized agenda on time, come to conclusions, use the inputs of everyone with something useful to say, manage those who want to dominate, bring in those who need to be involved but are reticent, end in action points and timed actions?

- Can you select people for interview and manage an effective interview in the spirit of equal opportunities and matching skills to roles?

- You need to make sure your personal problems don't interfere with your judgement.

- Do you have people you can trust to talk with, share ideas and successes/ problems with?

- You need to be able to take advice and cope with failure and think about what to do with both. Can you turn failure to positive and constructive ends?

These are just some of the questions to ask and issues to consider if you plan to enter management, stay there sucessfully and happily, and move on. Thinking about the good models and working out your responses to the questions is one move; seeking active development opportunities is another. You need to put yourself in the way of new responsible opportunities so that you get the chance to take responsibility and make decisions. As Van Velsor and Hughes (1990) have pointed out, putting yourself in the way of management-type activities makes others perceive you as management potential. It also gives you training on the job. You can later reflect on this, extrapolating factors contributing to success, and building on them, while finding out what went wrong and why, and avoiding this in the future.

Watching others, ensuring that you are there to take on responsibilities and make the move, in a prepared way, to manage activities, are all important training and self- development activities. Finding a mentor who can advise you and support your case helps women to become self-aware and develop as managers. You can also look out for women at managers training sessions which provide a structured version of self-examination, reflection, trialling, modelling, sharing and development of plans and action.

Learning from experience, developing self-awareness, moving towards self-actualization, finding skills and strengths and building on them, are all essential for the woman who wants to be a manager or leader. It is important to remember that much of what we have seen and been through can be reflected on to determine our ideas of good managers, and many of the necessary skills are latent within us, or practised daily. These need to be firmed up, developed and directed if we want to become effective managers without losing those important, varied qualities of being women. We must make the best of what we have and develop. Women can network and support each other, putting competition aside. They can also usefully share some of the understanding of successful management tactics. If we do not share, support and develop, the glass ceiling could well stay intact.

References

Al-Khalifa E (1989) 'Women teachers and school management', in *Women Teachers: Issues and Experiences*, H De Lyon and F Widdowson Mignivolo (eds) Open University Press, Buckingham.

Asplund, G (1988) *Women Managers: Changing Organizational Cultures*, John Wiley, Chichester.

Bown, G and Brady, K (1991) *Getting to the Top*, Women in Management Workbook Series, Kogan Page, London.

Chodorow, N (1978) *The Reproduction of Mothering*, University of California Press, Berkeley.

Gilligan, C (1982) *In a Different Voice*, Harvard University Press, Boston.

Massergill, D and di Marco, N (1979) 'Sex role stereotypes and requisite management characteristics. A current replication', *Sex Roles*, 5.

McLoughlin, J (1992) *Up and Running: Women in Business*, Virago, London.

Miller, J B (1976) *Towards a New Psychology of Women*, Beacon Press, Boston.

Morrison, A M, White, R P and Van Velsor, E (1987) 'Executive women: Substance plus style', *Psychology Today*, 21, 8, 18–26.

Nicholson, N and West, M (1988) *Managerial Jobs Change: Men and Women in Transition*, Cambridge University Press, Cambridge.

Pedler, M, Burgoyne, J and Boydell, T (1986) *A Manager's Guide to Self-Development*, 2nd edn, McGraw Hill, New York.

Schein, V E (1975) 'The relationship between sex role stereotypes and requisite management characteristics among female managers', *Journal of Applied Psychology*, 60.

Van Velsor, E and Hughes, M (1990) *Gender Differences in the Development of Managers*, Center for Creative Leadership, North Carolina.

Chapter 8

Assertiveness, Confidence-building and Positive Interactions

You don't need assertiveness training! You are aggressive enough already!

Several women attending sessions I have run on assertiveness have reported that their managers have either laughed at or felt threatened by their signing up to attend. Those managers are confusing assertiveness with aggression. But it actually takes a fair amount of assertiveness on the part of the woman requesting to attend to get agreement when such misapprehensions exist. Suggesting that you would benefit from assertiveness training perhaps looks like an admission of failure, or some kind of threat. It is neither. Everyone needs to recognize how to be assertive. It means being able to recognize and to stand up for your rights and the rights of others, without either being a passive victim or an aggressive bully, and managing awkward interactions without being manipulative. Running sessions for women enables them to share ideas about assertiveness, when it would be useful to them, what it is not, and how to handle becoming and being assertive so that negative, destructive responses are avoided yet situations changes and rights are respected. Learning how to be successfully assertive is really the key to success in all the other areas of work, from leadership to time-management to negotiating classwork with a group of students to gaining recognition for your achievements in appraisal sessions.

When asked 'What does assertiveness mean to you?' the women I have worked with have easily been able to discriminate between anger, aggression and assertiveness. They suggested they feel most assertive when they have the information they need, the responsibility and the power to do the job or make the decision, when they do not feel overawed by someone who is behaving manipulatively, and can find the right words and format (face to face, by phone, etc.) for the interactions. Often they need to be assertive because of the behaviour of the other people with whom they work. In this situation bosses who bully, whether openly or with a velvet glove, are high on the agenda for debate. Bullying is not usually based on greater size or height but seniority. It takes the form of extreme manipulation, constant negative responses to work, ignoring your work and your abilities, expecting too much too fast too often and not being able to take 'No' or negotiation for an answer. These are unreasonable behaviours in a manager; and many women, because they are in subordinate roles, suffer them daily. Andrea Adams' work on bullying (1986) considers a variety of bullying behaviours by mostly, but not always, male line-managers or colleagues. The bullying often continues for a long time and causes stress and deskilling. Women find they cannot perform to their full capacity, lose confidence, are silenced and get involved in a downward spiral involving marginalization and exclusion. All this prevents us from working well or enjoying our work. Assertiveness built up on a layer of confidence with proven achievements and rights helps us to tackle these negative interactions.

When working to produce an assertive response to a criticism or a difficult situation it is helpful to imagine that the response is needed to defend or assert the rights of *someone else*. Most of us are better at seeing the situation clearly and working out what to say when it is on behalf of someone else rather than ourselves. I find this helps me clarify where I stand, what to say, what not to say, what to gain agreement over and how to act in the future.

Getting a good inner dialogue

It is important to get a good inner dialogue and to objectify the problem which needs the assertive response. When faced by manipulation, confusion or rejection, it is useful to think through the situation, decide what your position is, and if you are in the right. Then work out why there is a difficult or hostile response coming from the person with whom you need to deal assertively. Decide on the kind of response you might construct, then try this out on your own or with someone you can trust to see whether it is too confrontational, too submissive, disorganized or just right. Hearing the planned words out loud often helps us proceed with deciding how to deal with the person and the situation. A neutral observer or friend can advise on the appropriate language. This also includes what you would say next if the person with whom you need to deal assertively should respond in certain ways. It is important to avoid personal remarks and divert those which come your way. Being objective rather than personal about a problem helps to solve it because no one's pride is overtly involved. The context of the assertive response or interaction is also important. Match body posture, ensuring that the other person is neither above nor below you or behind a desk. Look at ease, steering interactions into contexts where you can deal with them appropriately – neither in the corridor nor with someone behind their desk with you in a subordinated position.

Much of the role-play work in our sessions relates to giving and receiving criticism assertively. Listening to fair criticism involves listening carefully and then addressing different aspects of it, having acknowledged the truth and even thanking the critic, dealing with the other aspects and objectively coming to agreement. If the criticism is true but involves an additional personal element it is important to accept the criticism and work towards dealing with it: but point out the inappropriateness of personal comment: 'You are right, I have taken on too many things and not managed to do all of them as well as I would like. But it is not true to say that this is a bad habit of mine and always wrecks my work – I usually manage my time and tasks well.' Everyone dealing with such situations will need to find their own words. It is important not to be personal back which is inappropriate and puts you in the wrong. If the criticism is not true then you need to say so and to find supportive evidence from others before you approach the criticizer with your denial. If this criticism also involves a personal slight, point out its inappropriateness.

Some of the situations that require assertive responses can be long-term problem relationships with other people. For this a plan of campaign is necessary and also the support and evidence of others to make you feel secure that you have the assessment of the other person correct, have worked their situation out properly, and can handle it appropriately. Consistent responses of calm assertiveness are necessary to deal with manipulative or bullying people. It is also useful to seek others in whom you can confide. Sometimes it is necessary to start paper-based exchanges and if these have no response, to copy them appropriately upwards (but do not do this too early, it reduces the power of the interaction). Spending some time building up your own confidence by recognizing what you are good at, ensuring you work well and have it recognized by others is also important: you are going to have to maintain assertive responses with someone who no doubt feels threatened, likes bullying, is selfish, cynical, manipulative, stressed and blind to others' feelings.

Learning to say NO!

One of the most powerful ideas and practices people take away with them from assertiveness sessions is feeling that they have the right to say 'No!' and going off to say it. Obviously, I do not encourage everyone to say 'No' to every request or piece of work sent their way: only to being overloaded so that their professional job cannot be done, or being put upon by someone manipulative, or being bullied, or a similarly manipulative and destructive situation. If you know you really need or want to say 'No', because of manipulation or overload, then it is important to say it early in the exchange and get it out without contradictory body language. It is also important to repeat it, avoiding excuses but including explanations: 'No, it won't be possible to mark that amount of assignments in that short space of time while I am still teaching six hours a day. The time limit is unreasonable', should not be followed with 'Oh, all right, I'll try'. If you know you cannot do it, say so. It is surprising how many of one's male colleagues immediately respond to overload by insisting that it be removed and renegotiated, while women go on trying to fulfil obligations that are increasingly unreasonable, feeling guilty if they slip up. Warn the overloader of the consequences, and say 'No'. This should be usefully followed with a suggested alternative course of action. This helps others to manage their pride and gives them something to hold on to and negotiate with. We have the right not to be taken advantage of, overloaded, ignored, mismanaged; and we have the right to have our work recognized.

Speaking out in meetings

Women often find it difficult to speak out in meetings and be assertive. This is perhaps because there is often little opportunity to do so. Maybe we attend the meeting as a representative and, not in control, find it hard to intrude until it is 'our turn'. Maybe there is a culture which operates the 'speak, pause and speak again' response pointed out by Sandra Acker (Bristol University). This involves the meeting running on and everyone contributing. You or another woman speak. Everything freezes. Then without any response, it cranks back into action, as if you had not spoken at all. It is helpful then to say it again, have someone else to back you up, make your point clearly and assertively and to not be steamrollered into silence.

The broken record technique

This is another useful response when dealing with manipulative people who refuse to listen, or who keep on insisting on the impossible. It involves repeating yourself. Get out the statement you need to make straightforwardly. If they ignore it, repeat it. If they try to fob you off, repeat it again. Sometimes slightly different phrasing helps, but it is important to keep repeating it: 'Yes I know, but we do need to look at this further', ' Thank you for letting me know about that, but that does not solve this particular problem' and other phrases. This will help you to get the message across. Women often resist being assertive through lack of practice. Remember that you and others have rights. Practise assertive interactions with others – and stick to them.

Summary of strategies

Assertiveness is not aggression! Being more assertive means:

- knowing your rights;
- knowing and standing by the rights of others;
- not being put upon;
- learning to say 'No';
- not feeling guilty when it is not your fault, you haven't the information, you have been overloaded;
- learning to cope with making mistakes;
- learning to let some things go wrong or undone if you are under stress and explaining this, without feeling too guilty;
- learning to be heard;
- learning to take constructive criticism without collapsing, and identifying a positive course of action;
- learning to give constructive criticism and sticking to it;
- learning to refuse to take unfair criticism;
- being heard when your opinion and knowledge are relevant and valid;
- being heard when you have something to say and not being afraid to say it;
- learning to find ways to encourage people to treat you and others as human beings and individuals;
- not being railroaded into actions you will regret;
- learning to encourage others to deal with issues relating to you objectively and not personally so that criticism is not personally based;
- learning not to say 'Sorry' all the time, for example when refusing requests. Remember you are turning down the request not the person (and make this clear);
- learning to repeat requests, refusals, questions and statements when they are important and are clearly not being heard.

Assertiveness is all about rights, justice, responsibilities and good positive interactions. Learning to be assertive on one's own behalf and that of others is a key to all sorts of other positive behaviours, managing responsibilities, coping with stress, and a myriad of other factors.

References

Acker, S (1985) Personal communication.
Adams, A (1986) *Bullying at Work*, Virago, London.

Chapter 9

Leadership Issues

Where women are, power is not. (Rendel, 1980)

Educational leadership is helping to make effective teaching possible. Proficient academic leadership involves building a shared vision through establishing clear goals, improving communication, and creating challenge in an environment of collaborative decision-making and teamwork where each individual feels a responsibility for achieving excellence in teaching and learning. It involves engaging in a conversation or dialogue with the teacher. It implies encouraging staff to become involved in the process of evaluating and improving their teaching as a normal part of their work. Very importantly, it also implies putting ideas into practice through observable action – nothing is more disheartening than rhetoric about supporting good teaching that is not backed up by appropriate management behaviour that recognizes the value of good teaching. (Ramsden, 1994)

Why is leadership so important in higher education? Why would women want to be involved in it? Are there any specific gender-related issues and models of leadership? Not all of us want to be leaders and to many of us, men or women, the idea of leadership has too many unpleasant connotations of imposed power, arrogance, political wrangling and domination for it to be a role or set of behaviours we might wish to wholeheartedly embrace. Good leadership, however, is essential in any organization and any activity, whether it be a huge multinational or a small tutorial group. We need to widen and clarify the definition and appreciation of what leadership roles might be like in higher education, consider good models and effective leaders and move on to consider the development of women-oriented practices and models of good leadership behaviours. This way women in higher education can learn to be good leaders, to everyone's benefit.

Leadership Models and Roles

Within higher education many of us are involved in roles which we might not actually recognize as leadership roles, but which involve the activities, responsibilities and skills of leadership. For many women the idea of leadership is anathema: it has all the connotations of 'Over the top boys!', rallying the troops and captaining the squad. When I have run sessions on leadership inside and outside my university, I have found that women are frequently reluctant to identify their own roles and behaviours with those associated with leaders. Leadership sounds bossy, non-negotiating, a role available for the very few, not something with which we see ourselves involved.

If we want that absurd image of the leader to develop into a more woman-centred model, and a more positive, less thrustingly cut-throat or dully politically collusive model, we need to recognize what we do; train for it and do it well and differently. Typically, many of the things we do in the course of our work which require leadership qualities are:

- managing time;
- chairing meetings;
- supervising others;
- negotiating with and managing a team;
- providing academic or administrative-related leadership – being head in your field, involved in professional groups and activities, providing a model for others;
- taking decisions after due consultation, in context, realistically, and making sure they are actioned/actioning them;
- persuading others to do what you need and want;
- setting up work programmes and keeping people working;
- keeping discipline where necessary and handling awkward moments;
- giving bad news, negotiating attitude and behaviour change with those who are underperforming or upsetting the work;
- working to turn failure into success;
- selecting and recruiting others;
- managing the workload of others;
- appraising others and ensuring appraisal decisions are evaluated, planned and actioned;
- having an overall scheme or plan: negotiating realistically, taking decisions, taking action, evaluating and reflecting;
- resolving conflict.

Some, though not necessarily all, these activities and behaviours are present in the work of the higher education lecturer. Others are present in the work of the assistant, the member of secretarial staff or manager who supervises one or more other staff, the field leader who sets an academic role-model and works with their team, the administrator who does the same, and who negotiates difficult decisions up and down the hierarchy of the institution's structures, keeping informed, balanced and professional.

Higher education serves the wider world, for which it prepares new graduates. Some of what we do acts as a model. Our development of different versions of leadership qualities helps to change other people's lives, and the understanding of both the knowledge base and the basis for action in life outside the university. There is a real responsibility here.

> In academic work there is a high correlation between career- and life-satisfaction. The university, more than other places of employment, is highly influenced by life outside of work. In addition, universities are training grounds for future leaders and need to offer an effective model on how to balance family and career. (Hensel, 1991, p.vi)

Women learning to be leaders

Management studies have identified several significant similarities in the background and histories of those who have become high-fliers and leaders. Cox and Cooper (1988, p.129) suggest that successful people often obtain positions of responsibility at an early age. They trace women's recognition of significant changes and turning points which acted as springboards to their future success. 'I got thrown in at the deep end' is a common statement. Some who were forced into situations demanding management or leadership strategies initially felt a great fear of failure. They then discovered they were doing the job well, were behaving appropriately, were being recognized and rewarded for it, and subsequently felt greater self-esteem. Self-esteem based on self-awareness and success leads to the desire to build on this success and analyse what helped it. When management and leadership behaviours emerge from this analysis, women ensured these were reinforced. Self-awareness and self-monitoring, as well as seizing and working in a planned way through appropriate opportunities, all helped this development. Hall's notion of career growth is informative (Hall, 1976). He argues that as you gain competence relevant to your career role your career identity grows and you invest in it.

It is important that:

1. you set challenging goals for yourself;
2. you determine your own means of achieving these goals;
3. the goal is important to your self-concept; and
4. you actually attain the goals.

From success comes self-esteem, which fuels the development of competence. The women in the sample looked at by White *et al.*, 1992, followed these patterns, felt increased self-confidence moving towards more challenges to develop their competencies with success. Hennig and Jardim (1978) and Missiran (1982) found sucessful women had mentors who put opportunities for challenge and development their way and then recognized their success.

But the kinds of jobs we go into to some extent prevent development. Alston (1987) discovered fewer women lawyers went into private practice, Rycroft (1989) that women are more likely to be in finance, administration and personnel roles than line-managers.

Women are concentrated in support roles in universities as well as these more business-oriented examples. The success of searching for promotion or a job change which achieves the same result is largely predicted upon 'track record' (McCall and Lombardo, 1983), wide and appropriate successful experience which is sometimes hard for a woman in a support role to actually attain. White *et al.* (1992) note 'where women achieve equivalent status to men they do so through specialist routes' (p.133). Hennig and Jardim (1978), looking at successful American female executives, found they changed their jobs in the first two years because their companies would not let them do anything other than routine work. Some women will gain responsibilities early on in their careers, while others will gradually do so as challenges and opportunities arise.

Leaders or managers?

Leaders can be differentiated from managers because they are involved in a mission, motivation, creativity and change while managers concentrate more on organizations, time, space and people relationships, negotiating structures and systems. Middlehurst (1991) argues that in higher education the two roles need to merge to underpin the 'learning organization'. Ramsden (1994) has shown this demands good quality leadership and management to support teaching and research.

Leaders in higher education ideally:

- inspire;
- motivate;
- negotiate with those who work to them;
- negotiate with those who they work to, in context;
- are idealistic and realistic;
- are ethical;
- manage time well;
- supervise sensitively and with foresight and planning;
- recruit the right people;
- appraise others well and follow through;
- make decisions and ensure they are actioned/action them;
- know where they are at fault;
- make fair judgements;
- provide a model of behaviour, effort and production in their area of work/subject;

- care about those they work with;
- care about the work but do not let personal emotions interfere with good decisions;
- provide academic leadership: are up-to-date in their own subject and lead developments;
- recognize how important it is for others to be up-to-date, for others to recognize their suggestions for and work towards developments;
- have an overview of academic and institutional developments, resources, directions, constraints;
- have a sound knowledge of the context: institutional, systems, hierarchies, finances, resources;
- have a sound knowledge of current developments and thinking in the appropriate development and management groups;
- translate these deliberations, decisions and proposals to those they lead;
- negotiate positions with staff and test out responses in relation to constraints, cut-backs, developments, ideas, problems, benefits;
- listen;
- are available;
- are loyal;
- are honest;
- hear everyone's views but do not necessarily follow them (take the final reasoned decision and take the resultant responsibility);
- know where to delegate to the people with the right abilities and potential, to those who need these opportunities, to those with capabilities;

Some leaders are *action centred*. They:

- review the current situation, people, needs, resources;
- see ahead to developments, they plan and negotiate, motivate and direct;
- are team-oriented and task-directed: it is important to develop the team, and to work to get the task done;
- encourage and initiate evaluation to start the cycle up again;
- are not seen to be prejudiced for one person or against another;
- fairly represent the views of those whom they lead to higher management;
- have to convey bad news to those they lead, tactfully and appropriately;
- can manage change effectively without too much pain and with assured agreements;
- inspire;
- bring out the best in people;
- remain controlled and calm;
- can work both alone and in teams;
- are well aware of the importance of getting the team dynamics right for activity.

White *et al.* (1992) carried out studies of successful women and related these to various other studies of types at work, of how politics operate within power at work, and of women's typical behaviours and characteristics at work. Women, it is argued, often neither get involved in nor rate as important the informal (male-controlled) networks of relationships in their institution (Hennig and Jardim, 1978) believing that their work will be seen as good and they will be recognized and rewarded because of the way the system works. They have undergone socialization which from childhood relates them to community rather than agency. They are less likely to see themselves as active change agents, in need of being seen to do their job well, or self-advertising.

Kanter (1984) identifies successful women as a 'skewed group', a minority in a higher education or business culture where men are in the majority. Kanter believes that the recruitment of women and clustering them would help change organizational cultures. More fundamentally, the values and systems of organizations need changing:

> women will have little lasting impact on the culture of an organization unless the value systems incorporated in the informal networks of organizations are changed. Many women entering an organization identify to some extent with the prevalent male norms and values, and in doing so they limit their own sense of themselves as females. What needs to be addressed is 'How can women have the right to be women and to be valued? How can women gain respect for their female qualities, which can make a significant contribution to organizational life in their own right?' (White *et al.*, 1992, p.150)

White *et al.*'s interviews showed women acting less passively in the face of organizational culture, recognizing that you need to be seen to do a job well, to look out for opportunities and build good relationships with those to whom you are reporting so they can help you when you know what you want. Women need to recognize the political, informal systems at work, rather than viewing them as devious and immoral (Kakabadse, 1986).

Devine and Clutterbuck (1985) argue that advancement in organizations may seem too difficult using the informal political systems and games, so many women set up on their own instead (or remain doing a job well):

> advancement to senior management is still a tortuous process in large organ-izations... more women are circumventing these barriers and setting up their own ventures. (Devine and Clutterbuck, 1995)

Marshall (1984) considers awareness of gender in terms of success at work. She shows how some women operate a 'balancing act', muting their awareness of being different to men and seeing themselves as separate cases from the majority of women. They tend to become isolated, conforming to organizational socialization by suppressing thoughts and actions seen as divergent because they are female rather than male. Others underwent painful stress through challenging this more comfortable collusion. They had met prejudice and were gradually evolving new values. The third group she considered emerged from turmoil. They saw that being women in organizations needed acknowledgement and wanted to integrate gender and the demands of the job. They were often members of groups and networks which relieved isolation through friendships and contacts.

Academic leadership often depends on subject credibility. Considering the success of women publishing academically, Hensel points out that single women published at a slower rate than married women (Astin and Davies, 1985) but published more over their whole careers. The novelist Tillie Olsen commented on conflicting difficulties of being a carer and mother and a writer (1978). Other studies such as Widom and Burke (1978) found marital difference had little effect on scholarly activity but having children had a great effect. If you are to be a leader in your academic field, these kinds of findings may be troubling, since the effect of having children on a man's career and academic publishing life tends to be nil (White and Hernandez, 1985) but it makes a significant difference to women. Clearly, organizational structures as well as attitudes need to change to redress this imbalance.

Hunter and Kuh (1987) interviewed 18 prolific writers to determine what supported their writing. They found that participation in professional organizations, networks, support and the exchange of information and financial support; a mentor; and the ability to obtain large blocks of time all contributed to success in managerial and leadership roles. These are all necessary for successful women academic leaders, but some are in conflict with domestic demands.

Specific problems for women becoming leaders

Hensel (1991, p.49) argues of university life that it is 'not a system designed for people without wives'. One response to this is to suggest that women should not bother with leadership, management or academic roles, but instead choose family roles alone. Obviously, many do, but if you do not, and you wish to lead academically or managerially, the changing which needs to take place has to come from several sources – yourself, your family, your part of the university, the organization and culture and its behaviours as a whole and the perceptions of what good managers and leaders are and can be. With such changes, however gradual, women can not only move further into leadership roles, but change the nature of the behaviours associated with such roles, and so eventually spread change outside the university.

Successful women leaders

Marshall found that the largest number of successful women interviewed had 'integrated their femininity into their sense of identity'; that is, they were operating as 'creative individualists' (White *et al.*, 1992, p.168) They had learned to recognize the strengths they had as women and this gave them an inner power which integrated productively with their current structural constraints. Davies (1985) urges that management courses should change to recognize the need for women to integrate feminine behaviours and characteristics with management needs, and develop new styles:

> This is a challenge for management development courses to develop a strategy which will facilitate this combination of individual power and structural constraints. In other words, how can we help more women to become 'creative individualists'? (Davies, 1985, p.168)

Many successful women in the White *et al.* survey were seen to be:

> creative individuals, innovative with low concern for rule conformity, they could think then beyond existing paradigms and do things differently. The themes which emerge from both the measure of political and creative style is the potential to generate one's own values, giving the ability to think beyond the constraints of the position traditionally allocated to women at work... Rather than conforming to the 'male model of success', these women had integrated their femininity into a sense of identity while operating within structural constraints of the organization. These women have the ability to challenge the normative nature of power which has been postulated as one of the fundamental processes underlying women's under-representation in positions of authority. It is possible that this may be a vital characterstic for women entering the male-dominated worlds of business, commerce and industry. (White *et al.*, 1992, pp.180–81) (And, I would add, higher education.)

Your femininity should inform work within the university's structure and culture. Being a creative individualist means carving your own woman-oriented way through the jungles of the politics and practices of the university, but with the help of similar women within or elsewhere with whom you network, so as to reduce isolation.

The way to start to move towards being a good leader is to identify successful characteristics and behaviours of models, and recognize and reward your own performance of these in your daily work and in specific circumstances. Some role-play and case-study work help to develop awareness, as well as the discourses and behaviours appropriate to good leadership.

Some research-based tips on moving towards leadership/firming up your leadership practices and styles

- Reflect on your current leadership activities and define the successful characteristics.

- Define the successful characteristics of a variety of effective leaders you work with/have worked with.

- Reflect on your abilities to perform good leadership behaviours and roles. Analyse and concentrate on these behaviours.

- Seek opportunities to play a leader's role and prepare for them thoroughly.

- Let your successes be known.

- Find a mentor who will give you opportunities and advice.

- Step into crises and cope with them in a planned way.

- Remain sensitive to feelings and experiences, of yourself and of others.

- Practise good time-management, organizing yourself and the work of others, thinking about and helping to plan the work of those who work to you, rewarding, commenting, advising in a sensitive and structured way.

- Seek training and development opportunities in areas which you have decided you need to develop.

- Look ahead to changes in the university which will require your leadership skills with those who work to you.

- Keep well informed and have a reasoned view about developments.

- Make full use of formal and informal networks to keep informed; let your views be known; work to bring about positive developments.

- Ensure those who work with and to you have access to you in an appropriate way; stay in touch.

- Value and make known your needs to get the work done professionally, and the needs of others to get their work done professionally, and argue on your own or their behalf.

- Seek advice and explain why you do or do not use it.

- Own up to mistakes and explain them if you can.

- Seek out talented others and get them to work with you, use their skills.

- Do not use the role and aspects of it for self-aggrandizement but to do the job well, for the sake of the university and the people within it.

- Support and lead staff carefully through times of change.

Some of these ideas and practices can be stated as the positive character-istics of good leaders. Others can be teased out and focused on through work with case studies. Some of the behaviours are:

- responsible;
- action centred: sense of direction, planning to achieve aims, aware of skills needed and skills available;
- flexible: communicates and assesses responses, negotiates change and developments;
- accessible: others can come to talk, get in touch, air grievances, share ideas;
- ethical: fair to all, just in decisions, weighs up the information and seeks more if necessary, does not let emotions take over;
- caring: about how well the course group/team are working, how well the subject is being taught, whether resources get to the right place, whether the students are happy, how well the evaluation and monitoring of the course is developing.

It is also useful to look in depth at the different practices and behaviours associated with the variety of leadership roles we play, or could adopt, and focus on how to do these well, with an integrated sense of good practice and woman-oriented ways of behaving. Those to be focused on are: chairing meetings, supervisory practices, time-management, ensuring effective teamwork.

It is important to all of us to be and to have good leaders. For women, underrepresented in higher management, higher academic and leadership roles, we need to recognize how we can act as role models, to other women, both academic and support staff within the universities, and the students with whom we all work directly or indirectly. Gilbert *et al.* (1983) gathered evidence that 'same-sex role models were important to students' development professionally'. Women graduate students who identified women professors as role models viewed themselves as more career-oriented, confident and instrumental than students identifying with male models (O'Leary and Mitchell, 1990, p.68) while Tidball (1973) found that 'the number of career-successful women was directly proportionate to the number of (successful) women available in undergraduate institutions'.

Recognizing leadership abilities

Strategies and contexts which encourage women's success in their work and their subsequent success as leaders include seizing opportunities and challenges, moving on from merely routine work even though doing the job well is a reward of its own, having a mentor, and being self-aware and capitalizing on the qualities you develop which achieve success. The latter is important for all of us in higher education in particular. If as women we are doing mundane routine jobs and not exercising any leadership qualities, but wish to, then we need to seek opportunities for challenge and development, as well as mentors. Above all, though, we initially need to carry out an audit on the qualities we do have, the behaviours we have successfully practised, and the successful completion of competent leadership activities, recognizing what our achievements mean in terms of transferable behaviours:

- A successful recruitment and interviewing session producing the right candidate tells us about our abilities to discern, judge, make the right decisions in the context.

- A well-handled team meeting tells us about our time-management, negotiating skills, and ability to get the right decisions taken and actioned.

- A difficult piece of information, criticism or news conveyed to another member of staff which leads to their changing behaviour, agreeing to do what is needed, coping, shows us how well we have managed people, atmospheres, and the working relations of the group, to get the tasks done.

- A good class in which some awkward, boring or difficult work has been successfully taken on board by the students, who have worked actively, and shown they understand what we have been doing, tells us that we have managed discipline, time, people, and led academically so that others can learn actively.

- A decision made coolly, taking all the necessary context problems, personalities and resources into account, and then carried through with agreement, in a crisis, tells us how we can see, weigh up issues, lead people, ensure the right decisions are made and actioned.

- The achievement of a long-term task from start to finish with appropriate support and help, shows us we have planned well, negotiated well, seen the critical paths and stayed with them, and made careful and appropriate decisions. This could be a course development, a year's planning in a finance department, taking a course team through change and development and even dismantlement.

- These instances can be extrapolated into a variety of administrative/ support and academic scenarios and examples. Day-to-day teaching of a course provides endless opportunities for leadership as does day-to-day work with a few others in a team, in a supervisory capacity. It is up to us to recognize, reward and build on, evaluate and develop the skills and qualities of leadership which successful achievement of such activities illustrates.

As women who are leaders, it is important not to lose sight of gender, and of the learning which experience brings – exerience of sound role models, male and female, of mentors, of our own experiences as leaders in roles which we might not have so classified, and of ourselves and those we lead as people in a real world. A more sensitive and integrated experientially based mode of leadership with integration of good practices with real experience should then result. One feminist comment on women in positions of power, in a man's world, in fact, gives insight into the theory and morality of all this when Adrienne Rich says:

> To think like a woman in a man's world means thinking critically, refusing to accept the given, making conections between facts and ideas which men have left unconnected. It means remembering that every mind resides in a body; remaining accountable to the female bodies in which we live; constantly retesting given hypotheses against lived experience. (Rich, 1978, p.245)

Negotiating skills, skills related to sensitive interpretation of the needs, feelings and demands of others in a shared situation – whether a meeting, a departmental team, a crisis or a classroom – all inform our work as leaders. The recent, more person-sensitive management training books recognize this, recognize the need for women to credit and value some of the more social and personal experience-oriented behaviours which we quite often feel are denied in a role higher up the organization, because we so rarely see them in action in the leaders around us.

Good leadership helps everyone feel better, more clearly directed, aware of where they are going, and that their skills and individual personalities and beliefs are taken into consideration in the performance of the task. It helps us all to work well, happily, effectively, successfully, as well as bringing us, the leaders, and our team-members nearer to a real sense of our own effectiveness, our own self-realization.

References

Alston, A (1987) *Equal Opportunities: A Career Guide,* Penguin, Harmondsworth.

Astin, H (1978) 'Women and work', in *Psychology of Women: Future Directions of Research,* J Sherman and F Denmark (eds), Psychological Dimensions, New York.

Astin, H and Davies, D (1985) 'Research prductivity across the life and career cycles', in *Scholarly Writing and Publishing,* M Fox (ed.) Westview Press, Boulder, Colorardo.

Brodie, D and Partington, P (1992) *HE Department Leadership/Management: An exploration of roles and responsibilities,* CVCP, Sheffield.

Cox, C and Cooper, C L (1988) *High Fliers,* Blackwell, Oxford.

Davies, J (1985) 'Why are women not where the power is? An examination of the maintenance of power elites', *Management Education and Development,* 16, 3, 278–88.

Devine, M and Clutterbuck, D (eds) (1985) *Having a Mentor: A Help or a Hindrance? Business-women Present and Future,* Macmillan, Basingstoke.

Gilbert, L A, Gallesich, J M and Evans, S L (1983) 'Sex of faculty role model and students' self-perceptions of competency', *Sex Roles,* 9, 5, 597–607.

Hall, D T (1976) *Careers in Organizations,* Goodyear, Santa Monica, California.

Hayes, J (1984) 'The politically competent manager', *Journal of General Management* 10, 1, 24–33.

Hennig, M and Jardim, A (1978) *The Managerial Woman,* Marion Boyars, London.

Hennig, M, and Jardim, A (1977) 'Women executives in the corporate network', *Psychology Today,* January.

Hensel, N (1991) *Realizing Gender Equality in Higher Education: The Need to Integrate Work/Family Issues,* ASHE ERIC Higher Education Report 2, The George Washington University, Washington DC.

Hunter, D E and Kuh, G D (1987) 'The "write way"', *Journal of Higher Education,* 58, 4, 443–63.

Kakabadse, A K (1986) *The Politics of Management,* Gower, London.

Kanter, R M (1984) *Men and Women of the Corporation,* Basic Books, New York.

Marshall, J (1984) *Women Managers: Travelers in a Male World,* John Wiley, New York.

McCall, M W and Lombardo, M M (1983) 'Off the track: Why and how successful executives get derailed', *Technical Report 21,* Center for Creative Leadership, North Carolina.

Merriam, S (1983) 'Mentors and protégés: A critical review of the literature', *Adult Education Quarterly,* 33, 3, 161–73.

Middlehurst, R (1991) *The Changing Roles of University Leaders and Managers*, CVCP, Sheffield.

Missiran, A-K (1982) *The Corporate Connection: Why Women Need Mentors to Reach the Top*, Prentice-Hall, Englewood Cliffs, NJ.

O'Leary, V and Mitchell, J M (1990) 'Women connecting with women: networks and mentors in the United States', in *Storming the Tower: Women in the Academic World*, S Stiver Lie and V O'Leary (eds), Kogan Page, London.

Olsen, T (1978) *Silences*, Delacorte Press, New York.

Ramsden, P (1994) 'The research context', in *Improving Student Learning: Theory and Practice*, G Gibbs (ed.), Oxford Brookes University, Oxford, p.25.

Rendel, M (1980) 'How many women academics?' in *Schooling for Women's Work*, R Deem (ed.), Routledge & Kegan Paul London.

Rich, A (1978) 'Taking women students seriously', in *On Lies, Secrets and Silence: Selected Prose 1966–78*, A Rich (ed), Virago, London, p.245.

Rycroft, T (1989) *Survey of Women Managers*, Interim Report, British Institute of Management, London.

Tidball, M E (1973) 'Women's colleges and women achievers revisited', *Signs*, 5, 504–17.

University of Wisconsin Survey (1988) *Report of the Committee on Parental Leave Policy*, University of Wisconsin, Madison, WI.

White, A and Hernandez, N (1985) *Perceptions of Women and Men in Counselor Education about Writing for Publication*, ED, 265, 445, 15pp, MF-01.

White, B, Cox, C and Cooper, C (1992) *Women's Career Development: A Study of High Fliers*, Blackwell, Oxford.

Widom, C S and Burke, B W (1978) 'Performance, attitudes and professional socialization of women in academia', *Sex Roles*, 4, 4, 549–62.

Chapter 10

Women Chairing Meetings and Supervising Others

If the process of promotion and development were working properly, about 44% of senior management would be women. (Nicholson, 1986)

The present scenario of turbulence and change depicted in much current general management literature has resulted in enthusiasm for 'changing the culture' of organizations, and an advocacy of different management behaviour which is closer to behaviours typically associated with 'feminine' behaviours, notably collaborative and cooperative behaviours and humanistic values. (Al-Khalifa, 1989, p.93)

Taking the Chair

For women who are developing their skills in management roles, supervising others and the chairing of meetings are often the first signs that they are starting to 'arrive'. They are perceived as able to lead, control, encourage a group to make effective decisions, manage time and space, and enable action to take place.

However, for many if not most women in further and higher education, the opportunity to chair a meeting is simply not a realistic one; we will not get the chance, so we will not get the experience, so we will not get the training and the potential professional development and recognition to which these can lead. For many of us, too, the thought of chairing a large meeting brings out all those fears of making mistakes and performing unsatisfactorily. We fear being perceived as ineffectual while under public scrutiny, magnified because of the central and controlling nature of the role as defined largely by men, as men normally chair the big meetings because they hold the offices.

Taking a Chair

But chairing, ironically, is something we are likely to be good at. Women are often called on and prove extremely 'naturally' able in situations where they are required to negotiate, to summarize and to mediate between opposing factions. They find themselves able to be pragmatic, to ensure that decisions are made, responsibilities apportioned, times attached to the completion of roles and jobs assigned and accepted. We don't *all* run homes, though most of us manage our various-sized households – and these chairing behaviours are very like those practised by women in the home. There, too, we are balancing a variety of people's needs, time, demands and respons-ibilities which need sharing or shouldering. We get it all done efficiently and effectively without too many ruffled feathers. Like any other claim to 'natural' ability, this could be one which potentially reinforces stereotypes and marginalization, were it to depend on a 'natural' claim alone. Like mothering, though, managing, negotiating, ensuring decisions are taken and agreed and acted on are learned behaviours. The context of the home forces us to learn them. We also learn them elsewhere, and they transfer most usefully to chairing.

Enquire further and the women who hover around the role of chair or similar, claiming lack of practice, are found to run meetings outside their study or work. They run PTFA meetings, Guide meetings, local residents' meetings, charity and church gatherings. They organize jumble sales and raffles. They lobby local MPs about blocking and unblocking roads, they run local WEA groups. The skills are there and so is the practice. It is making the transfer and recognizing what can transfer that is so necessary.

Who's sitting in *my* Chair?

Most of our experiences of meetings are those with men in the chairing role. As with any management and training situation, we need to consider role models and the variety of practices available before deciding how we want to and can proceed in making our own the roles traditionally held by men.

We need to recognize the value of the skills of negotiation, control, direction, time-management, decision-making, sharing, action-planning and acting in ways which do not merely mimic those operated by the men currently chairing meetings in our institutions. We do not have to mimic men to succeed as managers, and we do not have to mimic men to be good chairpersons. Nor do we need to reinvent the wheel.

As women chairs we need to draw on our perceptions of good chairs we have experienced. We need to analyse the demands of the role of the chair, and train ourselves towards meeting these effectively and efficiently, without falling into the behavioural traps and modes we see around us. These are the bossy, dominant chair, the ineffectual chair, and so on.

The first step is to recognize that we do already have many of the skills, albeit in another sphere. The second is to begin to define how we are going to transfer the skills and manage this role, and what that will mean in terms of language, behaviour, relationships, expectations, decisions and actions.

Many of these are gender-free and just good practice. Others relate to models of behaviour associated with women as opposed to those associated with men: ensuring language is laundered of gender-related terms.

Taking your seat: becoming Chair

Many people dislike being called after an inanimate object, but equally find 'chairperson' ugly. You need to make your own choice, but I shall refer here to 'chair' for the sake of consistency.

Whether elected as chair, or asked to chair a meeting for a variety of reasons, you are immediately in the limelight. You are in a role of importance, guidance, decision-making and teamwork. It is essentially a role of leadership by negotiation. Many people forget this, preferring to use the role to give themselves a forum for their own views. If you really want space for your own views, becoming the chair is not the right place: stick to the role of meetings member where you can say more about what you personally think. Sometimes refusing to take the chair or abdicating for a while because your own agenda is pressing is a wise step. With good chairing the main aim is not to dominate the entire flow of the meeting with your own agenda and concerns.

For many, chairing is the sign of having arrived, being recognized as management potential. Chairing is good training for roles requiring decision-making and negotiating skills. Taking the opportunity of chairing is a wise decision, providing you are involved in or at least understand the issues of the meeting, and have knowledge of the directions the meeting could take, the people who are to be invited and the context. Information and the right to speak are important and empowering. Good chairing disseminates information, and enables appropriate, directed speech and decision-making. Bad chairing is chaos or an ego trip – and a few other disastrous things besides.

If you want to influence the kinds of issues which are to be discussed, and the kinds of actions taken, becoming a chair can help you. You need to show that you have knowledge, negotiating skills, linguistic skills, can make decisions based on lively discussion and can persuade people to take responsibility for actioning decisions. Showing these skills as a meetings member, being dependable, reasonable, articulate, imaginative, working towards resolutions and acting on decisions will mark you out as someone who could chair successfully.

Musical Chairs

Often in fairly egalitarian or democratic groups and meetings the role of chair is rotated. Women not in high office can gain experience in chairing meetings when this kind of non-hierarchical musical chairs is in operation.

It is important to be well aware of the issues to be discussed, decisions which need making, and the ways these meetings members are likely to behave in order to be an effective chair in a short-term capacity. It is good experience and should be embraced, though handled with care.

Collaborative course teams often rotate their chairs so that opportunities for chairing can be shared among many. Further and higher education institutions espouse equal opportunities. If you wish to gain the kind of training which being a chair provides, and to take part in the decision-making processes, suggest that chairs rotate.

The cycle of activities

Chairing is an activity with as much work in the production-planning, in the dressing-room, in rehearsal, in publicity and in staging and then clearing up and moving on to the next planning phase, as it is in the limelight 'on the night'. As chair you are in control outside the meeting as well as inside unless you have just been called in to take the chair for a specific, one-off purpose, or at the last moment. In these cases your influence extends through the meeting and in ensuring that actions are taken as a result of decisions made, but you will not be so tied up in the cycle of activities as the regular chair.

The regular chair

There are many kinds of meetings. There are small, informal meetings, information exchanges and updates, huge decision-making or/and central functional meetings, information exchanges, working parties, brainstorming and think-tanks, quality circles, team meetings, central college committees and local groupings. There are national and international meetings, meetings you attend as a representative, or which you attend because of your own role or specific qualities. All these meetings have similarities which relate to the rules governing behaviour and the need for preparation and action. They also have many differences in terms of the formality, numbers, length and the specific function within the organization, its structures and its planning cycles. All this needs taking into account when planning how you will chair the meeting and its outcome.

Being informed

As chair, you need to know the function of that particular meeting within the political and social structures of the institution, at that time, in that place, with those people. You must also be aware of such issues as what power the meeting has to make decisions, how crucial and effective it is. You need to know whether this particular meeting at this time will be influential, important or more routine.

Many of us have been successful in exchanging information, taking decisions and actioning them in informal settings and across networks. These skills are transferable, but the context is different. Sometimes a networking, informal style leads to a failure to insist on the proper support for meetings, which can produce confusion and waste time and energy. Insist that the meeting be supported by secretarial help, information sent to members in advance, and minutes sent promptly afterwards. A message is communicated to our colleagues that a meeting is unimportant if vital structures are not in place. If you end up taking the minutes or the notes yourself, you will not be able to chair the meeting effectively. You will not be able to concentrate on recording while introducing and refereeing.

Research and canvassing produce better attendance at a meeting than do lack of consultation and awkward timing. Missing out key people can make decisions powerless, and offend. Make sure you find out who should attend, whether regulars or guest specialists, and ask those who should come. If you have a hand in deciding who members are, ensure you have the right blend of skills. You need those with imagination and entrepreneurial flair, those with finishing skills, those who can help move the meeting on by summarizing and paraphrasing and those who will not only take on responsibilities but also action them.

Ensure you have booked a good-sized room which is warm, airy, light, with coffee and tea, and perhaps also water, at appropriate intervals or, in a longer running meeting, available throughout. As women, we are perhaps more aware of the importance of comfortable and suitable settings which we know will ensure that people can concentrate. I have seen meetings which have lost energy early on through lack of refreshment, poor lighting, cramped conditions, and others which have droned on and on, trapping their inmates eternally in an airless room while little intelligent conversation and decision-making can take place. We need to make sure that people want to come to our meetings, knowing that they are well-placed, well-thought-out and well-timed. Women frequently show the social skills which recognize these needs.

An agenda of timed items should be accompanied with exploration of expected outcomes, not just headings, which can be misinterpreted and vague. Members preparing for the meeting need to think beforehand and bring ideas and information. This will help the focus of discussion and use the skills and knowledge of all present.

Meetings members need important papers well in advance so that they can consider them and (except in emergencies) there should be a strict rule about not tabling papers at the meeting. Tabling long papers is a destructive political move based on the assumption that a quick decision can be made, brushing discussion aside. Or it shows lack of forethought and sloppiness. The exceptions to this are last-minute results and emergency information. If these are rare additions, they will be given the attention they deserve.

Running the Meeting

The chair is responsible for seeing that the meeting starts on time. Members feel that a brisk, well-organized meeting is about to begin if you start on time and, like any other activity, it signals to latecomers that they need to make sure they get there on time next time, or they will miss something. With a timed agenda it is clear that items will be considered, decisions made and an end is in sight. This tends to galvanize people into thought and action. Check that the order is satisfactory, and move items, with agreement, should they need key members present or demand particular focus and attention.

The chair's role is to *chair*: keep the meeting moving; attend to the items; time them and ensure that everyone who needs to or/and wants to speak gets the chance. The most difficult elements are controlling the garrulous and self-important professional meetings people who want to dominate everything, and drawing in the people with vital things to say who are hanging back for whatever reason (shyness? silent aggression? cannot see how to break into the flow? lack of practice?).

- Body language is initially helpful to suggest that someone has gone on too long, swifter nodding and shifting eye contact, followed if necessary by a hand held slightly out as if to prevent a train running you down. All this suggests that the speaker needs to hold back. It is like physical refereeing because you are beckoning people in, recognizing desires to speak with a gesture and adding these up, and holding off, cutting out or down, repetitive or long-drawn-out contributions A 'free-for-all' hampers decisions, encouraging apathy – and the meeting will be hijacked.

- It is essential that the items get covered. Deferring too much of the agenda to another time indicates stagnation. It might also be important that the decisions are made on that particular day. You need to know all this and to ensure that even if it means some juggling of the agenda, key items are discussed, leading to decisions, even if they are about future discussions. It is essential that decisions are built upon full and free discussion to encourage ownership and action. Here the skills of negotiation and management enter. As chairs we need to make sure we are able to encourage decisions but avoid railroading.

- Ensure that you give everyone the chance to speak. Do not let the discussion lapse into small talk and sub-conversations or energy and focus will get lost.

- Keep the pace moving from item to item, summarize, assume and test out decisions, and move on. Do not rush and steamroller people, but also do not let them waffle and lose energy. Reiterate questions, sum up and suggest that answers or decisions are reached by agreement which will then need active support. Make and mention assumptions that these are the feelings of the meeting.

- Do not be steamrollered by bullies, or upstaged by those wishing to use this forum as another space to pull their weight. *You* are in control, with the agreement of several people, and you need to remember this. Let it be known with such phrases as 'I don't think we can give much more time and space to that item', 'Thank you for your contributions. Now I think we need to get on with the next item,' and so on. These are polite, but firm and prevent the meeting being hijacked.

- Ensure that decisions are clearly signalled, and that individuals or groups take appropriate responsibility for actioning them. Ask the minuter to record action points, named persons, and dates by which tasks will be completed, meetings set up of working parties and progress reports sent in so that the future is clear in everyone's mind.

- It is invaluable to set the date of the next meeting at this stage, too, so that time is not wasted circulating time slots. This enables you to ensure that key figures can be present next time, and make some suggestions about the meeting's subject.

- Finally, do end on time. Everyone appreciates this. It ensures that most people will be able to stay to the end, contributing as necessary, rather than rushing off without being able to discuss key items into which they might have valuable input.

Tidying the chairs away and setting out the next session

The work done after the meeting by the chair and the minute-taker is just as important as the preparation. Immediately after the meeting the chair needs to sit with the minuter and go through the minutes, ensuring that the interpretation placed on major points and decisions is correct.

Model Chairs

It is useful to think of models of good chairs, male or female, and to determine their characteristics. Many women at my 'women as managers' sessions can produce gender-free characteristics of timing, management, involving people, relevance, keeping the pace going, ensuring action takes place. They also find it useful to think of specific good *women* chairs they have known, deciding how their behaviours can be adopted.

Sally Brown's termly publications committee meetings attract people from all over the UK. We have agenda and papers in advance and refresh ourselves with constant tea and coffee. We know that the agenda will end on time with decisions negotiated and agreed on, action points with names and dates beside them, so that we all have a task to do after the meeting. Sally handles moments of committee decision-making sensitively and briskly. She has even had us making design decisions one after another through assembling examples of our choices well in advance, saving weeks of mailing. Items are ticked off, logically covered and everyone is invited to discuss. Larger new ideas are given an early airing and sub-groups are set to work to prepare more for next time, circulating ideas in the meantime. There is a formal space for necessary informal discussion among widely dispersed colleagues. Sally shakes up the action-centred meeting with brainstorming sessions, freeing up our creative thinking using flipcharts and groups to develop ideas. This helps to maintain energy and enables the meeting to have both a developmental and a business function.

The idea of breaking up a formal meeting with creative activities is a novel one, lending itself to negotiating and sharing. It really uses the resources of the group, and allows the chair to both facilitate and to join in. Maidi Brown's validation meetings are a model for a formal meeting. These last all day, proceeded often by an evening meeting and the reading of heavy validation tomes of documentation. One of Maidi's main skills is identifying the different agendas of the meeting's members, and drawing an agenda from what we perceive as the main items to address. Items are discussed and specific ones allocated to team members to raise with the course team. The actual day is well-orchestrated with pre-meetings to define agenda, main meetings with all or parts of the management team, regroupings of the validation team to reset the scene and decide on emerging items. It is as highly formalized as a dance, but also responsive to the immediacy of the situation, allowing for the drawing-up of main items, changing, developing, refocusing as needs be. It is important that everyone is kept both mellow enough to be sensible and not hot-tempered, and on their toes enough to ask and answer the questions in a partnership exchange. It is important also for the chair to spot developments and answers of importance at every turn, adding these to the overall jigsaw of the validation. Refocusing and maintaining the energy levels, good humour and stamina of the team are essential. (I have seen Maidi doing all of this, even with a heavy cold.)

It is difficult to argue that these are specifically female styles. They are successful and take strength both from the stamina women must maintain when faced with organizing homes after a full day's work, and the creative play of energy many develop when meeting ossified routines which refuse thought and creativity. It is useful to look both at the qualities of good chairs, in every context, and at the qualities of women who manage well, communicate, negotiate, plan and carry out actions well, thoughtfully, appropriately and effectively. The skills are similar. We can all embrace and adopt *our own* versions of them, to suit our own contexts and personalities. In order to be well-planned, well-controlled and effective, chairs who get the best out of their energized meetings members, we do not have to turn into mimic men, harridans or a soap-opera queen. We have to recognize and work on the strengths and skills we operate in other contexts and focus on chairing. For many of us taking the chair effectively is the first step towards other management roles, if we want them, and in itself it is most rewarding. A good job can be seen to be done. It is based on people communicating, negotiating, creating, sharing, deciding and agreeing to act. This is the foundation for effective day-to-day and longer-term work in higher education. As women it is certainly high time that more of us were taking the chair rather than being sat on!

Women Supervising Others

Many women play roles of a supervisory nature. It is interesting to consider how we play these roles, what characteristics are in our favour, what we need to learn to do without sacrificing difference and integrity, in order to be good supervisors and, subsequently, good senior managers.

As women we can identify the aspects of the role we feel we can best operate, some aspects of which are gender-free, others gender-specific. We can emphasize the equal importance of these aspects as any of those more traditionally associated with male managers or supervisors. The model is changing in these times of turbulence and redefinition, and will change further as more of us play the roles according to our negotiation with and interpretation of the 'rules' of the role. Interestingly the association of masculinity with management spills over into conceptions about the 'managed'. Management tasks relating to the curriculum, staff development and devaluation are conceptualized as if gender-neutral, or with masculinity as the silent yardstick in measuring staff and pupil needs. Knowledge and experience of gender-linked issues are not normally the required preparation for management.

It is particularly important to recognize the variety and value of supervisory skills within management and a management training context which aims to develop women in higher education. Research on women's roles and advancement within higher education, as within other institutional contexts, suggests that women are more likely to be skilled in the various techniques and considerations associated with supervisory skills, such as communications, liaison, interpersonal relations, cooperative working structures. For many women the advancement to a role which depends on supervisory skills is the first real step towards full managerial responsibility. Many will not want to move anywhere else, finding fulfilment in the range of roles offered here.

Whatever the promotional desires, it is primarily this skills area which forms the focus and locus for women's management training. Women need opportunity to train for careers in senior management, where they still constitute only a small minority (Vaughan and Lasky, 1991).

I have run courses on supervisory skills to small, mixed-gender groups using what appeared to be gender-free materials. In practice, however, I have found that many of the assumptions, the do's and don'ts of such (actually rather male-oriented) materials often seem to contradict the working styles with which I and other women were happy. I have come to the conclusion about the inappropriateness of many materials which do not suit us as women. We need our own, which will have some similarities, and some differences. Some supervisory skills include:

- coaching and training;
- communicating;
- motivating;
- delegating;
- time-management;
- counselling;
- appraising;
- negotiating workloads, deadlines, achievements, solutions to problems;
- giving bad news and criticism;
- recognizing and rewarding;
- liaison 'up' to superiors/managers, the hierarchy, and 'down' to the supervisee/trainee/those who work to us.

On more careful reflection, many of the skills and assumptions underlying the role raised gender-related questions and issues in terms of how well they accorded with practices which seemed widespread among women staff, the strengths and weaknesses we felt we had, the developmental needs we spotted and the demands of the role in the institutional context. Some conflicts of role and some positive characteristics which women in particular seem to have were not being fully recognized and harnessed productively. They need recognizing, valuing and developing further.

Supervisory skills or team work?

> Leadership characteristics and the masculine sex role correspond so closely that they are simply different labels for the same concept. (Marshall, 1984)

What's in a name? What do supervisory and management roles signify to us?

The first problem was with the term 'supervisory' because, as one woman course member pointed out, what we really need is 'team building'. And here is the nub of the difficulty. Supervisory roles imply a conscious hierarchy and a maintenance of hierarchical divisions, while team-building suggests sharing, working in a group with mixed roles without emphasizing the hierarchical elements.

Positive and negative role images

Faced with negative stereotypes perpetuated by others, internalized by us, we need to establish a different image, one which accords with our own various ways of working and seeking and maintaining support from those we supervise. While we seek some positive models, we need to bear in mind the *other* conflicts which are inherent in this role for women. Supervisory skills might be the management area most likely to attract women, but it might then be tinged with that nurturing image which seems to denigrate women's hard work.

According to Quince and Lansbury (1988), women managers have been handicapped in another way by their sex-role conditioning: namely, by being steered – even if seemingly by their own free choice – towards the nurturing roles found mainly in human resources management. 'Unfortunately, this specialization has lower status, less influence and lower average salaries than most others in management (Knockly, 1990). The warning is clear. A revaluing of supervisory skills must include the valuing and training of nurturing skills, recognizing their equal importance to the 'harder headed' management skills of financial management.

Characteristics of a good woman supervisor

Communicating and liaison

A supervisor liaises between the various members of the hierarchy, decision-makers and supervisees. Keeping informed is important, as is communicating needs and doubts, problems and strategies backwards and forwards between those in layers of responsibility to the supervisee. As supervisor, you need to be accessible, responsible and knowledgeable, to know where to find the information even if you do not have it yourself.

Communication skills are central to this function and also to the immediate relationships with the supervisee and they are skills that women often have. The ability to determine covert and overt messages, read body language, read between the lines in directions, questions or complaints are only too familiar. We are constantly reading the body language of others at work and at home and acting on it, recognizing the gap between what people say and what their bodies express. This can help us determine what our supervisees really feel and understand about conditions, practices and tasks at work. Work is much more likely to be done well when clearly understood, so we can use this important raft of verbal and non-verbal communication skills to ensure it is fully understood and agreed. Feedback on quality, changes, developments and future work must also be given, received and acted on appropriately. Sometimes this involves praise and sometimes constructive criticism, which we must not shirk even if we feel awkward giving it. The expression of recognition of a good job well done can seem patronizing. In a positive model of women's practices, the team spirit and networking, the nurturing and other social skills give us inroads into praising and recognizing good work openly from a basis more akin to equality than hierarchy. Some women I work with have established group routines for such recognition of work well done which are not patronizing, and which reflect the path the woman (or man) concerned plays in the team working together within the institution.

The role also involves giving constructive criticism in a positive way. You need to be able to:

- give bad news, point out mistakes, and encourage the reflection and practice which lead to overcoming problems and mistakes;

- reward and recognize good work without seeming patronizing;

- be sympathetic without appearing weak and merely bending to a variety of excuses and problems with which your supervisees face you;

- be responsive to needs and the different personalities of those who work with and to you;

- be aware of body language, overt and covert communications;

- be able to listen attentively and respond sensitively and appropriately to questions, aired problems and suggested needs.

Communicating: ensuring the completion of tasks

We all have different personal communication styles. These need to adapt to time and place. If we want to make sure we have an adult, reasonable exchange, it is as well to avoid vague orders, such as 'I think you ought to be working a bit harder', because unless this is used as a friendly rallying or the gentle first of a series of increasingly more explicit warnings, the recipient won't really know what the issue is and will feel confused. Bribes such as offers of time off are often an admission of weakness. If genuine offers can be fulfilled special requests are reasonable, but not too often. If it is necessary to ask people to work long hours because there is a special emergency, then offer time off or whatever is realistically reasonable. Threats of telling the line-manager if a task is not performed or not performed to standard can seem hollow if you do not have the power to back them up. They can seem an admission of weakness. If someone has had explicit warnings, and bad practices have not changed as a result, possible repercussions and procedures need pointing out.

Pleading 'Please do this or I shall get in trouble' is a weak way of managing. It should only be used when there is a real favour needed for the work to be completed. This is an exchange which is more on a personal than a professional level, so using it too much actually reduces professional credibility.

Reasoned, explicit requests are preferable to orders. Give clear reasons for asking for work, set in contexts and against objectives which have been explained, with clear and negotiated time and resource constraints. The supervisee will feel their views have been sought. They know why they are being asked to do something, and they know the difficulties which could arise if it is not done. They have not been made to feel threatened, patronized, or forced by pleading and bribery into doing more and different tasks from what is expected of them. While it is difficult to remember to comply with these sorts of guidelines, they should make for a more honest, adult working relationship with mutual respect.

Evaluation and Appraisal

The role carries with it elements of appraisal, evaluation, feedback and redirection. You need to be able to advise those who are clearly in the wrong job, or carrying out dangerous, incorrect, inappropriate practices, and to suggest alternative ways of working to overcome these problems and faults. You need to have a good close eye on the emotional responses of those who work with and to you and, while not letting these dominate, nonetheless recognize their importance and how they affect work. For many of us as wives, mothers, daughters, sisters, we are used to interpreting the needs of others and responding to them, as we are also used to discussing and sharing the problems of others with a view to helping sort them out mutually, in a sharing manner. These skills are all transferable to the supervisory role, with the necessary 'edge' added that the context is one of work, not friendship. If there are problems about transferring these communication and sharing skills, they might well fall into two areas: first, the inability to recognize that the skills of dealing with supervisees are actually like those we use in the family and among friends, but with that harder edge: it is someone's job, it is the needs of the institution we are considering. Second, we cannot afford to let sympathy and friendships cloud our judgement, since to do so will not be in anyone's interest in the end. We must make sure we are clear, firm, responsive, appropriately directed and professional.

Delegation: cooperation not competition. Sharing and collaborating

For many women, the image of management projected by practitioners and selectors is not compelling. It is not just a lack of knowledge or training which serves to create barriers for women but their rejection of these elements of the role which they see as masculine. In particular, women managers pinpoint aspects for management practice which they find repugnant or dysfunctional: namely, aggressive, competitive behaviours, an emphasis on control rather than negotiation and collaboration, and the pursuit of competition rather than shared problem-solving. Some of the chacteristics of management roles, including that of supervisory skills, need redefining to avoid these negative role models.

In a hierarchical system, one which is arguably more likely to be man-made, created and run, concerns with maintaining a superior position, pride and hierarchical divisions sit oddly with the networking and sharing skills of women. We are probably less likely to feel that we can delegate as a matter of course and expect all aspects of the work to be carried out without question. But delegation is part of the role, so how should we manage it to maintain good relations which are not overpowering, and not so very friendly and equal as to make it difficult to request that tasks be carried out?

You need to be firm and flexible, reasonable and objective, not to delegate excessively and hand over the responsibility which is yours, thus shirking that responsibility and perhaps leaving those who work to you in a vulnerable position. Similarly, you must ensure that you do not hang on to each piece of responsibility, denying access to it to others.

The aggressively competitive, controlling behaviours Al-Khalifa (1989) identifies with masculine role norms are not the only ways to delegate. We can recognize the individual skills of others, help nurture and train these, and then delegate appropriately, with no need to feel competitive with the person to whom we have delegated, nor to jealously guard all the responsibilities to ourselves.

Delegating is not just a matter of offloading the nasty bits of one's work on to someone else. It is actually a very necessary part of time and task management. It is also a contributing factor to the supervisor's coaching and training work. In order to delegate you must be able to define the skills of those working to you, and match these up with the appropriate tasks, ensuring that the supervisee does not merely do the mundane tasks, but sometimes the tasks you would like to do yourself, and the pleasant ones, the ones which might stretch and help develop their abilities. It is unfair to delegate tasks for which the load of responsibility is so great that the supervisee is put in a potentially awkward position. You have the responsibility: delegation is a responsible, negotiated activity with tasks being chosen within the organizational context, according to clear objectives in relation to skills. So how can women move on in management roles ?

Coaching and Training

'When women change administrative positions they are more likely to move within the institution, whereas men are more likely to be recruited from outside it' (Johnsrud, 1991). Management research such as that carried out by Johnsrud indicates that women are more likely to gain promotion within institutions, and men are more frequently recruited from outside, but that within institutions for higher level positions, staff are usually selected for their similarity to the current postholder or (usually) his colleagues. 'Similarity to self' is not very helpful to women seeking promotion when the self in question is usually male. Vaughan and Lasky (1991) argue the importance of women's accessibility to management training since this can equip them with the appropriate qualifications and confidence to apply for those higher level jobs. For those thinking about those staff who work to us, their own training and coaching needs must be catered to as far as they relate to the institutional context. Like our probably male managers loftily above us, we carry much of the power to limit or help expand their choices, their flexibility, their directions.

Coaching and training are other key features. For many women the sharing of information and skills and the pooling of work tasks are things with which we are all familiar and skilled. Under this model, though, it is possible to forget the specific training needs of our supervisees, because we are aware of how we all pull together to get a job done, rather than aware of their individual professional development, even as we might well ignore our own in the concentration of getting the job done, as a team. You need to be aware of the performance and the training and education and professional development needs of others, and to help clarify these, rendering them realistic and helping them ensure they start to become real when it is possible.

Develop a coaching and training plan, agreed with those you supervise. Set times and tasks to enable them to be trained, coached, taught new tasks and their progress monitored. Opportunities for appropriate outside courses or workshops all need spotting and passing on. Keep an eye on which kinds of training and development are personal and which professional, to get a good balance.

Motivating

One central role of the supervisor is to act as motivator. It is difficult to motivate staff when you are in recession, or the institution, faculty, department or section have bad relationships. It is important then to concentrate on sorting out problems, trying to set up and maintain good relationships, and giving people the opportunity to air their grievances and fears. Then move on to think about the importance of doing a professional job well.

You need to be able to motivate even when you feel unmotivated yourself. Develop an *objective* outlook which enables you to weigh up the good and bad points and work together with others to concentrate on the good. Develop enthusiasm and clarify goals, deal with fears and difficulties and move on. Encourage the demotivated who cannot see the relevance of their job to get a sense of belonging and direction in professional terms, as well as in social terms, so that the team can work harmoniously together. These skills are like the ones we employ as a good friend: a spot of direct talking, a lot of cheering up and some objective goal-planning. They should be easily and genuinely transferable to the work situation.

People are motivated by different things at different times. If we are motivated by professional satisfaction, or prestige, for example, we might not understand why someone who works to us could be motivated by the enjoyment of working in a good social atmosphere, or the need to get a living wage, to work in comfortable surroundings, or to get personal and professional satisfaction out of doing a job as perfectly as possible. We need to work with those in the team to determine the motivating factors and ensure they are fulfilled; then the institution's needs, as well as the team's, will be better satisfied.

Relationships

It is difficult to maintain hierarchical positions if you believe that networking and information-sharing are good models for teamwork. It is important for women supervisors to build on these networking skills when they move into a different relation of power. The most successful networking of women I ever experienced was in an intensely hierarchical organization which depended on divisions of power between the men, and assumed that such divisions would be paralleled by the women staff. These ranged much more widely between typists and secretarial staff, office managers, lecturers and research managers. We networked well. Being honest about the specific needs of the organization, we shared these and divided up the work. We shared problems as and when they arose and we did not keep unnecessary secrets to retain power. This made for flexible working and some fantastic rallying and sharing when various elements of the job became tough.

Straightforward dealings and *networking* are major characteristics of successful women supervisors. *Clear information channels* and *sound communication practices* also help to clarify what work needs to be done and what needs to support the work and the team members. Work tasks must be explained and agreed, and if anyone is worried or blocked by these they must seek out advice and help sort out the problems. *Clear negotiated tasks* and *mutual support* are the main features.

Conclusions

Our nurturing characteristics, our flexibility, cooperation, collaboration, networking, sharing and problem-solving are *the* skills for supervisors and managers of the future: 'It is the variety of roles carried by women at present and their openness to different levels of experience in daily life which is a positive model to adopt and adapt for a full and richer life for all in the future' (Hughes and Kennedy, 1985). In a time when 'turbulence and change' characterize the revaluation and rewriting of management roles, women's flexibility and movement into these roles can cause a radical change in accepted practices and role redefinitions. It is not necessary to denigrate characteristics associated with caring and sharing, nor need we adopt masculine, outdated models. It is important to share our ideas and practices in women-only groups in the first instance and, out of the confidence that such sharing affords us, to feel secure in the development of our women-centred supervisory practices. Such a positive move might even start to redress that gender imbalance in the senior management ranks. Who knows?

References

Al-Khalifa, E (1989) 'Women teachers and school management' in *Women Teachers: Issues and Experiences,* H De Lyon and F Widdowson Mignivuolo (eds) Open University Press, Buckingham, p.93.

Hughes, M and Kennedy, M (1985) *New Futures: Changing Women's Education,* RKP, London, p.17.

Johnsrud, L (1991) 'Administrative promotion', *Journal of Higher Education,* 12, 2, March/April.

Knockly, D (1990) 'Salary surveys reveal top jobs', *Australia,* 10 February, 35.

Marshall, J (1984) *Women Managers: Travellers in a Male World,* John Wiley, Chichester.

Nicholson, B (1986) in his Speech as the Chairman of the Manpower Services Commission.

Quince, A and Lansbury, R (1988) 'Two steps forward but going nowhere: Women in management in Australia', *Employee Relations*, 10, 6, 26–31.

Vaughan, E, and Lasky, B (1991) 'How will women manage? A speculation on the effects of equal opportunities in management training', *Journal of General Management*, 16, 4, 53–60.

Chapter 11

Managing the Balancing Act

If you want a job doing well, give it to a busy person.

Might it be that we could use the opportunity created by the increasing numbers of women entering management, with the possibly different approach that they may bring to the organizational culture, to reassess the nature and balance of the work and non-work sphere of our lives, to produce a healthier society? (Alban Metcalfe, 1987, p.195)

The old adage about giving jobs to busy people certainly rings true when we think about the variety of tasks and roles we have to balance as women in our daily jobs within higher education. Recently I visited a Russian circus. I was impressed with the female clown's setting to and managing the balancing of whirling plates on sticks, just catching each plate and giving it an extra twirl at the exact moment when it looked as though it was about to fall off its perch. I really identified with her!

Being able to manage a variety of roles and tasks at any one time is an example of that famous female flexibility and diversity. We do have to be careful, however, that it does not become a millstone around our necks and that we do not hamper our own rise to power or our own management of stress as we take on more roles, intent on proving ourselves to be super-women. We need to practise stress and time management, identify the roles and needs which are in the balancing act for each of us. We need to learn to support each other and develop coping and planning strategies for ourselves and others. We also need to learn to say 'No' when we cannot do a professional job and will become overwhelmed, and learn to prioritize so that we do not find all those plates collapsing on top of us.

What is in the balance?

Most women working in higher education balance at least two roles. They have a job, full- or part-time, and a set of domestic responsibilities to family, parents, partners and sometimes a host of pets and close friends besides. Many of us also balance various roles within our jobs, coping with the complexities of teaching, administration and research. Increasingly, more demands are being made on us to take on and develop the various roles related to our jobs. If we are women academics there is increasing pressure to research. If we want to further our careers, we all have to take on more administrative responsibilities whether or not we also teach and research. Other balancing acts include balancing the demands made by the various people to whom we report, and those whom we supervise, as well as those with whom we work closely. We balance working with administrative and support staff, personal assistants, secretarial, clerical and technical staff, and other teaching staff on modules, course schemes, working parties and quality groups. Within the complex institution of a university, we have many relationships at work and many responsibilities. The tensions and demands of these often build up simultaneously, so that we are faced with a variety of heavy demands at particular points during the year.

Varieties of roles and activities

In order to consider the variety of role demands and various elements in the balancing act, it is useful to review where our particular responsibilities and activities, where our strengths, rewards and demands lie. One way of doing this is initially to look at the skills, activities, roles, demands and pleasures identified under the categories of home, work and other related activities (see Figure 11.1).

Once you have started to fill in your own version of this figure, you need to ask yourself some questions.

What skills, problems, demands, strengths or rewards appear in each of the circles? What overlaps are there? Are there any strengths and enjoyments which appear in one area which could be usefully developed and used in

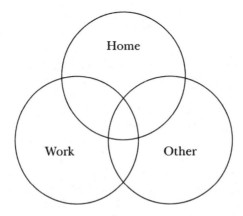

Figure 11.1 *Balancing responsibilities*

another, such as a skill in out-of-home activities, for example, running a PTA or a Guide group, which shows strengths not yet being fully recognized or used at work, which could be built on. Then ask yourself whether there are any specific outlets and relaxation areas, personal development and enjoyment areas which appear in home or 'other' which can balance some of the tensions and demands of work. Perhaps they let you develop such skills or provide an opportunity to do something completely different. The clue is to decide what kind of part they play in your life and whether the unstressful, sporting or social activities, or alternative demanding roles, help to offset the stresses and demands of work, those of work the demands of home, and so on. If you find there is an overload of similar demands or of damagingly conflicting demands in the various different strands and areas of your life, you will need to think about changing things, about coping with the clashes. Often it is the recognition of differences and balances which offset tensions which actually helps us to see the benefits of the different areas. If you discover there is nothing else than work, consider developing other activities, a hobby or sport, which can help you divert stress away from work, develop differently or help you to escape. What suits one person will not suit another, but we can also learn from discussing our completion of these areas with others. With a colleague, try to match the ways in which you have filled in the area. This is just the beginning of a personal development plan. From this audit of interests, skills potential and pressures you can start to decide which areas to work on, which to integrate, which to set off against each other and which to avoid.

Balancing rather than collapsing under the stress

The kinds of balancing acts we can cope with will vary as much as our personalities. Recognize what you thrive on and what to avoid. I thrive on variety but with some overlap. If I am involved in many different activities, some of which have a common theme of skills or interest, I can carry out a certain balancing. The overlap and interfaces will help me keep various activities running simultaneously. There are dangers in everything being connected and relying on the same skills and contacts, producing the same demands and responsibilities. Everything could fail at the same time. The same kinds of stresses could emerge simultaneously in each area of your life. If you can manage to keep separate some activities in your work, home or other areas of your life you have something totally different to turn to should disaster strike. If you play squash, go riding or enjoy listening to classical music, there is no reason why that should be affected by a particular manager finding fault with your work, blocking your new idea, or removing from you an area of work you enjoy, or whatever currently causes work problems. Some of the most balanced people can maintain a home life which provides an escape from their work demands, or a work life which provides an escape from home.

Sometimes outside pursuits can be more stressful than home or work. If we compete in sport, dancing, painting, poetry or dog showing, there are other stresses and rewards. It is up to us to decide where skills shown elsewhere, ignored at work, can be recognized, developed, used and rewarded at work. From chairing local committees we can move to chairing university meetings. From time managing and organizing families and local groups we could transfer these skills to management at work, whether it be of classroom activities and teaching/learning strategies with students, or the running of an office or unit, or both. The important consideration is whether we want to transfer and develop these skills at work, and how and where to do so. First we need our own personal skills and directions audit.

Balancing research and teaching

If you are expected to carry out both research and teaching, you will probably also have those other domestic and outside responsibilities to consider. There are contradictory findings about the success of various balancing acts. Margherita Rendel's research (1986) suggests that women with domestic responsibilities actually produce proportionally more research and published papers than do single men: an interesting example of a successful balancing act which gives you heart! This is contradicted by Over (1982) in his study of psychologists, but there are subject differences which could account for the overall differences in these findings. Shirley Fisher (1994) comments that domestic responsibilities may play a big part in the discrepancies found between the publication and research rates of men and women: 'The difference in publication rates may reflect the dual role of women in that rearing children even with back-up services may create overload' (Fisher, 1994, p.58).

However, there are growing loads currently being placed on both men and women. In higher education we are increasingly being asked to publish and research and always on top of heavy teaching and administrative loads. Fisher (1994) considered the difficulties university staff have in managing the different demands on their time. She divided up groups of academic staff in relation to their expectations and their role demands and the stress these caused. Staff were grouped according to their sense of identity as researcher/administrator/teacher, teacher/administrator/researcher or administrator/researcher/teacher, each role balance reflecting how the staff member saw their priorities and the demands of the job. Asking academics what caused stress for them in this complex balancing act, Fisher found that research was frequently prioritized as the activity academics most wished to be involved in, but which caused most stress because it could only be performed in congenial circumstances. As demands increased to produce research output under the research assessment exercises, pay-offs increased, but stress did too. Changes in academic life produce different expectations and stress in staff.

Administrative and support staff balancing acts

Administrative or support staff manage different kinds of balancing acts against a different background to their academic counterparts. Often they are responsible for the running of an office or unit, and they are also likely to be working closely with other support and academic staff who either directly or indirectly require their support services. Here a balancing role emerges as the staff member has to deal with the different demands of those to whom they work and with whom they work, balancing the mass of demands from different staff, and sometimes also from different students, often in a work atmosphere and setting which makes concentration and people-oriented skills difficult. The busy departmental secretary or office manager will have constant phone calls and demands from staff and the various administrative units within the university such as finance, student administration and academic standards, as well as students often physically crowding round them as they try to undertake their daily paper-based activities and phone calls.

Organizational skills are essential for this balancing act, or the different elements of the work will spill into each other. The longer-term paper-based demands will go unfulfilled as you concentrate on the immediate problems of the student or staff member in front of you. Keeping your temper, remaining calm, obtaining the necessary information within a set time rather than being harassed into feeling confused on the spot, are all necessary skills to maintain simultaneous activities running smoothly. In departmental offices staff often call in for a chat and expect both a friendly face and a sense of bustle. They can escape and you cannot. While their relaxing chat goes on, you have the mountain of paperwork at the back of your mind and the middle of your field of vision. Handling people politely and warmly without letting their demands take your working life over are skills most support staff learn fast and well.

Changing the university's culture to reward our diversity and balancing

Organizational cultures within universities are rarely geared to recognize the variety of roles which women are particularly likely to perform as equally valuable and essential. For many women in higher education administration, teaching and research loads are added to by being responsible for students' counselling and support needs. Further research into the experiences of women academics suggests that we are more likely to be singled out for support and counselling, even if we are not directly responsible for individual students, and that students will also seek women as supervisors for independent study and dissertations (sympathetic/empathetic male colleagues report similar experiences). Some aspects of these roles are similar to counselling and support activities. The downgrading and ignoring of pastoral roles is closely related to the devaluing and ignoring of much (socially necessary and essential) 'women's work', including housework and childcare. If these roles are part of our portfolio, they need to be recognized and rewarded, not assumed as a kind of social activity low on the scale of importance when it comes to promotion and the overall recognition of valued activities and skills within the department/faculty/unit/school. Within our varied roles in universities, and especially as we increase management responsibilities, it is important that we work to change the culture of academic establishments so that the varied roles women do perform, and perform well, are properly recognized and valued. We need to highlight the importance of the flexibility, diversity and balancing strengths which so many of us have, ensuring these are seen not as 'butterfly' behaviours, rushing from bitty task to ill-completed bitty task, but the awe-inspiringly well-organized, timed and balanced flexible range of performances they are.

Balancing and/or prioritising

Stewart and Salt (1981) make a case for the benefits of a complex balancing act. They suggest that working women who are married and have domestic reponsibilities are likely to be better able to balance their varied demands, and to be in better health than those who are either single or full-time at home: 'their results suggest that working women who are married generally fare better in terms of well being and health than those at home in traditional roles and those who are single and work' (Fisher, 1994, p.58).

But domestic responsibilities take away the physical time for work preparation, research and publishing. They also prevent many women from undertaking their research work at all because the facilities they need are outside the home and they cannot stay late in the lab, pop in on Saturdays or work through the school holidays. Single-mindedness might well be the characteristic which enables the setting up and completion of complex experiments. Fisher suggests that the single-minded male with or without domestic responsibilities (but not a first-line carer) will probably find it easier than a woman with responsibilities at home to indulge his need for this concentration. Women, on the other hand, are probably more likely to be

144 Empowering Women in Higher Education

snatching moments of study and working wherever available. A favoured workplace for many women is the kitchen or dining-room table.

As women we must be careful not to be the victims of that famous versatility. While Stewart and Salt (1981) suggest there is a 'buffer' around women with multiple roles, the stresses of work being offset by demands of home, nonetheless 'defocusing because of multiple roles may be beneficial in many ways but may hit productivity rather harder' (Stewart and Salt, 1981). We need to harness this diversity and balance to our own ends – sanity and productivity.

Balancing the demands of academic life and domestic responsibilities: how can higher education change?

The difficulties of the integration of domestic and work responsibilities, styles of practice and pressures are, as for women students, partly caused by our socialized expectations of women's performance of domestic roles. They are partly caused or exacerbated by the men-centredness, not women-centredness, of academic insitutions. Noble and lauded are the male academics sometimes to be seen trailing children into their offices at the end of school. Criticized as poor managers, obviously unable to give of their all to the university, seen as confirming the 'pin money' version of working women, are the women academics who actually hide their children, racing around to ensure there are no reasons for criticism about the lack of 100% concentration on the ever-extending working day.

Nancy Hensel (1991), looking specifically at American higher education strategies, argues that few studies have considered the relationships betwen marriage/parenthood and scholarship. Using an economic or availability model, she suggests that the climate in higher education must change to enable women to achieve their full potential, 'if higher education is to solve issues of faculty diversity and the impending shortage of qualified teachers' (Hensel, 1991, p.v). She foresees a shortage of academics. The UK does not. But her suggestions for change in HE to accommodate women academics with domestic responsibilities are a model. I am always wary of an economic argument. One which encouraged women returners because of potential job-market shortages would just as easily have packed them back to the kitchen sink with rising unemployment. Human potential and equal opportunities are stronger arguments. Women also provide particular modes of behaviour, models and skills which higher education cannot afford to ignore. For these reasons it should strive to enable its talented and skilled women staff to perform well, and to fulfil domestic responsibilities without being desperately torn apart and stressed.

Hansel's suggestions are sweeping but logical and they are sensitive to the needs and requirements of women academics. There should be changes to:

1. address inequities in hiring, promotion, tenure and salaries of women;
2. 'family responsiveness' evaluation of university practices and policies should be conducted to eliminate factors of work/home conflict and see where support is needed;
3. a recruitment and hiring policy responsive to dual-career couples;
4. a maternity policy which actually enables women to take leave without too much disruption to students' study, for example by rearranging modules in certain semesters, and not disadvantaging the women academics;
5. a family leave policy should be developed and both parents encouraged to take advantage of it;
6. allow new parents to reduce their teaching loads for a designated period;
7. look at the provision of on-campus childcare;
8. reduce the number of early morning and late evening obligations and so enable academics to have a life outside the university;
9. review examining, teaching and research expectations for everyone.

These are wonderful suggestions. In order to work they must be accompanied by changes in attitudes so that there is no stigma attached to women with children dealing with domestic demands, particularly at certain points in their own and their children's lives. The humanizing element of integrating domestic and work thoughts and activities should not be ignored. Women should be rewarded for being better when they are better, with the more obvious nurturing counselling roles having an equal standing with research and teaching roles. It is important that all women academics are recognized, valued, promoted, supported and able to act.

Successful women in higher education: the universities' need for innovative balancing acts

Mona Wasow (1992) has grave concerns about women staff and students in higher education. Wasow looks at the pressure to produce fast and argues that this works against reflection and quality:

> Most original, complex ideas evolve over many years and develop out of passions, beliefs and dreams, as well as rigorous scholarship. All this takes time... constant compromise can do a lot to destroy a person's self-confidence, desires and dreams... there has always been pressure for excellence, for getting publications out, and for making a name for oneself. It is a question of degree. (Wasow, 1992, p.486)

Breda Gray (1994) looks at Wasow's work in her argument that women in higher education and especially within women's studies have created space to question and develop definitions of academic knowledge but have not developed the space to allow reflective and challenging practices in their own work. Academic life absorbs all energies: 'In order for women to develop their presence in higher education, a life of dedication is required' (Gray, 1994, p.78). This leaves few options open. Some women for whom this is a job but not their total life commitment will find themselves alienated and falling behind. Others will want to compete within the academic system and seek success in the research ratings. If they are successful they might or might not extend the practices and power of this success to other women, through enabling practices. Some recognize that this success is on the terms of a system which actually excludes the variety of their lives, shuts out and prevents anything domestic and much that is creative other than work. Others will not collude and feel torn both ways. Still others dedicate their lives to challenging the system and finding alternatives. Most women probably fall between these different categories. Gray talks about many women becoming 'ambivalent academics' as a result of these tensions and balancing acts.

Qualities women in academic and managerial roles have to offer – why universities should be more flexible

Data from studies on women in successful management roles suggests creativity generated by flexibility, diversity and innovativeness, from being able to see from many angles and many experiences in solving problems, can help women's success. Kirton (1976) discusses the innovative nature which enables the crossing of boundaries and adaptation. He makes a correlation between women's success in the male-oriented worlds of work and their initial ability to recognize the need to make changes in attitudes and practices to become involved in the male-oriented world in the first place. Their first step is a response to challenge. They are likely to perceive established ways of working as ingredients for useful change. Another (male), who began in a position of power, may believe that maintaining that *status quo* (which after all has recognized and rewarded their conformity) is safer and more productive.

In the long run, organizations do not benefit from such stasis. Universities, like other organizations, need well-thought-out change, innovation, flexibility and creativity. Innovative, flexible and creative women who start to succeed are immensely useful if they are recognized and enabled. This is currently even more true in universities than before, with the rapidity of changes in terms of delivery styles, student group and conditions as well as the constant internal/external demands for information and quality assurance. Considering women's innate and developed flexibility within organizations which can be used to fuel change, Kirton:

> speculated that people who are most willing to cross boundaries of any sort are likely to be innovators. The more boundaries there are, and the more rigidly they are held, the more innovative the individual must be to cross them. This speculation has relevance to women working in male-dominated realms of work. It is plausible to suggest that women will need the ability to look beyond the existing paradigm which dominates thinking about the role of women in society. So as such, we would expect women who succeed in the world of work to be highly innovative. Evidence to support this may be drawn from a small-scale study of women managers and entrepreneurs. (White, 1989, p.172)

White (1989) carried out a small-scale study of female managers and entrepreneurs to see how their work patterns and successes related to Kirton's (1987) adaption-innovation inventory. The results (White, 1989) confirm the belief that successful women in organizations are adaptable and innovative, that organizations need these skills and that (for the successful women at least – a roundabout argument) they are rewarded. Cox and Jennings (1990) discovered that in comparison to élite entrepreneurs, successful women conformed less to rules, while successful women had a slightly lower score than the élite entrepreneurs on the scale which showed proficiency of ideas and ability to accept precision. Overall, successful women were found likely to innovate, to be creative and to resist conformity to rules and groups: 'The sucessful women are highly innovative. The above average scores... on each sub-scale indicate a preference for a proliferation of ideas and ability to cope with uncertainty and imprecision and a willingness and ability to resist rules and group pressure' (White *et al.*, 1992).

Major predictions are that even in a more stable world both men and women should be more adaptive in work behaviours. Women working in predominantly male-dominated worlds such as universities are likely be more innovative than men. Innovation and creative changes are the lifeblood of organizations, as are flexible work behaviours. Women need to question what is considered normative behaviour if they are to succeed, although they do not have to sacrifice either rigor or efficiency in the cause of innovation and creativity. Ryecroft (1989) has pointed out that top managers fulfil a variety of roles and flexibility is their key, thus matching the kinds of balancing behaviours we find in some people within universities.

Recognizing the value of our flexibility, innovative insights and behaviours is first of all our responsibility. Next we must persuade our line-managers and university organizations to recognize these valuable skills. Universities need us to be flexible, diverse and to manage a balancing act. We have to make sure we wish and know how do this, without buckling under the conflicts, contradictions and stresses produced by the sheer complexity of balancing or others' doubts of our abilities. The female clown in the Russian circus balancing the plates caused gasps of disbelief and wonder. Some did not believe she was really controlling them all at once and looked for wires. There weren't any wires: she was just creative, well-organized, flexible and clearly enjoying her ability to keep it all spinning. She got a big round of applause, too, when they had all been caught safely at the end of the act.

References

Alban Metcalfe, B (1987) 'Male and female managers: An analysis of biographical and self-concept data', *Work and Stress*, 1, 209–19.

Cox, C, and Jennings, R (1990) 'The foundations of success: The development, work experience and characteristics of British entrepreneurs and intrapreneurs', paper presented at the ENDEC International Entrepreneurship Conference, Singapore.

Fisher, S (1994) *Stress in Academic Life*, SRHE and Open University Press, Buckingham.

Gray, B (1994) 'Women in higher education: What are we doing to ourselves?' in *Changing the Subject*, S Davies, C Lubelska and J Quinn (eds), Taylor & Francis, London.

Hensel, N (1991) *Realizing Gender Equality in Higher Education: The Need to Integrate Work/Family Issues*, ASHE-ERIC Higher Education Report 2, The George Washington University, Washington DC.

Kirton, M J (1976) 'Adaptors and innovators: A description and a measure', *Journal of Applied Psychology*, 61, 5, 622–9.

Kirton, M J (1987) *KAI Manual*, 2nd edn, Occupational Research Centre, Hatfield.

Over, R (1982) 'Does research productivity decline with age?' *Higher Education*, 11, 511–20.

Rendel, M (1986) 'How many women academics 1912–1977?' in *Schooling for Women's Work*, R Deem (ed.), Routledge, London, pp142–61.

Ryecroft, T (1989) *Survey of Women Managers – Interim Report*, British Institute of Management, London.

Stewart, S and Salt, S (1981) 'Life stress, life styles, depression and illness in adult women', *Journal of Personality and Social Psychology*, 40, 6, 1063–9.

Wasow, M (1992) 'What are we doing to ourselves?' *Social Work*, 37, 6, 485–7.

White, B, Cox, C and Cooper, C (1992) *Women's Career Development: A Study of High Fliers*, Blackwell, Oxford.

White, B L (1989) 'A study of the characteristics of female managers and female entrepreneurs', unpublished MSc dissertation, UMIST.

Chapter 12
Conclusion

We women staff and students within higher education need to be empowered by our practices and processes and those of our universities if our full potential and flexible, creative practices are to be realized. Much ground has been won and many successful strategies and course processes have been embedded. There is a need to extend the practices of women's studies courses and the defined skills of women managers into higher education more generally if we are to move into the next century with full awareness of, and reward for, the flexibility, creativity and imaginative emotional responses which women staff and students have to offer higher education and employment.

Women who break like Alice through the 'glass ceiling' of higher education hierarchical positions often seem noticeably reluctant to lean back and help others up there with them, arguing that they achieved this position against all the odds by themselves, or that ability always wins out in an ultimately harsh, political but fair system. The women managers in academia, academic or support staff, might not always be the best advocates for other women, but they must be persuaded to reflect on their successful practices and pass their strategies on to others. Some successful women have had either to collude with a patriarchal system or define their own success within this system as a product of fitting into established structures and practices. They have become confused about the strengths they might share specifically with other still-ambitious women, and might also feel they have had to turn themselves into 'honorary men' and must further adopt and develop the behaviours of successful men to stay in position. It would be very naïve to have such an idealized view of women in higher education that assumes we are all aiming at equality and sisterhood – just like the arguments that insist if women were in control, war would be impossible.

The tone of this book on empowering women in higher education avoids such naïvety and equally pointless positions of negativity and cynicism. It is positive and useful. It is a discussion of women in higher education, both students and staff. It considers the ways in which, through recognizing structures, problems and contradictions, and through building upon strengths and successful strategies, we can work together as women and men to change higher education to better enable women. Universities should develop, confirm and build upon the knowledge and experience of those who have succeeded in making strategies, practical and attitudinal changes in their own and in institutional practices and provisions.

Curriculum and cultural change should be widespread. The balancing act must be helped by changes in practice, behaviour and provision. Women insist on bringing their social commitments to teaching and other activities within the university, but that change must be part of a general reconceptualization of the university role in society. And the competitive and hierarchical bureaucracy of the university, supportive only of personal ambition rather than cooperative work and communal goals, must make way for each new way of living and working in an academic community. In each of these cases a feminist scholarship may represent the beginning of a flowering of the humanities and a rehumanization of humanities' study. But to be truly revolutionary, these new ideas must permeate the whole life of the university. Women's freedom must be won, but so also must human freedom. The cultural change encompasses every subject and people at all levels of the university's structure.

Higher education needs to build upon and benefit from the flexible and successful practices of women staff and students. It needs to change behaviours, practices and cultures at all levels in all ways not just to accommodate women, but to recognize that they bring a flexibility and an experientially based, multiple-perspective, creative response to the demands of higher education and the labour market.

Index

INTEGRATED MATHEMATICS SCHEME

M2/N2 Answers

Bell & Hyman

First published 1985 by BELL & HYMAN
an imprint of Unwin Hyman Limited
Denmark House, 37-39 Queen Elizabeth Street,
London SE1 2QB

Reprinted 1987

Note: answers requiring diagrams are not provided

ISBN 0 7135 2529 0

Typeset by Advanced Filmsetters (Glasgow) Ltd.
Printed and bound in Great Britain by Thetford Press Limited,
Thetford Norfolk.

Exercise 1·1

Drawing

Exercise 1·2

A 1. $2/3 = 8/12 = 0.666$
$7/9 = 35/45 = 0.777$
$5/8 = 15/24 = 0.625$
$12/15 = 4/5 = 0.8$

2. $3/10 = 15/50 = 0.3$
$8/15 = 40/75 = 0.5333$
$1/2 = 124/248 = 0.5$

3. $4/5 = 16/20 = 0.8$
$8/20 = 2/5 = 0.4$
$70/100 = 35/50 = 0.7$
$3/9 = 1/3 = 0.333$

4. $5/6 = 75/90 = 0.8333$
$15/25 = 9/15 = 0.6$
$28/50 = 14/25 = 0.56$
$8/18 = 4/9 = 0.444$

B 1. True; $3 \times 10 = 5 \times 6$
4. True; $7 \times 8 > 9 \times 6$
7. True; $2 \times 8 > 3 \times 5$

2. True; $8 \times 3 = 12 \times 2$
5. False; $7 \times 4 > 3 \times 9$
8. True; $3 \times 15 > 4 \times 11$

3. False; $15 \times 8 \neq 40 \times 5$
6. True; $7 \times 7 > 10 \times 4$
9. True; $16 \times 80 > 25 \times 45$

C 1. 3/4
4. 1/3
7. 9/10

2. 7/15
5. 3/11
8. 81/194

3. 9/11
6. 9/20
9. 18/23

Exercise 1·3

A 1. 5/6
4. 10/21
7. 13/40

2. 3/4
5. 11/100
8. 12/27

3. 11/30
6. 12/20
9. 14/48

B 1. 1 1/15
4. 1 11/45

2. 1 1/8
5. 24/35

3. 39/40
6. 26/30

C 1. 5/6
4. 8/10 (= 4/5)
7. 13/16

2. 17/20
5. 47/40
8. 1 11/20

3. 1 1/24
6. 19/20
9. 4/5

D 1. 1/4
4. 3/8
7. 1/10

2. 3/10
5. 1/2
8. 23/90

3. 1/2
6. 1/4
9. 7/20

Exercise 1·4

A 1. 3 1/2
4. 9 19/20
7. 7 5/8

2. 6 1/4
5. 11
8. 4 4/15

3. 5 4/5
6. 5 1/6
9. 6 3/10

B 1. 1 1/4
4. 1 5/6
7. 1 9/20

2. 7/8
5. 1 3/4
8. 2 11/12

3. 3/4
6. 2 7/10
9. 2 11/15

C 1. $^3/_4$ in.   2. $6^3/_8$ in.   3. $30^1/_2$ min.   4. 1 hour, $34^1/_4$ min.
5. (a) $2^1/_4$ hours   (b) $2^5/_8$ hours   (c) 3 hours   (d) $1^7/_8$ hours

Exercise 1·5

A 1. 3/8
4. 4/25
7. 1/20

2. 1/12
5. 1/5
8. 12/40

3. 1/2
6. 8/15
9. 4/15

B 1. 0.083 33, 1/12
4. 0.093 75, 3/32
7. 0.3125, 5/16
10. 0.4666, 7/15

2. 0.4, 2/5
5. 0.12, 3/25
8. 0.4666, 7/15
11. 0.375, 3/8

3. 0.2, 1/5
6. 0.234 375, 15/64
9. 0.656 25, 21/32
12. 0.35, 7/20

C Drawing

D 1. 4
4. 2
7. 20/27

2. 4
5. 3
8. 2/3

3. 7 1/2
6. 1 1/10
9. 3/4

1

Exercise 1·6

A **1.** 6 1/4   **2.** 4 3/8   **3.** 2 17/32
    4. 6 3/16   **5.** 4 2/3   **6.** 8 1/6
    7. 11 1/9   **8.** 3 9/10   **9.** 2 11/40
    10. 5 31/40   **11.** 7 13/20   **12.** 16 4/5

B **1.** Drawing

2. (a) 2/7   **(b)** 4/9   **(c)** 10/13   **(d)** 1 1/4
    (e) 5/11   **(f)** 3/4   **(g)** 10/37   **(h)** 8/27

3. (a) 3   **(b)** 9 1/2   **(c)** 7 1/2
    (d) 3 3/4   **(e)** 2 4/9   **(f)** 8/15

Exercise 1·7

1. 3 9/10 kW   **2. (a)** $1^3/_4$ lb   **(b)** $2^1/_8$ lb
3. 15/16 in.   **4.** $1^1/_4$ in.   **5.** 16
6. (a) £8   **(b)** £10.33   **(c)** £9.33   **(d)** £18.93
7. No, there are 340 passengers travelling.
8. (a) 13.6 km   **(b)** 15 miles   **9. (a)** $24^3/_4$ Deutschmarks   **(b)** £18.89

10. (a) Several examples will show that the new fraction lies between the other two.
        The proof is simple (but will need discussion).

Step 10 $\frac{a}{b} < \frac{c}{d}$ where a, b, c and d are whole numbers

Step 20   Deduction $ad < bc$ (cross multiplication)

Step 30   Consider $\frac{a + c}{b + d}$, we want to show (i) $\frac{a}{b} < \frac{a + c}{b + d}$ (ii) $\frac{a + c}{b + d} < \frac{c}{d}$

Step 40 $\frac{a}{b} < \frac{a + c}{b + d}$ if $a(b + d) < b(a + c)$ i.e. if $ab + ad < ab + bc$
                    i.e. if $ad < bc$,   which is the case (Step 20)

Step 50 $\frac{a + c}{b + d} < \frac{c}{d}$ if $(a + c)d < (b + d)c$ i.e. if $ad + cd < bc + cd$
                    i.e. if $ad < bc$,   which is the case (Step 20)

Step 60   END

(b) If $\frac{a}{b} < \frac{c}{d}$ and both are less than 1, $\frac{ac}{bd}$ will be less than $\frac{a}{b}$.   Other results may be discovered.

Exercise 1·8

A **1.** $\frac{1}{-2}$ **2.** $\frac{3}{2(x + 2y)}$ **3.** $\frac{2ac}{b}$

    4. $\frac{a + b}{ab}$ **5.** $2 + \frac{a}{b} - \frac{b}{a}$ **6.** $\frac{x^2 - y^2}{2y}$

    7. 2   **8.** $\frac{p^2 + q^2}{p}$ **9.** $\frac{2x^3}{y}$ **10.** $\frac{a}{(b - c)}$

B **1.** $t = -14$ **2.** $m = \frac{29}{21}$ **3.** $z = \frac{4}{3}$ **4.** $p = \frac{-1}{5}$

    5. $x = -1$ **6.** $z = -4$ **7.** $x = -4$ **8.** $y = 3$

Exercise 2·1

A **1.** 20   **2.** 230   **3.** 36   **4.** 48
    5. 512   **6.** 369   **7.** 854   **8.** 773
    9. 450   **10.** 700   **11.** 1520   **12.** 4850
    13. 272   **14.** 445   **15.** 3207   **16.** 452

Exercise 2·1 *(cont.)*

B
1. 3	**2.** 4.2	**3.** 5.23	**4.** 4.87
5. 0.35	**6.** 0.482	**7.** 8.865	**8.** 180.3
9. 0.23	**10.** 0.144	**11.** 3.6	**12.** 45.2
13. 78	**14.** 0.0426	**15.** 0.0031	**16.** 0.1524

C
1. False	**2.** True	**3.** False	**4.** True
5. False	**6.** True	**7.** False	**8.** False

Exercise 2·2

A
1. 1.51×10^8	**2.** $1.00(8) \times 10^2$	**3.** 5.79
4. 5.94×10^1	**5.** 9.98×10^3	**6.** $3.06(3) \times 10^{-8}$

B
1. 1.75×10^1	**2.** 7.82×10^{-2}	**3.** 1.91
4. 1.33×10^7	**5.** 2.05×10^{-6}	**6.** 2×10^1

[handwritten: 1·8, 7·8, 1·9, 1·3, 2·1]

[handwritten right margin: 2 sig figs required]

C
1. 4.56×10^{-2} tonnes per person (45.6 kg) **2.** 2.66×10^{-2} tonnes per person (26.6 kg)
3. 1.752×10^4 litres; 9.636×10^{11} litres **4.** 5×10^7 cells
5. 5.321×10^{22} protons

[handwritten: 5·32.]

D
1. 1.23×10^{-2}	**2.** 1760	**3.** 1.6×10^4
4. (c) 2.56×10^2	**5.** 3.301×10^3	**6.** 9.3×10^7
7. 3.5×10^2; 3.5×10^{-2}	**8.** 2.649×10^9	

Exercise 2·3

1. Lengths: 11 mm, 2.3%; 8 mm, 2.2%. Area: 32 mm², 0.02%   **2.** 324, 3.5%
3. 120 m, 1.2%   **4.** 2610, 35.3%   **5.** 6.44 mpg, 15.3%
6. 536.5 m², 7.7%   **7.** 1.54, 2.5%
8. A0: 4%; A1: 3.9%; A2: 3.8%; A3: 3.8%; A4: 3.8%   **9.** A = 79.01 cm²
10. (a) 0.47 cm²   **(b)** 0.6%
    (c) Yes; the ancient result is equivalent to using 256/81 as an approximation of π.

Exercise 2·4

A
1. 386.98	**2.** 2.825 531	**3.** 1572.482 014
4. 2.089 401 828	**5.** 0.391 491 545	**6.** 26.494 289 24

B
1. Estimate: $2 \times 1 \times 11 = 22$; calculation: 17.644 45
2. Estimate: $(3 + 2) \times (14 + 26) = 200$; calculation: 210.3775
3. Estimate: $(1.5)^2 = 2.25$; calculation: 2.239 209
4. Estimate: $(5 \div 1) \times (6 \div 1) = 30$; calculation: 38.807
5. Estimate: $(63 \times 3)/8 = 24$; calculation: 21.579
6. Estimate: 160 000; calculation: 137 770
7. Estimate: $27 - (3 \times 9 \times 2) = -27$; calculation: -19.6218
8. Estimate: $19^2 = 361$; calculation: 379.2278
9. Estimate: $64\,000 \times 80 = 5\,120\,000$; calculation: 6 321 479
10. Estimate: $169 + 144 + 16 = 329$; calculation: 314.0525

Exercise 2·5

A
1. 99.95 – 100.04 m
2. 5.05 – 5.14 cm
3. 2.645 – 2.654 cm
4. 586.775 – 586.824 km
5. 24.995 – 25.004 kg
6. 4.45 – 4.54 tonnes
7. 7.245 – 7.254 tonnes
8. 4 h 25 min 25 sec – 4 h 25 min 34 sec

[*Note:* the same argument applies to the last measurement. Thus the 99.95 could in fact be 99.945 so we can *never* express the *exact* measurement. Think about it!]

9. 4.05 – 4.14 min (4 min 3 sec – 4 min 8 sec)
10. $484.5m – $485.4m

Exercise 2·5 *(cont.)*

B 1. $19.8025 - 20.6116 \, \text{cm}^2$ 2. $12.075 - 15.576 \, \text{cm}^2$ 3. $25.43 - 25.59 \, \text{cm}^2$
   4. $5.1875 - 5.6816 \, \text{cm}^2$ 5. $1520.9 - 1906.6 \, \text{cm}^3$ 6. $209 \, 562 - 221 \, 232 \, \text{mm}^3$
   7. $3817.3 - 3896.1 \, \text{cm}^3$ 8. $0.152 - 0.164 \, \text{m}^3$ 9. $1.858 - 2.120 \, \text{m}^3$
   10. $39 \, 888 - 40 \, 503 \, \text{cm}^3$

C 1. (a) anything between 105.4 and 135.4 miles (b) between 109.1 and 130.9 miles
   2. $£10 \, 150 \, 000 - £5 \, 750 \, 000 = £4 \, 400 \, 000$ 3. $188.5 - 201.5 \, \text{cm}^3$; $0.875 \, \text{g/cm}^3$

Exercise 3·1

A 1. (a) 1.3 cm, 2.5 cm (b) 1 cm, 2.9 cm (c) 1.5 cm, 1.9 cm
   (d) 1.3 cm, 2.9 cm (e) 1.6 cm, 2.5 cm (f) 4 mm, 28 mm
   (g) 20 mm, 35 mm (h) 12 mm, 25 mm (i) 4.4 cm, 7.5 cm
   (j) 2.8 cm, 6.3 cm (k) 1.5 cm, 3.5 cm
   2. (a), (b), (e), (g), (i), (j), (k)
   3. (a) 10 mm (b) 14 mm (c) 13 mm (d) 20 mm (e) 16 mm
   (f) 19 mm (g) 23 mm (h) 30 mm (i) 16 mm (j) 15 mm
   (k) 18 mm; (k) (g) has the greatest height
   4. (d) has almost equal diagonals.

C Make a class competition out of finding all the trapezia. [Lettering the diagrams will help.]

Exercise 3·2

A 1. $8 \, \text{cm}^2$ 2. $12.2 \, \text{cm}^2$ 3. $9.62 \, \text{cm}^2$ 4. $8.75 \, \text{cm}^2$ 5. $6.4 \, \text{cm}^2$
   6. $18.48 \, \text{cm}^2$

B 1. (a) $17.325 \, \text{cm}^2$ (b) $21.06 \, \text{cm}^2$ (c) $1.853 \, \text{cm}^2$
   2. $28.739 \, \text{cm}^2$ is the calculated area. [The drawing will require considerable skill.] Construct the 6.2, 5.7, 4.5 cm
   triangle first.

C 1. $75 \, \text{cm}^2$ 2. $a = 36 \, \text{cm}$ 3. $b = 12 \, \text{cm}$ 4. $h = 5 \, \text{cm}$
   5. The four areas are 224, 336, 624 and 416 mm^2

Exercise 3·3

A 1. $A = 0.5 \, \text{m}^2$, $B = 1.35 \, \text{m}^2$, $C = 1.9 \, \text{m}^2$, $D = 2.25 \, \text{m}^2$, $E = 2.5 \, \text{m}^2$,
   $F = 2.65 \, \text{m}^2$, $G = 2.65 \, \text{m}^2$, $H = 2.5 \, \text{m}^2$, $I = 2.25 \, \text{m}^2$, $J = 1.9 \, \text{m}^2$,
   $K = 1.35 \, \text{m}^2$, $L = 0.5 \, \text{m}^2$.
   $A + B + C + D + E + F + G + H + I + J + K + L = 22.3 \, \text{m}^2$
   2. $0 + 1.0 + 1.7 + \ldots + 1.7 + 1.0 + 0 = 22.3$
   3. $65.5 \, \text{m}^2$
B 1. $1563 \, \text{mm}^2$ 2. $1596 \, \text{mm}^2$ 3. $1424 \, \text{mm}^2$ 4. $1637 \, \text{mm}^2$
   [It would have been hard to put them in order of size by guessing.]

C 2. 0 mm, 30 mm, 40 mm, 46 mm, 49 mm, 50 mm, 49 mm, 46 mm, 40 mm, 30 mm, 0 mm.
   3. $150 \, \text{mm}^2$, $350 \, \text{mm}^2$, $430 \, \text{mm}^2$, $475 \, \text{mm}^2$, $495 \, \text{mm}^2$, $495 \, \text{mm}^2$, $475 \, \text{mm}^2$, $430 \, \text{mm}^2$, $350 \, \text{mm}^2$,
   $150 \, \text{mm}^2$. Total $= 3800 \, \text{mm}^2 = 38 \, \text{cm}^2$.
   4. Estimate for $\pi = 38 \div 12\frac{1}{2} = 3.04$. [Low because every trapezium loses some of the area.]
   5. It should agree.

4

Exercise 3·4

Region	Base (measured)	Offset 1 (measured)	Offset 2 (measured)	Area	Working
A	21 m	0 m	16 m	168 m²	← ½(0 + 16) × 21
B	17 m	16 m	17 m	280.5 m²	← ½(16 + 17) × 17
C	19 m	17 m	17 m	323 m²	← ½(17 + 17) × 19
D	14 m	17 m	0 m	119 m²	← ½(17 + 0) × 14
E	17 m	0 m	18 m	153 m²	← ½(0 + 18) × 17
F	17 m	18 m	17 m	297.5 m²	← ½(18 + 17) × 17
G	16 m	17 m	13 m	240 m²	← ½(17 + 13) × 16
H	11 m	13 m	13 m	143 m²	← ½(13 + 13) × 11
I	10 m	13 m	0 m	65 m²	← ½(13 + 0) × 10
				1789 m²	

2. Compare results around the class.
3. Scale is 1 mm ↔ 20 metres. The area is in the region of 200 hectares.

Exercise 3·5

A 1. False   2. True   3. True   4. True
   5. False   6. False   7. False   8. True

B, C Practical work

Exercise 3·6

A 1. 18 square units   2. 31½ square units   3. 34½ square units
   4. 40½ square units   5. 270 square units   6. 100 square units
   7. 4/3 square units   8. 42 square units

B 1. $A = \frac{1}{2}x_1(mx_1 + 2c) = \frac{mx_1^2}{2} + cx_1$

Exercise 3·7

1. 30 km   2. 450 nautical miles   3. 232 miles
4. 113 yards   5. 1.875 km (runway)   6. 720 km
7. (a) 40.05 m/sec, 98.1 m/sec, 147.15 m/sec, 196.2 m/sec   (b) 122.6 m   (c) 367.9 m
8. 515.5 m   9. 68.4 yards   10. No: her stopping distance is 80 m.

Exercise 4·1

A 1. The higher the price, the less you can buy.
   2. The greater the thickness, the less the number of stitches.
   3. The longer the lengths cut, the less the number of lengths cut.
   4. The greater the area, the less the depth (or vice versa).
   5. The greater the number of winners, the less money received.
   6. The more industrialised, the more calories eaten (direct variation), but, for Third World countries, a high population growth means less calories per person.
   7. The more oil burned, the less time it will last.
   8. The greater the pressure, the less the volume.
   9. Many possible examples.

Exercise 4·2

A
1. 300 men. Not realistic because other things affect the time.
2. (a) 25 lengths (b) 50 lengths (c) 40 lengths
3. £250; £50. People form syndicates to do the pools. 4. £112.
5. 3⅓ weeks (just over 23 days) 6. 684 tiles
7. 12 days 8. (i) 600 h (ii) 100 h

B
1. (a) 300 h (b) 6000 h (c) 30 000 h (d) 600 h
2. (a) 1500 days (b) 750 days (c) 600 days (d) 200 days
3. (a) 7.33 m (b) 15.28 m
4. £1.71 per metre
5. (a) 7½ h (b) 3¾ h (c) 3 h 13 min
6. (a) 5 h (b) 6 h 40 min (c) 20 h

C
1. (a) 5 h (b) 2½ h (c) 1¼ h (d) 24 min
2. (a) 36 days
   (b) 9 days; the limit on the number of harvesters is the number that can operate without getting in each others way.
3. (a) 100 days (b) 50 days (c) 16.66 days
4. (a) 6.4 days (b) 38.4 days (c) 80 days (d) 30 days
5. (a) 4200 litres (b) 4097 litres (c) 4667 litres (d) 2979 litres

Exercise 4·3

A
1. 6.4 cm (± 0.4 cm) (b) 5.3 cm (± 0.3 cm)
2. Drawing 3. 32 people
4. (a) (i) 24 amps (ii) 12 amps (iii) 5 amps
   (c) (i) 12 amps (ii) 1½ amps (iii) 3 amps (iv) 2 amps
   (d) Current rises to 24 000 amps; 5760 kW of energy is released.

5.

Substance	Density (kg/litre)	Volume of 1 tonne (litres)	
Gold	19.64	$1000 \div 19.64 =$	50.9
Silver	11.09		90.2
Iron	7.64		130.9
Granite	3.00		333.3
Brick	2.00		500.0
Coal	1.25		800.0
Water	1.00		1 000.0
Pine	0.55		1 818.2
Cork	0.24		4 166.6
Air	0.0012		833 333.3*

*Note: It will not be possible to show the point corresponding to air on the graph.

Exercise 4·4 INVESTIGATIONS

Exercise 5·1

A
1, 2, 5, 6, 8, 9 Drawing
3. 25.136 cm 4. 6.366 m, 31.83 m² 7. No
10. (a) a pair of intersecting circles (b) two circles, one inside the other
    (c) two circles, one inside the other touching at one point (d) two separate circles touching at one point

B
1. (a) diam. 45 mm; circum. 141 mm; area 1590 mm² (b) diam. 29 mm; circum. 91 mm; area 660 mm²
   (c) diam. 56 mm; circum. 176 mm; area 2463 mm² (d) same as (a)
2. Drawing and investigation
3. (a), (b) Drawing
   (c) PR will be parallel to QS and PS will be equal to RQ, i.e. PRSQ will always be an isosceles trapezium. For proofs, join P, Q, R and S to the centre. Consider symmetry.
4. Drawing 5. Yes. 6. Ratio is 6 : 1.
7. (a) (i) kite (ii) axis of symmetry (iii) they are the bisectors of the three angles
   (b) (i) yes (ii) yes (iii) it is not always possible (e.g. think of a long, narrow trapezium)
8. Drawing

Exercise 5·2

A 1. (a) AX = XB = CY = DY =10.5 mm   **(b)** CX
  2. Draw two chords on the curve PQ and find where their perpendicular bisectors meet: this will be the centre of the whole circle.
  3. DC; equal chords subtend equal angles at the centre.
  4. The axis of symmetry passes through the centre of the circle; AC and BD are both chords; hence they must be perpendicular to the axis of symmetry, and will be parallel to each other.

B 1, 2 Drawing
  3. **(a)** they are equal   **(b)** AC and BD are parallel; AD and BC are equal
  4. **(b)** at the midpoint of AB
  5. **(a)** they all meet at one point   **(b)** where the perpendicular bisectors meet
  6. The point where the perpendicular bisectors of AB, BC and AC meet would give the centre of a circle touching A, B and C.
  7. **(b)** they do not form a triangle (e.g. three points on a straight line)

Exercise 5·3

A 1. **(b)** and 2. **(c)** yes, they should be, allowing for inaccuracy of measurement
  3. **(a)** 16.67 mm   **(b)** 9 mm   **(c)** 5.66 mm; use Pythagoras or $(9.8 - x)(9.8 + x) = 64$
  4. **(i)** 3 cm   **(ii)** 4 cm   **(iii)** 6.5 cm
  5. 43.63 cm (use Pythagoras and check by the product of chords)
  6. 169.4 m
  7. **(a)** This is a special case of XA.XB = XC.XD where C, D are co-incident
   (b) If XS is the other tangent $(XS)^2 = XA.XB = (XT)^2$ so XS = XT
  8. **(a)** 125.9 miles   **(b)** 488.5 miles   **(c)** 982.6 miles
  9. **(i)** 15.9 km   **(ii)** 25.2 km
  10. An interesting problem which I leave to you.

Exercise 6·1

A 1. **(b) (i)** $\hat{Q}$ **(ii)** $\hat{P}$ **(iii)** $\hat{R}$
  2. **(b) (i)** $\hat{B}$ **(ii)** $\hat{C}$ **(c)** XZ
  3. **(b) (i)** LN   **(ii)** LM   **(c)** $180° - (\hat{A} + \hat{B}) = 180° - (\hat{M} + \hat{N}) = \hat{C} = \hat{L}$
  4. **(b) (i)** $\hat{R}$ **(ii)** $\hat{P}$ **(iii)** $\hat{Q}$

B 1. ABX ≡ ACX (RHS)   2. ABC ≡ CDA (AAS)
  3. PRS ≡ QSR (SAS) and many others   4. ABD ≡ CBD (SSS) and others
  5. ABC ≡ CDA (SAS)   6. PTU ≡ QRS (RHS)

C 1. AOP ≡ AOS; DOS ≡ DOR; BOP ≡ BOQ; COR ≡ COQ 2. OPA ≡ OPC, OQC ≡ OQB, ORB ≡ ORA
  3. BCD ≡ EDC   4. FBC ≡ ABX, MBC ≡ AYC

Exercise 6·2

All of these proofs depend on choosing a pair of triangles, proving them congruent by one of the rules and then deducing the equal sides or angles.

Exercise 6·3

A 1. 28°, 62° and 90°   **2.** 84°   **3.** 140°   **4.** 120°   **5.** 64°
  6. $r = 21°, s = 51°, t = 60°$

B, C Different proofs can be expected for these questions.

Exercise 6·4

These questions are basically investigations. In question 2, the congruent triangle method of proof needs two stages. First prove the base angles to be equal by constructing a parallelogram. Then use congruent triangles.

7

Exercise 7·1

A **2.** $a = 80°$, $b = 65°$
    3. $B\hat{A}D = 108°$ and since $B\hat{A}P = 180° \Rightarrow P\hat{A}D = 72°$
    4. Angle at Q = 30°, at R = 40°, at P = 40° and 70°. Angles at the centre are 40°, 100°, 100°, 120°.
        (a) $S\hat{O}Q = 2 \times S\hat{R}Q$ **(b)** $P\hat{O}R = 2 \times P\hat{S}R$
    5. This generalises question 3.
    6. (i) 80°   **(ii)** 80°   **(iii)** they are equal (third angles in the triangles)

B **1.** 80°, 110°, 100°, 70°, 80°. Triangles XBC and XAD are similar
    2. CBPQ; APXQ   **(i)** PAQ + PXQ = 180°   **(ii)** PQC + PBC = 180°
      (iii) PAQ = PXB   **(iv)** AQP = ABC
    3. Use circumcircle method. It will always be possible to draw such a circle unless all three points are in a straight line.
    4. Opposite angles must add up to 180°; the quadrilateral must be cyclic. There will be pairs of equal angles when the diagonals are drawn.
    5. △'s XBC, XAD are similar and so are △'s YDC, YBA. Angle properties follow.
    6. (c) rhombus (unless a square) and **(d)** parallelogram, since they do not have equal diagonals.

Exercise 7·2

A **1.** Drawing
    2. (a) 40°   **(b)** 36°   **(c)** 52°
    3. (a) $A\hat{Q}B = A\hat{P}B$ **(b)** $A\hat{X}Q = B\hat{X}P$ **(c)** $Q\hat{A}X = X\hat{B}P$, △'s AXQ and BXP are similar
    4. (a) 25°   **(b)** 115°   **(c)** 65°
      (d) 90°   **(e)** 90°   **(f)** 65°
    5. △ ABF and △ CDF; △ EBC and △ EDA.
    6. (a) 85°, 95°   **(b)** 95°, 85°   **(c)** 65°, 65°

B **1.** $A\hat{O}B$ is $2x + 2y$, while $A\hat{P}B$ is $x + y$.
    2. (a) 50°   **(b)** 90°   **(c)** 100°   **(d)** 150°
    3. (a) 36°   **(b)** $A\hat{O}B$ is twice $O\hat{P}B$ and $O\hat{B}P$ **(c)** 72°
    4. Start with $A\hat{P}B = x$, the rest follows. Note this proves the theorem for *all* angles.
    5. (a) $A\hat{D}B = 20°$, $B\hat{D}C = 70°$ **(b)** 12.57 cm²
    6. (a) $A\hat{C}B = 30°$ **(b)** 14 cm   **(c)** 102.6 cm²
    7. (a) $A\hat{B}D = 90°$ **(b)** $B\hat{O}C = 70°$ **(c)** $B\hat{D}C = 35°$ **(d)** 11.47 cm
    8. (a) $P\hat{S}R = 130°$ **(b)** $P\hat{Q}R = 50°$ **(c)** $P\hat{O}R = 260°$

Exercise 7·3   These are open-ended questions and the results should be compared as part of the lesson.

Exercise 8·1

A **1. (a)** both hands are moved simultaneously; a sound is emitted
      (b) you jump and move your wrists simultaneously
      (c) you and the bike move simultaneously
      (d) you move your arms and legs simultaneously.
      (e) two batsmen run simultaneously
    2. Many possible answers.

B **1.** $x = 4$, $y = 4$ **2.** $x = 4$, $y = 4$ **3.** $x = 4$, $y = 1$
    4. $x = 2$, $y = 6$ **5.** $3x = 4$ **6.** $x + y = 14/3$

Exercise 8·2

A **1.** $x = 3$, $y = 2$ **2.** $x = 1\frac{1}{2}$, $y = 2\frac{1}{2}$ **3.** $x = 2\frac{1}{2}$, $y = 4\frac{1}{2}$
    4. $x = 1\frac{2}{3}$, $y = -\frac{1}{3}$ **5.** $x = 1$, $y = 2$ **6.** $x = 2$, $y = 1\frac{1}{2}$

B **1.** $x = 4$, $y = -1$ **2.** $x = 1$, $y = 1$ **3.** $x = 3$, $y = 1$
    4. $x = 1$, $y = 1$ **5.** $x = 3$, $y = 2$ **6.** $x = -6$, $y = -5$

C **1.** $x = 2.6$, $y = 0.6$ **2.** $x = 3.73$, $y = 0.54$ **3.** $x = 2.46$, $y = 0.85$
    4. $x = 1.6$, $y = 6.8$

Exercise 8·3

A **1.** $x = 3, y = 2$ **2.** $x = 2\frac{1}{2}, y = 4\frac{1}{2}$ **3.** $x = 3, y = 1$
 4. $x = 5, y = -3$ **5.** $x = 1, y = 1$ **6.** $x = 3, y = 1$
 7. $x = 4, y = -1$ **8.** $x = 3, y = 2$ **9.** $x = 1, y = 2$
 10. $x = -6, y = -5$ **11.** $x = 5, y = 2$ **12.** $x = 3, y = -1$

B **1.** $a = 3, b = 4$ **2.** $c = 24, d = 4$ **3.** $c = 2, d = 7$
 4. $p = 2, m = 3$ **5.** $s = 3, t = 8$ **6.** $p = 2, q = 12$
 7. $c = 3, d = 4$ **8.** $y = 3, z = 221$

Exercise 8·4

A **1.** 7 and 12 **2.** 14 and 25 **3.** 17 and 14 **4.** 12 and 24
 5. $\hat{A} = 96°, \hat{B} = 32°, \hat{C} = 52°$ **6.** 65p

B **1.** $s = 12, f = 44$ **2.** Miranda is 15, Gill is 13 **3.** 5 10p coins, 30 5p coins
 4. 57 km/h and 63 km/h **5.** £1.80 **6.** Potatoes 10p/lb, apples 25p/lb

D **1.** (a)

x	-6	0	6
y	-4	2	8

 (b) $x = -4\frac{1}{2}, y = -2\frac{1}{2}$
 2. $x = -3, y = 5$ **3.** $x = \frac{1}{2}, y = -2$ **4.** (a) **5.** $x = 2, y = -1$ **6.** $p = \frac{1}{2}, q = -2$
 7. Return fare £5.80, single £4.95 [to the nearest 5p].

Exercise 8·5

A **1.** $\begin{bmatrix} 6 & 8 \\ 8 & 4 \end{bmatrix}$ **2.** $\begin{bmatrix} 4 & -3 \\ 2 & 0 \end{bmatrix}$ **3.** $\begin{bmatrix} 14 & 10 \\ -6 & 6 \end{bmatrix}$
 4. $\begin{bmatrix} 2 & 2 \\ -2 & -2 \end{bmatrix}$ **5.** $\begin{bmatrix} 48 & 37 \\ 6 & -1 \end{bmatrix}$ **6.** $\begin{bmatrix} 1 & 0 \\ 0 & 1 \end{bmatrix}$

B **1.** (a) -2 (b) 1 (c) 1 (d) -1 (e) -2 (f) 1 (g) 1 (h) 1
 2. (a) $\begin{bmatrix} -6\frac{1}{2} & 2 \\ 3\frac{1}{2} & -2 \end{bmatrix}$ (b) $\begin{bmatrix} 3 & -4 \\ -2 & 3 \end{bmatrix}$ (c) $\begin{bmatrix} 1 & 0 \\ 0 & 1 \end{bmatrix}$ (d) $\begin{bmatrix} -1 & 0 \\ 0 & 1 \end{bmatrix}$
 (e) $\begin{bmatrix} -\frac{1}{2} & 1\frac{1}{2} \\ 1 & -2 \end{bmatrix}$ (f) $\begin{bmatrix} 1 & -1 \\ -1 & 2 \end{bmatrix}$ (g) $\begin{bmatrix} -2 & 1 \\ 3 & -2 \end{bmatrix}$ (h) $\begin{bmatrix} -1 & 0 \\ -1 & -1 \end{bmatrix}$
 3. Each does.
 4. $\begin{bmatrix} \dfrac{ad - bc}{\Delta} & \dfrac{-ab + ba}{\Delta} \\ \dfrac{cd - cd}{\Delta} & \dfrac{-bc - ad}{\Delta} \end{bmatrix} = \begin{bmatrix} \dfrac{ad - bc}{ad - bc} & \dfrac{0}{ad - bc} \\ \dfrac{0}{ad - bc} & \dfrac{ad - bc}{ad - bc} \end{bmatrix} = \begin{bmatrix} 1 & 0 \\ 0 & 1 \end{bmatrix}$
 5. $\begin{bmatrix} \dfrac{ad - bc}{\Delta} & \dfrac{bd + bd}{\Delta} \\ \dfrac{-ac + ac}{\Delta} & \dfrac{-bc + ad}{\Delta} \end{bmatrix} = \begin{bmatrix} \dfrac{ad - bc}{ad - bc} & \dfrac{0}{ad - bc} \\ \dfrac{0}{ad - bc} & \dfrac{ad - bc}{ad - bc} \end{bmatrix} = \begin{bmatrix} 1 & 0 \\ 0 & 1 \end{bmatrix}$

C INVESTIGATIONS

Exercise 8·6

A **1.** (a) $\begin{bmatrix} 1 & 1 \\ 1 & 2 \end{bmatrix} \begin{bmatrix} x \\ y \end{bmatrix} = \begin{bmatrix} 2 \\ 3 \end{bmatrix}$ (b) $\begin{bmatrix} 1 & 3 \\ 1 & -1 \end{bmatrix} \begin{bmatrix} x \\ y \end{bmatrix} = \begin{bmatrix} 4 \\ 3 \end{bmatrix}$ (c) $\begin{bmatrix} 2 & -5 \\ 1 & 2 \end{bmatrix} \begin{bmatrix} x \\ y \end{bmatrix} = \begin{bmatrix} 13 \\ 6 \end{bmatrix}$
 (d) $\begin{bmatrix} 2 & -3 \\ -2 & 1 \end{bmatrix} \begin{bmatrix} x \\ y \end{bmatrix} = \begin{bmatrix} 5 \\ 1 \end{bmatrix}$ (e) $\begin{bmatrix} 1 & -1 \\ 2 & -3 \end{bmatrix} \begin{bmatrix} x \\ y \end{bmatrix} = \begin{bmatrix} 6 \\ 0 \end{bmatrix}$ (f) $\begin{bmatrix} 3 & -2 \\ -3 & 1 \end{bmatrix} \begin{bmatrix} x \\ y \end{bmatrix} = \begin{bmatrix} -5 \\ 6 \end{bmatrix}$
 2. (a) $3x + 4y = 4$ (b) $2p - 3q = -2$
   $5x + 6y = 2$ $p - q = -3$
 (c) $5y - 3x = 7$ (d) $3b - a = 1.5$
   $2x - y = 0$ $0.5b = 2.2$

9

Exercise 8·6 *(cont.)*

A 3/4		Matrix		Inverse		Δ	Solution
(a)		2 1		−1 −1		−3	$x = 4$
		1 −1		−1 2			$y = -1$
(b)		2 −1		1 1		−1	$x = 3$
		−3 1		3 2			$y = 1$
(c)		2 1		1 −1		1	$x = 5$
		1 1		−1 2			$y = -3$
(d)		2 −3		−1 3		1	$x = -6$
		1 −1		−1 2			$y = -5$
(e)		4 −2		−2 2		−2	$x = 19$
		3 −2		−3 4			$y = 23$
(f)		3 4		−2 −4		−10	$x = 3$
		1 −2		−1 3			$y = -1$

B   **1.** $x = 3.18, y = 2.347$ **2.** $x = 6.752, y = 5.507$
     3. $x = 23.26, y = 6.82$ **4.** $x = 31.77, y = -17.2$

Exercise 9·1

A   **1. (a)** <   **(b)** >   **(c)** >   **(d)** <   **(e)** >
     (f) >   **(g)** <   **(h)** <   **(i)** <   **(j)** <
     (k) <   **(l)** >   **(m)** >   **(n)** <   **(o)** >
     2. (a) $n = 5, 6, 7, 8, 9, 10, 11, 12, 13, 14, 15$ **(b)** $x = -4, -3, -2, -1, 0, 1$
     (c) $y = -6, -5, -4, -3$ **(d)** $-4, -3, -2, -1, 0$
     (e) $4.1, 4\frac{1}{2}, 4.99, 4.0003$, etc.   **(f)** $w = 3, 4, 5, 6, 7$
     3. (a) true   **(b)** false   **(c)** false   **(d)** false
     (e) true   **(f)** false   **(g)** false   **(h)** true, only if x is positive
     4. (a) true   **(b)** false   **(c)** true
     (d) false   **(e)** true   **(f)** true

B   **1. (a)** <   **(b)** >   **(c)** >   **(d)** >
     (e) >   **(f)** >   **(g)** >   **(h)** >
     2. (a) see answers to previous question   **(b)** they should! . . . but what about negatives?
     3. (a) false   **(b)** true   **(c)** true
     (d) false   **(e)** true   **(f)** true
     4. (a) false   **(b)** true   **(c)** true
     (d) true   **(e)** true   **(f)** true

Exercise 9·2

A   **1.** Set of numbers < 2.   **2.** Set of numbers < 3.   **3.** Set of numbers < −3.
     4. Set of numbers < −5.   **5.** Set of numbers < 3.   **6.** Set of numbers < −1.
     7. Set of numbers < 0.   **8.** Set of numbers < 2½.   **9.** Set of numbers < 1.

B   **1.** Set of numbers > 5.   **2.** Set of numbers > −7.   **3.** Set of numbers > − 10.
     4. Set of numbers > 12.   **5.** Set of numbers > 2.   **6.** Set of numbers > −1.
     7. Set of numbers > 2.   **8.** Set of numbers > 2.   **9.** Set of numbers < 2.

C   **1** $x > 3, x > 4, x < 10$ **2.** $x > 30$ **3. (a)** $w > 20$ **(b)** $w < 20$
     4. (a) $t < 21$ **(b)** $t > 21$, but could be between 15° and 21° and not have come on!
     5. $a < 29\,000, a > 35\,000$ [It would not have been 'ordered' if it was already flying in the band.]
     6. $f > 149.75, f < 149.84$ **7.** Many possible answers.

Exercise 9·3

A 1. **(a), (b)** Drawing   **(c)** $x > 2, y < 3$ **(d)** none
    (e) points of form $(x < 2, y > 3)$
2. **(a), (b)** Drawing   **(c)** $(2, 0), (2, -1)$ **(d)** $x + y < 1, y > x$
    (e) points which satisfy $x + y < 1$ and $x > y$, e.g. $(1, -3)$. They will not be in the completely unshaded area.
3. **(a), (b)** Drawing   **(c)** $y < x + 1, y < 3$
    (d) any points which satisfy **(c)** e.g. $(3, 2)$
4. Drawing   5. Investigation

B 1. $y > 3$
2. $-2 < x < 3$
3. $x + y < 4$
4. $y > x - 3$

[*Note:* It is usual to shade the area which does *not* satisfy the inequality, blanking it out. It is not wrong to shade in the area which does satisfy the inequality but great care should be taken with examination questions.]

C 1. $x < 4, y < 3$
2. $y < x, y > -1$
3. $x + y > 6, x < 3$
4. $x < y, 5x + 4y < 20$

D INVESTIGATIONS [A reminder may be needed about the simple nature of vectors.]

Exercise 10·1

A $1, 4, 5, 7, 8, 9, 10$

B 1. $a = 1, b = 2, c = 3$ 2. $a = 1, b = -3, c = 2$ 3. $a = 1, b = -5, c = -5$
4. $a = 2, b = -3, c = -7$ 5. $a = 1, b = -7, c = 0$ 6. $a = 4, b = -5, c = 0$
7. $a = 3, b = 0, c = 5$ 8. $a = 2, b = 0, c = -7$ 9. $a = -3, b = 0, c = 0$

C 1. $x^2 - 2x + 5$ $a = 1, b = -2, c = 5$ 2. $-x^2 + 3x - 2$ $a = -1, b = 3, c = -2$
3. $2x^2 - x - 4$ $a = 2, b = -1, c = -4$ 4. $-3x^2 + x + 1$ $a = -3, b = 1, c = 1$
5. $x^2 - 2x + 2$ $a = 1, b = -2, c = 2$ 6. $2x^2 - 2x - 12$ $a = 2, b = -2, c = -12$
7. $x^2 - 2x + 2$ $a = 1, b = -2, c = 2$ 8. $-x^2 + x - 1$ $a = -1, b = 1, c = -1$
9. $x^2 - 2x - 8$ $a = 1, b = -2, c = -8$

Exercise 10·2

A 1. $x = 5, x = -5$ 2. $x = 9, x = -9$ 3. $x = 0.8, x = -0.8$
4. $x = 3.873, x = -3.873$ 5. $x = 5.196, x = -5.196$ 6. $x = 1.844, x = -1.844$
7. $x = 31.623, x = -31.623$ 8. $x = 27, x = -27$ 9. $x = 15.62, x = -15.62$

B 1. $x = 4.47, x = -4.47$ 2. $x = 2.45, x = -2.45$ 3. $x = 3.16, x = -3.16$
4. $x = 1.58, x = -1.58$ 5. $x = 1.5, x = -1.5$ 6. $x = 3.46, x = -3.46$

C 1. $x = 1, x = 0$ 2. $x = -3, x = 0$ 3. $x = 1.58, x = -1.58$
4. $x = 0, x = -1.75$ 5. $x = 0, x = 2$ 6. $x = 0, x = 2.5$
7. $x = 0, x = -5$ 8. $x = 0, x = 1$ 9. $x = 0, x = 7$

D 1. **(a)** $x^2 = 2x; x = 0, x = 2$ **(b)** $x^2 + x = 0; x = 0, x = -1$ **(c)** $2x^2 = \frac{2}{3}x; x = \frac{1}{3}$
2. No real solutions; the calculator will not give $\sqrt{-5}$
3. **(a)** $x = 1, x = 2$ **(b)** $x = 1, x = -5$

Exercise 10·3

A 1. $x = -2$ 2. $x = 2$ 3. $x = 2$ 4. $x = -3$
5. $x = -\frac{1}{2}$ 6. $x = 1$ 7. $x = \frac{1}{2}$ 8. $x = \frac{1}{3}$

B 1. $x = 1, x = 2$ 2. $x = 3, x = 3$ 3. $x = 3, x = -1$ 4. $x = 2, x = -1$
5. $x = 4, x = 3$ 6. $x = 1, x = -\frac{1}{2}$ 7. $x = -1, x = 1\frac{1}{2}$ 8. $x = 3, x = -2\frac{1}{2}$

C 1. $2x^2 - x - 1 = 0; x = 1, x = -\frac{1}{2}$ 2. $x^2 - 5x + 6 = 0; x = 2, x = 3$ 3. $x^2 - x - 2 = 0; x = 2, x = -1$
4. $2x^2 - x - 3 = 0; x = -1, x = 1\frac{1}{2}$ 5. $x^2 - 2x - 3 = 0; x = -1, x = 3$ 6. $x^2 - 3x + 2 = 0; x = 1, x = 2$

Exercise 10·4

A
1. $x = -1, x = -3$
4. $x = -3, x = -7$
2. $x = -2, x = -4$
5. $x = -5, x = -7$
3. $x = -3, x = -5$
6. $x = 1, x = -3$

B
1. $x = -1, x = -2$
4. $x = -2, x = -5$
2. $x = -1, x = -4$
5. $x = -4, x = -5$
3. $x = -2, x = -3$
6. $x = -2, x = -7$

C
1. $x = -3.414, x = -0.586$
4. $x = -9.472, x = -0.528$
2. $x = -5.236, x = -0.764$
5. $x = -2.618, x = -0.382$
3. $x = -7.742, x = -0.258$
6. $x = 0.618, x = -1.618$

[*Note:* Sum and product of roots give an easy check here and lead to discussion.]

Exercise 10·5

A
2. (a) $x = 2, x = -2$
(d) $x = 0, x = -1$
(g) $x = 0, x = -2.67$
(b) $x = 3, x = -3$
(e) $x = 0, x = 1.5$
(h) $x = 2.3, x = -1.3$
(c) $x = 2.35, x = -2.35$
(f) $x = 0, x = -2$
(i) $x = 3.24, x = -1.24$

B
1. True.
2. True.

Exercise 10·6

A
1. $x = -1, x = 2$
4. $x = 3.45, x = -1.45$
2. No real solutions.
5. $x = 1.54, x = -4.54$
3. $x = 7.123, x = -1.123$
6. No real solutions.

B
1. $x = 2.303, x = -1.303$
2. $x = 2.732, x = -0.732$
3. $x = 1.56, x = -2.56$

Exercise 10·7

A
1. $x = 0.796, x = -8.796$
4. $x = -1.17, x = -6.83$
7. $x = -0.86, x = -8.14$
2. $x = 1, x = 5$
5. $x = -1, x = -2$
8. $x = 0.32, x = -9.32$
3. $x = 0.29, x = -10.29$
6. $x = -1.38, x = -3.62$

Exercise 10·8

A
1. $x = 0.54, x = -5.54$
4. No real solutions.
2. $x = 3.56, x = -0.56$
5. $x = 0, x = \frac{2}{3}$
3. No real solutions.
6. $x = 1.175, x = -0.425$

B
1. $x = 2\frac{1}{2}, x = -1$
4. $x = -1.3, x = 2.3$
2. $x = 7.242, x = -1.242$
5. $x = 1.264, x = 0.264$
3. No real solutions.
6. $x = 1.618, x = -0.618$

Exercise 11·1

1. (a) $A = \{A, B, C, \ldots, Z\}$
(b) $B = \{A, B, C, D, E, K, M, T, U, V, W, Y\}$
(c) $S = \{$python, anaconda, boa constrictor, adder, etc.$\}$
(d) $C = \{$France, Germany, Spain, Italy, Liechtenstein, etc.$\}$
(e) $G = \{$hockey, squash, badminton, netball, soccer, swimming, etc.$\}$
2. (a) false
(e) true
(i) true
(b) true
(f) false
(j) false!
(c) true
(g) false
(d) false
(h) true
3. (a) true
(e) true
(b) false
(f) false
(c) true
(g) false
(d) true
(h) true
4. Drawing
5. (a) $\{x : x = 5n\}$
(d) $\{x : x = 2n - 1\}$
(b) $\{x : x = n + 1\}$
(e) $\{x : x = 3n - 1\}$
(c) $\{x : x = 10n\}$
(f) $\{x : x = n^2\}$
If n takes the values $1, 2, 3, \ldots$ in turn, the set will be arranged in order.

Exercise 11·2

A **1. (a)** fruit **(b)** green things **(c)** cities with over 5 million people
   (d) big cats **(e)** three-letter words
   2. (a) the set has 3 in it: lower-case letters and numbers
   (b) the set includes a trapezium: closed figures made from straight lines
   (c) the set includes a circle: closed figures
   (d) the set has 1 in it: powers of 2
   (e) the set has 5 in it: factors of 60
   3. (a) lion, tiger, baboon, elephant, etc. **(b)** 2, 3, 5, 6, 7, 8, 10 . . .
   (c) 3, 4, 5, 6, 7, . . . **(d)** three, letter, word
   4. (a) true; this is not a very good choice as a is usually taken to be a member of set A
   (b) true **(e)** false . . . but see (a) above
   (c) false **(f)** false
   (d) false **(g)** true **(h)** true
   5. (a), (b) in the region of B
   (c) B takes up all the elements of E which are *not* in A. Thus B and A′ are the same set
   (d) odd numbers **(e)** the numbers which are not multiples of 7
   (f) the set of whole numbers over 50 (including 50 itself)
   (g) $\{x: x \leqslant 100\}$, A is the same set **(h)** many possible answers

Exercise 11·3

   1. 2 boys are in both teams **2.** 4 girls are in both teams
   3. (a) 6 members; 16 members **(b)** $A \cap B = \{2, 4, 8, 16, 32\}$; 5 members
   (c) $A \cup B = \{1, 2, 4, 6, 8, 10, 12, 14, 16, 18, 20, 22, 24, 26, 28, 30, 32\}$ [same as set B plus 1]
   4. (c) ambidextrous people [using both hands equally well]
   (d) everybody left- or right-handed **(e)** people with no hands!
   [*Note:* This question depends on what you mean by 'right-handed'. There may be some argument!]
   5. (a), (b) Drawing **(c)** square **(d)** Drawing **(e)** yes **(f)** yes
   6. 13
   7. (a) true **(b)** false **(c)** true
   (d) true **(e)** true **(f)** true
   (g) true **(h)** true **(i)** true
   (j) true **(k)** false **(l)** true
   8. Drawing

Exercise 11·4

A **1.** Many possible answers.
   2. (a) any two of stare, east, star, rate, tear, rat, tea, set, sat, at, as, era, sate, tar, rest (possibly more)
   (b) maths, mites, mates, steam, ethic, chime, haste, caste, chase, smite, times, heats, etc.
   3. (a) bad **(b)** bog **(c)** deaf **(d)** ode **(e)** fade **(f)** code
   5. (c) and (f)
   6. (a) true **(b)** true **(c)** false **(d)** true **(e)** true

B **1.** Drawing
   2. (a) left-handed old people; females and left-handed males; female old people; everyone
   (b), (c) Drawing

Exercise 11·5 INVESTIGATIONS

Exercise 12·1

A **1. (a)** 1.10 sec **(b)** 1.42 sec **(c)** 0.78 sec **(d)** 1.19 sec
   (e) 0.70 sec **(f)** 1.20 sec **(g)** 0.92 sec **(h)** 1.47 sec
   2. (a) 11.0 sec **(b)** 14.2 sec **(c)** 7.80 sec **(d)** 11.9 sec
   (e) 7.00 sec **(f)** 12.0 sec **(g)** 9.20 sec **(h)** 14.7 sec
   3. No, it should be 1.06 sec. Sarah should check the length of the pendulum and the time of the swing.
   4. A straight line would not fit the facts for shorter lengths. One more point would probably show that a straight line is only an approximation.
   5. (a) 1.68 sec **(b)** 1.80 sec **(c)** 2.01 sec

Exercise 12·1 *(cont.)*

B **1.** Time and distance.
   2. 1 cm ↔ 1 minute; 1 cm ↔ 50 km
   3. The graph suggests a linear relationship except, perhaps, for the first minute.
   4. **(a)** 70 km (approx.)   **(b)** 150 km (approx.)   **(c)** 215 km (approx.)
   5. As time proceeds the graph gets less reliable. Variations in weather and change in mass due to the use of fuel will affect the speed.
C There are many different things to discuss in these graphs but no right answers.

Exercise 12·2

B **6.** **(a)** quarter-circle   **(b)** quarter-ellipse

Exercise 12·3

A **1.** **(a)** 15 min   **(b)** 30 m/min   **(c)** 35 min
      (d) the swimmer reduced speed after 10 min to 20 m/min
   2. **(a)** many facts can be obtained from the graph
      (b) between 4.1 and 4.2 hours after starting, 260 miles from London.
      (c) about 63 mph **(d)** about 65 mph   **(e)** car: 72 mph; coach: 65 mph
   3. **(a)** **(i)** 20 m/sec   **(ii)** 40 m/sec   **(iii)** 40 m/sec
      (b) 40 m/sec in 6 sec; i.e. $(6^2/_3$ m/sec)/sec   **(c)** no acceleration, speed stays the same
      (d) **(i)** 40 m   **(ii)** 80 m   **(iii)** 120 m
   4. **(a)** this means the ball is returning to earth
      (b) **(i)** 25 m   **(ii)** 40 m   **(iii)** 45 m   **(iv)** 40 m

B **1.** 49 m/sec   **2.** 147 m/sec
   3. 196 m/sec downward speed! (not considering its original flying speed)
   4. 122.5 m   **5.** 1960 m   **6.** Just over 45 sec.
   7. 442.7 m/sec (nearly 1600 km/h)
   8. **(a)** 3.19 sec   **(b)** 31.26 m/sec   **(c)** 112.32 km/h

C **1, 2.** INVESTIGATIONS
   3. **(a)** she flies over the handlebars **(b)** it decreases very quickly to zero
   4. 88 sec; 7744 ft (1.47 miles)   **5.** 8 sec; $^2/_3$ mile

D **1.** They meet at a point approximately 7.7 km from one home (2.3 km from the other) after 23 min.
   2, 3. INVESTIGATIONS
   4. Approx. 450 miles north at 12.20 a.m.   **5, 6.** INVESTIGATIONS

Exercise 13·1

A **1.** **(a)** quadrilateral **(b)** pentagon   **(c)** hexagon   **(d)** nonagon   **(e)** 16-gon
      (f) 27-gon
   2. **(a)** 6   **(b)** 8   **(c)** 8
      (d) yes; every time a new side is added, a new vertex is added
      (e) start with a triangle, 3 sides, 3 vertices; keep adding sides 1 at a time
   3. **(a)** 298°   **(b)** 130°, 140°   **(c)** 62°
   4. **(a)** 184 mm   **(b)** 30 mm
   5. **(a)** 5; yes   **(b)** 9   **(c)** 20
      (d) there are $\dfrac{n(n-1)}{2} - n$ diagonals for n vertices   **(e)** 4850
   6. Compare answers in class.

Exercise 13·2

A **1.** **(a)** 55°, 85°   **(b)** 40°, 40°   **(c)** 80°, 100°
   2. Proof: Extend BC to D. Let $A\hat{C}D = x$. It follows that $x + c = 180°$, $a + b + c = 180°$, so $x = a + b$.
   3. $a + b + c + d = 360°$, but $a = b = c = d$, so $a = b = c = d = 90°$.
   4. **(a)** 110°   **(b)** 48°, 48°, 132°   **(c)** top down, 40°, 145°, 35°, 110°, 70°
   5. 360°   **6.** Cannot be done! The figure does not close.

B **1.** Any hexagon can be divided into two and only two quadrilaterals, each with internal angle sum 360°; hence internal angle sum of a hexagon is 720° [or use triangles].

2. Drawing

3. **(a)** 1080° **(b)** 1440° **(c)** 4140°

4. 360°; 360°

5. 5; yes

6. INVESTIGATION—could lead to $\dfrac{n(n-1)}{2} - n$, or some equivalent form.

Exercise 13·3

A

Polygon	No. of sides	Vertex angle	Length of side	Largest diag.
Eq. triangle	3	60°	8.66 cm	7.5 cm
Square	4	90°	7.07 cm	10.0 cm
Pentagon	5	108°	5.88 cm	9.5 cm
Hexagon	6	120°	5.00 cm	10.0 cm
Heptagon	7	128.6°	4.34 cm	9.7 cm
Octagon	8	135°	3.83 cm	10.0 cm
Nonagon	9	140°	3.42 cm	9.8 cm
Decagon	10	144°	3.09 cm	10.0 cm

B **1.** **(a)** 144° **(b)** 162° **(c)** 172.8° **(d)** 176.4°

Exercise 13·4 INVESTIGATIONS

Exercise 13·5

A **1.** **(a)** 5.88 m; 2.38 m² **(b)** 83.47 m; 479.43 m²

2. radius = 27.51 m; perimeter = 161.73 m

3. radius = 6.81 cm; area = 110.3 cm²

4. **(a)** 60 cm, 259.8 cm² **(b)** 150 cm, 1623.8 cm²

(c) 216 cm, 3367.1 cm² **(d)** 300 cm, 6495.2 cm²

5. 6.57 cm **6.** 4156.9 m²

7. 514 tiles, if no part is wasted **8.** 120.7 mm²

B **1.**

n	r	C	sin C	$A = \frac{1}{2}nr^2 \sin C$	Area $\div r^2$
5	1	72°	0.951	2.377 5	2.377 5
10	1	36°	0.588	2.938 9	2.938 9
20	1	18°	0.309	3.090 2	3.090 2
100	1	3.6°	0.063	3.139 5	3.139 5
360	1	1°	0.017	3.141 4	3.141 4
3 600	1	0.1°	0.002	3.141 590 4	3.141 590 4
36 000	1	0.01°	0.000 2	3.141 592 6	3.141 592 6 ... π

2, 3. INVESTIGATIONS

Exercise 14·1

A **1, 2.** Drawing

3. **(a)** true **(b)** true **(c)** false **(d)** true

4. **(a)** false **(b)** false **(c)** true **(d)** false **(e)** false

5. **(a)** false **(b)** false **(c)** true **(d)** true **(e)** true

6. **(a)** false **(b)** false **(c)** false **(d)** true

B **1.** **(a)** equal **(b)** yes

(c) experiment will show the theorem to be true; it can be proved by drawing another intersecting line through Y and then using congruent triangles

2. **(a)** BX, CY, DZ **(b)** BC, CD **(c)** BD **(d)** XY, YZ **(e)** WY **(f)** yes

3. AY = YC; follows as a special case of question 1(c).

Exercise 14·1 *(cont.)*

C 1. (a) (i)/(ii) obvious by turning figure
  (b) $\{C\hat{X}B + C\hat{X}A = C\hat{X}B + B\hat{X}D = 180°\} \Rightarrow C\hat{X}A = B\hat{X}D \dots$
 2. (a) it takes the same amount of turning to rotate XY about X into the AB direction as it does to rotate XY about Y into the CD direction (AB//CD)
  (b) $A\hat{X}Y, X\hat{Y}D, C\hat{Y}M$ (c) $C\hat{Y}X, Y\hat{X}B, L\hat{X}A$
  (d) (i) 180°   (ii) 180°   (iii) 180°
 3. Mark all the angles x or y; the result follows.
 4. The stick will have been rotated until its direction has been reversed. Since a whole turn is 360°, the half turn is 180°.

Exercise 14·2

A 1. The parallelogram is formed by simple translation of one side. Thus opposite sides are equal.
 2. See question 3 of Exercise 14·1 C.
 3. A triangle can be translated from one side of the parallelogram to the other, forming the rectangle whose area is base × height.
 4. Rotate about the centre.
 5. The parallelogram is formed by translation.
 6. Difficult to *prove* by translation or rotation. Simpler to draw diagonal and use component triangles.

B 1. Follows from question A 6.
 2. The figure has 2 axes of symmetry which divide the angle at the centre into 4 equal parts.
 3. It is a rectangle, anyway.
 4. The rectangle (ABCD, centre O) is symmetrical. Thus AO = AD, BO = OC. Therefore AC = BD.
 5. Divide into two triangles or use external angles.
 6. Yes. There will be an axis of symmetry perpendicular to the parallel sides.

C INVESTIGATION

Exercise 14·3

 1. The perpendicular bisector of AB is an axis of symmetry of the figure and therefore passes through the centre of the circle. Two perpendicular bisectors of chords will therefore meet at the centre.
 2. OCD can be rotated over AOB. The property can also be deduced from the axis of symmetry of the figure, which will be the perpendicular bisector of BC.
 3. Join the centre of the circle to the point on the circumference, making 2 isosceles triangles with base angles x and y respectively. It follows that $2x + 2y = 180°$ so $x + y = 90°$.
 4. Symmetry again.
 5. $2x + 2y + 2w + 2z = 360°$ = $x + y + w + z = 180°$.
 6. Follows from 5, by fixing one vertex of a cyclic quadrilateral and moving the opposite one round the circle. This can also be deduced from question 7.
 7. Use exterior angles of $\triangle OAX$ and $\triangle OBX$.

Exercise 14·4

A 1. (a) $\dfrac{YZ}{XZ} = \dfrac{QR}{PR}$ (b) $\dfrac{BX}{QP} = \dfrac{YZ}{QR}$ 2. No. A simple example is a rectangle.

Exercise 14·5

A 1. All true
 2.

	R	L	A	I
R	A	I	L	R
L	I	A	R	L
A	L	R	I	A
I	R	L	A	I

 3. (a) true   (b) false: $I^2 = I$ (c) true
  (d) true   (e) true   (f) false, except for **I**

B INVESTIGATIONS

Exercise 15·1   Many answers are possible in this exercise.

Exercise 15·2

A **1. (a)** there were 21 thefts per 100 cyclists   **(b)** by multiplying by 10
   2. (a) 4   **(b)** halfway between £51 and £60
      (c) 4 bikes stolen at an average value of £55 = £220
   3. (a) £82.38
      (b) basic: £17.30 (plus a figure which covers insurer's costs, profit, etc.)
      (c) £17 300, or thereabouts
   4. Many answers possible: % rates according to value of bike, higher premiums if bikes have already been stolen
      from owner, etc.

Exercise 15·3

A INVESTIGATIONS

B **2. (a)** 4   **(b)** 12 700 didn't vote
   3. Three girls and two boys, or two boys and three girls are equally most likely
   4. No! The door frame and floor must form a parallelogram as well.
   5. (a) there is none that is longer than the other two combined
      (b) for any stick there will be two which, combined, are longer
         The above restrictions enable you to search for patterns. For example
         (1 2 3); (1 2 4); (1 2 5) . . . are all impossible
         (2 3 5); (2 3 6); (2 3 7) . . . are all impossible
         If we limit the length by the size of the box it is possible to work out all possible lengths for the sticks.

C **1. (a)** add 2; $n \rightarrow 2n + 1$; 100th number = 201 (straight line)
      (b) add 3; $n \rightarrow 3n$; 100th number = 300 (straight line)
      (c) add 3; $n \rightarrow 3n - 2$; 100th number = 298 (straight line)
      (d) add on one more each time (triangle numbers); $n \rightarrow \frac{1}{2}n(n + 1)$; 100th number = 5050 (parabola)
      (e) square; $n \rightarrow n^2$; 100th number = 10 000 (parabola)
      (f) double; $n \rightarrow 2^n$; 100th number = 1.267×10^{30} (exponential curve)
      (g) multiply by 1.1; $n \rightarrow 1.1^n$; 100th number = 13 780.61 (slow exponential curve)
      (h) add previous two numbers of sequence; start with 1, 1, . . ., (Fibonacci)
      (i) ratios formed from (h) by dividing each term by the previous one
      (j) same as (h) but start with 4, 7; then divide each term by the next
   2. $x^2 + y^2 = 25$
   3. Area of largest shape = combined areas of two others.
   4. They all lie on the same circle.
   5. The shape comes from a 16-square grid.

Exercise 16·1

A **1, 2.** Model-making
   3. (a) cube: 8, tetrahedron: 4   **(b)** cube: 6, tetrahedron: 4   **(c)** cube: 12, tetrahedron: 6
   4. There are only two ways of colouring the cube under these conditions.
   5. Three ways.
   6. Yes. Mirror images give 2 different colourings.
B **1.** AE, ACGE, ABFE, ACDBFE, ACGHFE, ACDHGE, ABDHFE, ABDHGE, ABDCGE,
      ACDHFE, ACDBFHGE, ABDCGHFE, ACGHDBFE, i.e. 13 routes without going through any
      point twice.
   2. 5 routes: AB, ACB, ADB, ACDB, ADCB

Exercise 16·2

A **1. (a)** V = 6, E = 12, F = 8   **(b)** no
      (c) 16 (without going through a vertex twice)
   2, 3. Model-making

B **1, 2, 3, 4, 5.** Model-making
   6. (a) V = 20, F = 12, E = 30   **(b)** 5 × the length of one edge   **(c)** 108°, 109.466° (dihedral angle)
      (d) 12 × the area of each pentagon

Exercise 16·3

A **1.** V = 12, F = 20, E = 30   **2, 3, 4, 5, 6.** INVESTIGATIONS

Exercise 17·1

A **1.** (a) Elisabeth Jones   (b) Elisabeth Jones and Christine Elton
   (c) Christine Elton
2. Ruth Gordini grew 4 inches between 1983 and 1984
3. Gary Hill
4. Brett Allen, Chris Crittall, Gary Hill, Steven King, John Prince
5. *Boys:* 0.8 in, 1.7 in, 2.1 in   *Girls:* 1.2 in, 1.5 in, 1.6 in
6. *1981:* Brett Allen, Thomas Archway, Chris Crittall, Gary Hill, Mitch Howe, Steven King, Brian Lennox,
   John Prince
   1984: Brett Allen, Chris Crittall, Gary Hill, Mitch Howe, Steven King, Brian Lennox, John Prince

B **1.** *Term 1:* 5.6 h   *Term 2:* 8.1 h   *Term 3:* 6.6 h
2. *Batch 1:* 11.1 h   *Batch 2:* 10.3 h   *Batch 3:* 11.3 h   *Batch 4:* 11.9 h
3. (a)

A	B	C	D	E	F	G	H	I	J	K	L
191	190.3	182	178	180	183.7	189.3	182	181.7	181	172.7	185.3

   (b) *1st jump:* 182.7   *2nd jump:* 183.5   *3rd jump:* 183.1
   (c) half the jumpers recorded their best score on the first jump, but the best average was for the second jump
4. *14 years:* 5.56   *15 years:* 7.56   *16 years:* 7.16   *17 years:* 6.36
5. Tomatoes: 44.83; apples: 29.5
   Tomatoes: Jan–Mar + Oct–Dec: 52.5; Apr–Sept: 37.17
   Apples: Jan–Mar + Oct–Dec: 29.0; Apr–Sept: 30.0
6. (a) coach: 105.25 km/h; lorry: 87.90 km/h; car: 114.72 km/h; bike: 110.00 km/h   (b) yes

C **1.** (8, 7, 5, 4),   (9, 8, 4, 3),   (10, 9, 3, 2),   (11, 10, 2, 1),   (12, 11, 1, 0),   (13, 12, 0, −1), . . . etc. Many
   possible answers, especially if you allow negative or decimal values.
2. (0.9, 0.7, 0, −0.7, −0.9),   (0.8, 0.4, 0.2, −0.6, −0.8), . . . etc.
3. (a) the score is 6 each time; no other possibilities
   (b) scores could be (1, 5, 5, 5),   (1, 5, 6, 4),   (2, 6, 6, 2),   (2, 5, 5, 4),   (2, 6, 5, 3),   (3, 3, 5, 5),   (3, 3, 6, 4),
      (3, 4, 4, 5),   (4, 4, 4, 4)
4. (10, 10, 10, 10),   (9, 10, 10, 11),   (9, 8, 12, 11),   (9, 9, 11, 11), . . . etc.
5. (a) between 3 and 4 (average of 1 + 2 + 3 + 4 + 5 + 6 = 3.5)
   (b) 7 (average of 2 + 3 + 4 + 5 + 6 + 7 + 8 + 9 + 10 + 11 + 12 = 7, even though these are not equally likely)
6. The second train should be faster to make up for the stops.

Exercise 17·2

A **1.**

May–Oct	June–Nov	July–Dec
35	35.8	37.5

   2. Gradually increase again to over 50p.
3. 3.8, 4.0, 3.4, 3.4, 3.2, 2.8, 3.0, 3.8, 3.6, 3.0, 3.6, 4.0, 3.8, 3.8, 4.2, 3.6, 3.0, 3.2.
   [*Note:* It is best to calculate all the 5-totals first and then divide to obtain the moving average.]
4. The same.
5. 3.8, 3.5, 3.1, 3.3, 3.5, 3.3, 3.5, 3.6, 3.5, 3.1, 3.2, 3.5, 3.8, 3.7, 3.6, 3.6, 3.5, 3.5.

B **1.**

Week	1	2	3	4	5	6	7	8	9	10
Moving av.				6.5	6.75	6	5.75	6.75	7.25	7.75
Week	11	12	13	14	15	16	17	18	19	20
Moving av.	7	5.75	6.25	6.75	8.25	9.5	9.5	10.0	10.0	9.5

2.

	Jan–Mar	Feb–Apr	Mar–May	Apr–Jun	May–Jul	Jun–Aug
England	91.7	72.0	59.0	56.3	68.7	76.7
Scotland	142.7	107.3	86.0	53.7	66.3	89.7
	Jul–Sept	Aug–Oct	Sept–Nov	Oct–Dec		
England	71.3	48.0	42.3	82.3		
Scotland	125.7	128.7	158.0	151.0		

[*Note:* This work can be done very easily with careful planning.]

3. 7.1, 6.9, 7.0, 7.0, 6.9, 6.9, 6.6, 6.4, 6.5, 6.4, 6.3, 6.3, 6.2, 6.1, 6.2, 6.4, 6.4, 6.4, 6.4, 6.3, 6.7, 7.1, 7.0, 7.1, 6.9, 6.7, 7.0, 6.8, 6.8, 6.7, 5.9, 5.5, 5.5, 5.5, 5.5, 5.5, 5.6, 5.5, 5.7, 5.8, 5.9.

4. *The Sun:* Average daily sales: 54.5
Moving averages: 55.0, 54.7, 53.8, 58.0, 57.2, 58.8, 63.0, 64.0, 65.0, 64.2, 63.3, 61.7, 56.7, 52.7, 49.5, 47.0, 45.7, 41.5, 43.2
The Mirror: Average daily sales: 43.2
Moving averages: 42.0, 44.2, 43.8, 43.2, 46.5, 45.3, 42.8, 42.3, 42.0, 44.7, 46.7, 48.0, 47.0, 47.0, 48.3, 44.0, 38.5
The Guardian: Average daily sales: 21.1
Moving averages: 18.7, 19.0, 19.7, 22.0, 23.7, 25.3, 23.3, 25.2, 26.5, 25.8, 24.8, 24.2, 23.8, 22.0, 20.3, 18.0, 18.5, 17.8

C **1.** To iron out the daily variations and concentrate on trends.
  2. Burning of coal is restricted and industrial pollution is controlled.
  3. About 160 h (a very rough estimate).

Exercise 17·3

A **1.**

No. of exams passed	No. of people	Cumulative frequency
0	11	11
1	12	23
2	8	31
3	12	43
4	10	53
5	11	64
6	8	72
7	6	78
8	10	88
9	12	100

2.

Hours of paid work done	No. of people	Cumulative frequency
0	21	21
1	3	24
2	10	34
3	8	42
4	5	47
5	2	49
6	1	50

3.

No. of hours watched	No. of students	Cumulative frequency
0–4	3	3
5–9	8	11
10–14	13	24
15–19	11	35
20–24	16	51
25–29	8	59
30–35	1	60

4.

Amount of rent paid	No. of families	Cumulative frequency
0–£9.99	4	4
£10.00–£19.99	14	18
£20.00–£29.99	13	31
£30.00–£39.99	13	44
£40.00–£49.99	6	50

Exercise 17·3 (cont.)

A   6.

Response	No. of people	Cumulative frequency
SA	18	18
A	12	30
U	12	42
D	14	56
SD	13	69

(a) 51 people did not strongly agree with CND
(b) 24 people agreed or were uncertain

Exercise 18·1

A   1, 2. INVESTIGATIONS
3. $x = 9.35$ cm, $y = 9.03$ cm
4. $x = 9.08$ cm, $h = 10.62$ cm, $\beta = 58.8°$
5. (b) (i) $45°, 45°$ (ii) $63.4°, 26.6°$ (iii) $67.4°, 22.6°$ (iv) $53.1°, 46.9°$

B   1. $\hat{C} = 53°$, AB $= 12$ cm, AC $= 9$ cm
2. $\hat{X} = 32.1°$, $\hat{Z} = 57.9°$, XZ $= 50.77$ cm
3. $\hat{R} = 46°$, PQ $= 12.2$ cm, PR $= 11.8$ cm
4. $\hat{L} = 47.3°$, $\hat{N} = 42.7°$, LN $= 17.7$ cm
5. $\hat{E} = 53°$, EG $= 1.56$ m, FG $= 2.08$ m

C   1. $w = 42.9$ mm   2. $a = 22°$
3. (a) CD $= 100$ m, AB $= 200$ m (b) $B\hat{A}C = 15°$ (c) $\sqrt{20\,000} = 100\sqrt{2}$
   (d) (i) $\dfrac{1}{\sqrt{2}}$ (ii) $\dfrac{\sqrt{3}}{2}$ (iii) $\sqrt{3}$ (iv) $\sqrt{3} - 1$
4. (a) true   (b) false   (c) true   (d) false   (e) true
5. 13 m   6. 14.4 cm   7. 15 838 feet
8. 41.8°   9. 11.28 cm; also 11.28 cm
10. (a) 51.14 m   (b) 77.72 m   [This solution assumes that A and B are at the same level as the motorway.]

Exercise 18·2

A   1. roof 30°; mast 70°; cliff $\simeq$ 27°; sun 31°; slide 32°
2. 10.89 km   3. 2549 m (2.55 km)   4. 9.285 km
5. 42.6°   6. At 55.1 km, a weather satellite.
7. When the pilot reported he was 48.1 km from one radar station and 39.3 km from the other.
8. 428 m (plus the height of the control tower).

C   1. 21.8°   2. 49.6 m   3. 1 : 1.376
4. (a) 0.6   (b) 31°
5. (a) 7   (b) 81.87°   (c) 28.8°
6. (a) 0.07, 0.06
   (b) the gentlest slope is due East from the top of the hill; the steepest is North and South
7. 31°
8. AB has slope 1, BC has slope -3, AC has slope $-\frac{1}{3}$. The product of their slopes is 1.
9. The product of their slopes is -1.
10. (a) (i)   (b) (iv)   (c) (iii)   (d) (ii)

Exercise 18·3

1. (a) (i) 0.996   (ii) 0.643   (iii) 0.017   (iv) 0.737
   (b) (i) 85°   (ii) 40°   (iii) 1°   (iv) 47.5°
2. (a) (i) -0.139 (ii) -0.940 (iii) -0.707 (iv) -0.940 (v) -0.707
   (vi) 0.5
   (b) θ between 90° and 270° will give a negative cosine

Exercise 18·3 *(cont.)*

3. (a) (i) −1.327 **(ii)** 0.176 **(iii)** −0.7 **(iv)** 0.364 **(v)** 2.747
  (vi) −1.111 **(vii)** −0.7
  (b) (i) none **(ii)** 20° **(iii)** none
  (c) 90° < θ < 180°, 270° < θ < 360° will give a negative tangent

4.

θ	sin θ	cos θ	tan θ	θ	sin θ	cos θ	tan θ
10°	0.174	0.985	0.176	190°	−0.174	−0.985	0.176
20°	0.342	0.940	0.364	200°	−0.342	−0.940	0.364
30°	0.500	0.866	0.577	210°	−0.500	−0.866	0.577
40°	0.643	0.766	0.839	220°	−0.643	−0.766	0.839
50°	0.766	0.643	1.192	230°	−0.766	−0.643	1.192
60°	0.866	0.500	1.732	240°	−0.866	−0.500	1.732
70°	0.940	0.342	2.747	250°	−0.940	−0.342	2.747
80°	0.985	0.174	5.671	260°	−0.985	−0.174	5.671
90°	1.000	0.000	∞	270°	−1.000	0.000	∞
100°	0.985	−0.174	−5.671	280°	−0.985	0.174	−5.671
110°	0.940	−0.342	−2.747	290°	−0.940	0.342	−2.747
120°	0.866	−0.500	−1.732	300°	−0.866	0.500	−1.732
130°	0.766	−0.643	−1.192	310°	−0.766	0.643	−1.192
140°	0.643	−0.766	−0.839	320°	−0.643	0.766	−0.839
150°	0.500	−0.866	−0.577	330°	−0.500	0.866	−0.577
160°	0.342	−0.940	−0.364	340°	−0.342	0.940	−0.364
170°	0.174	−0.985	−0.176	350°	−0.174	0.985	−0.176
180°	0.000	−1.000	0.000	360°	0.000	1.000	0.000

Exercise 18·4

Calculator values are given below. Estimates should agree to one significant figure.

A 1. (a) 0.407 **(b)** 0.829 **(c)** 0.978 **(d)** 0.342
  (e) −0.139 **(f)** −0.788 **(g)** −0.951 **(h)** −0.829
2. (a) 17.5°, 162.5° **(b)** 36.9°, 143.1° **(c)** 64.2°, 115.8° [*Note:* Some calculators will give −ve
  (d) 191.5°, 348.5° **(e)** 203.6°, 336.5° **(f)** 233.1°, 306.9° angles instead of values between 0° and 360°.]
4. (a) 0.914 **(b)** 0.559 **(c)** −0.208 **(d)** −0.940
  (e) −0.990 **(f)** −0.616 **(g)** 0.309 **(h)** 0.559
5. (a) 66.4°, 293.6° **(b)** 53.1°, 306.9° **(c)** 25.8°, 334.2°
  (d) 98.6°, 261.4° **(e)** 110.5°, 249.5° **(f)** 138.6°, 221.4°
6. (a) true **(b)** true **(c)** true **(d)** false **(e)** false
7. INVESTIGATION
8. (a) 38.7°, 218.7° **(b)** 58.0°, 238.0° **(c)** 116.6°, 296.6° **(d)** 105.9°, 285.9°

Exercise 18·5

A 1. Drawing
2. (a) (i) + **(ii)** + **(iii)** + **(iv)** −
   (v) − **(vi)** − **(vii)** − **(viii)** −
   (b) (i) + **(ii)** − **(iii)** − **(iv)** +
   (v) − **(vi)** + **(vii)** + **(viii)** −
   (c) (i) − **(ii)** − **(iii)** − **(iv)** −
   (v) − **(vi)** + **(vii)** − **(viii)** +
3. (a) 0, 1, 0, −1, 0 **(b)** 1, 0, −1, 0, 1 **(c)** 0, no value, 0, no value, 0
4. (a) false **(b)** true **(c)** true **(d)** false **(e)** true
   (f) false **(g)** true **(h)** true
5. (a) − **(b)** − **(c)** + **(d)** − **(e)** +
   (f) − **(g)** + **(h)** +

Exercise 19·1

A 1. 15, 18; f: $x \rightarrow 3x$
2. 4, 5; f: $x \rightarrow x - 1$
3. 11, 13; f: $x \rightarrow 2x + 1$
4. 14, 17; f: $x \rightarrow 3x - 1$
5. 26, 37; f: $x \rightarrow x^2 + 1$
6. 3, 2; f: $x \rightarrow 8 - x$

B 1. Output: 0, 4, 8, 12, 16
2. Output: 0, 4, 16, 36, 64
3. Output: −2, 1, 4, 7, 10
4. Output: 0, 3, 8, 15, 24
5. Output: 0, −1, −2, 1, 2
6. Output: 1, 3, 9, 3, 9
7. Output: −6, −3, 0, 3, 6, 9
8. Output: 2, 6, 12, 0, 0

C 1. Input: 7, 9
2. Input: 12, 14
3. Input: 10, 50
4. Input: 7, 10
5. Input: 20, −35
6. Input: 5, 7
7. Input: 10, 29
8. Input: 3, 7

Exercise 19·2

[Students will not know why log −1 gives E etc. but some of the E's can be accounted for.]

Input → Function	0	1	10	90	0.5	0.05	−1	−10	−90	−0.5
$x \rightarrow x^2$	0	1	100	8100	0.25	0.0025	1	100	8100	0.25
$x \rightarrow 1/x$	E	1	0.1	0.0111	2	20	−1	−0.1	−0.0111	−2
$x \rightarrow \sqrt{x}$	0	1	3.16	9.487	0.7071	0.2236	E	E	E	E
$x \rightarrow \sin x$	0	0.017	0.174	1	0.009	0.0009	−0.017	−0.174	−1	−0.009
$x \rightarrow \cos x$	1	0.999	0.985	0	0.999	0.9999	0.999	0.985	0	0.999
$x \rightarrow \tan x$	0	0.017	0.176	E	0.009	0.0009	−0.017	−0.176	E	−0.009
$x \rightarrow -x$	0	−1	−10	−90	−0.5	−0.05	1	10	90	0.5
$x \rightarrow \log x$	E	0	1	1.954	−0.301	−1.301	E	E	E	E
$x \rightarrow \ln x$	E	0	2.303	4.500	−0.693	−2.996	E	E	E	E
$x \rightarrow x!$	1	1	3 628 800	!	E	E	E	E	E	E

! = (approx.) 3×10^{138} [The largest number that most calculators will show is 10^{100}.]

B 1. $1/x$
2. $\sqrt{x}$
3. x^2
4. $x!$
5. $\sin x$
6. $\log x$
7. $-x$
8. $\cos x$
9. $\sqrt{x}, \log x, \ln x, x!$
10. $\tan x$

C 1. Input: 12
2. Input: 0
3. Input: 2.25
4. Input: 25, 155
5. Input: 45, 315
6. Input: 45, 315
7. Input: −0.8
8. Input: 31.62
9. Input: 0, any negative number
10. Input: 0.5

Exercise 19·3

A 1. Royals. f: $x \rightarrow$ wife of x.
2. Clothes and materials. f: $x \rightarrow$ substance x is made of.
3. Colours, instructions (traffic lights).
4. Sports, gear.
5. Many possible answers

B 1. Set of names; set of natural numbers; alphabetical order.
2. Set of names; set of years; year each person was born [or weights in kg?].
3. Set of cities; set of distances; how far each city is from London.
4. Set of names; set of telephone numbers; each person's number.
5. Set of towns; set of area codes; codes for each town.
6. Set of Kings/Queens of England; position in alphabet of last letter of name.

C 1. $x \rightarrow 2x$
2. $x \rightarrow x - 1$
3. $x \rightarrow 2x + 1$
4. $x \rightarrow 3x - 1$
5. $x \rightarrow x^2 + 1$
6. $x \rightarrow x^3 - 2$
7. $x \rightarrow \sin x$
8. $x \rightarrow 1/x$
9. $x \rightarrow \sqrt{x}$

Exercise 19·4

A **1** (a) 100, 0.01   (b) 0.25, 4   (c) 12.25, 0.0816   (d) 0, E   (e) 9, 0.111
     2. 25, 625, 390 625, $1.525\,878\,9 \times 10^{11}$
                                    3. $^1/_8 \,(= 0.125)$, 8, $^1/_8$, 8 . . .
     4. (a) probably 5 times   (b) 4 times   **5.** As many times as you like.
     6. Yes.
     7. [Working down left hand column first.]
         (a) 7   (b) 0.1677   (c) E
         (d) 1.0627   (e) 0.9889   (f) -1.9 (g) E

B **1.** (a) $f: x \to \frac{1}{2}x$ (b) $f: x \to x - 3$ (c) $f: x \to x + 3$
       (d) $f: x \to \frac{1}{2}(x - 3)$ (e) $f: x \to x/3 + 2$ (f) $f: x \to \sqrt{x} - 1$

Exercise 19·5

A **1.** INVESTIGATION
     2. (a) $41.30°$ (b) $4.59°$ (c) $21.10°$ (d) $28.03°$
         (e) $74.93°$ (f) $60.66°$ (g) $11.48°$ (h) $88.85°$
         (i) $28.81°$ (j) $37.95°$ (k) $52.85°$ (l) $77.68°$
     3. (a) $29.74°$ (b) $24.62°$ (c) $56.94°$ (d) $27.95°$ [Working
         (e) $55.77°$ (f) $48.19°$ (g) $36.53°$ (h) $31.26°$ across page]
     4. $-1 \leqslant x \leqslant 1$, $-1 \leqslant x \leqslant 1$, $9 \times 10^{99} \leqslant x < -9 = 10^{99}$ for a full scientific calculator.

Exercise 19·6

A **1.** 729   **2.** 437.8939   **3.** 35 831 808   **4.** 4.660 957
     5. 923 521   **6.** 0.107 374 2   **7.** 0.000 002 373   **8.** $2.713\,659 \times 10^{11}$

B **1.** false   **2.** true   **3.** false
     4. false   **5.** false   **6.** false

Exercise 20·1

A **1.** (a) £38.50   (b) £151.20   (c) £115.00   (d) £135.40   (e) £436.80
         (f) £748.80
     2. (a) £1.44   (b) £3.33   (c) £3.85   (d) £6.17
     3. (a) £350   (b) £408.33   (c) £450
     4. £6864
     5. A tiny bit less (there are 52 weeks and 1 day in a year).
     6. £160

B **1.** (a) £4.81   (b) £5.78
     2. First job pays £99.36; second pays £75
     3. £22 256
     4. (a) £3.85 per hour; £153.85 per week   (b) £6 per hour; £132 per week
         (c) £2.88 per hour; (approx.) £115.20 per week
     5. (a) £201.60
         (b) (i) £162 per week   (ii) £226.80 per week   (iii) £7.02 per hour
              (iv) £6048 per year   (v) £11 016 per year
     6. (a) £364   (b) £655.20   (c) £1033.33

Exercise 20·2

	Date	Incoming		Outgoing		Balance
1	Jan 1	in hand	£240			£240
	Jan 4			TV	£4.50	£236.50
	Jan 8	wages	£121	personal	£50	
			£95	food	£35	
				drink	£12	
				video	£6	£349.50
	Jan 11			TV	£4.50	£345
	Jan 12			car HP	£95	
				new tyre	£38.50	£211.50
	Jan 15	wages	£216	weekly spending	£103	£324.50
	Jan 17			gas bill	£49	£275.50
	Jan 18			TV	£4.50	£271
	Jan 22	wages	£216	weekly spending	£103	£384
	Jan 25			TV	£4.50	£379.50
	Jan 28			electricity	£52.50	£327
	Jan 29	wages	£216	weekly spending	£103	£440
	Jan 31			rent	£178	
				rates	£42	£220
	Feb 1			TV	£4.50	£215.50
	Feb 5	wages	£216	weekly spending	£103	£328.50
	Feb 8			TV	£4.50	£324
	Feb 9			telephone bill	£27.50	£296.50
	Feb 10			car service	£37.60	£258.90
	Feb 12	wages	£216	weekly spending	£103	
				car HP	£95	£276.90
	Feb 15			TV	£4.50	£272.40
	Feb 18			car repair	£26	£246.40
	Feb 19	wages	£216	weekly spending	£103	£359.40
	Feb 22			TV	£4.50	£354.90
	Feb 26	wages	£216	weekly spending	£103	£467.90
	Feb 28			rent	£178	
				rates	£42	£247.90
	Mar 1			TV	£4.50	£243.40
	Mar 5	wages	£216	weekly spending	£103	£356.40
	Mar 8			TV	£4.50	£351.90
	Mar 10			car tax	£42	£309.90
	Mar 12	wages	£216	weekly spending	£103	
				car HP	£90	£327.90
	Mar 15			TV	£4.50	£323.40
	Mar 16			insurance	£125	£198.40
	Mar 19	wages	£216	weekly spending	£103	£311.40
	Mar 22			TV	£4.50	£306.90
	Mar 26	wages	£216	weekly spending	£103	£419.90
	Mar 29			TV	£4.50	£415.40
	Mar 31			rent	£178	
					£42	£195.40
						£195.40

Exercise 20·3

A 1. Workers' wages, heating, lighting, rent, machinery, depreciation, rates, taxes, research, advertising, accounting.
2. Distribution costs, storage, transport, taxes, wages, advertising, sales force.
3. Fewer overheads: no charges for light, heat, advertising, minimal rent. Quick turnover so stock does not have to be held.
4. Wholesaler's profit: 62.5%; retailer's profit: 66.2%.

Exercise 20·3 *(cont.)*

B 1. 28.6% 2. 38.6% 3. 39.3%; 46.2%
    4. 66.7% 5. 33.3% 6. 28.6%
    7. 33.9%, 23.8%, 8.3%, 44%
    8. **(a)** manufacturer's profit: 255.6%; wholesaler's profit: 68.8%; shop's profit: 48.1%
       (b) 29.6% **(c)** 13.8%
    9. **(a)** 23.6% **(b)** 37.5% **(c)** 7.7% **(d)** 35.9%
   10. Many possible answers

Exercise 20·4

A 1. £4.00 2. £20.35 3. £19.80
    4. £27.60 5. £50.40 6. £187.50

B 1. £107 2. £492.75 3. £69.98
    4. £401.41 5. £905.08 6. £5050.61

C 1. £84.25 2. £692.93 3. £793.44 4. £5746.05
    5. **(a)** £3060 **(b)** £2952 **(c)** £2844

Exercise 20·5

A 1. **(a)** £288 **(b)** £360 **(c)** £528 **(d)** £576 (there is £288 difference)
    2. **(a)** £558 **(b)** £691.92

Exercise 21·1

  1. **(a)** F **(b)** B **(c)** centre of OA **(d)** D **(e)** C
    (f) centre of DE **(g)** E **(h)** centre of base **(i)** centre of rectangle
    (j) centre of BP
  2. **(a)** on the 'floor' of the rectangle **(b)** along the z-axis **(c)** along the y-axis
  3. **(a)** **(i)** P **(ii)** the centre of the ceiling
    (b) (0, 0, 0), (0, 0, 4), (0, 6, 0), (0, 6, 4), (8, 0, 0), (8, 6, 0), (8, 0, 4), (8, 6, 4)
    (c) **(i)** (4, 0, 2), (4, 6, 2), (0, 3, 2), (8, 3, 2) **(ii)** (4, 3, 0)
      (iii) (0, 0, 2), (0, 6, 2), (8, 2, 0), (8, 6, 2)
  4. **(a)** latitude, longitude and height **(b)** latitude, longitude and depth **(c)** floor, ward, bed

Exercise 21·2

  1. **(a)** A (0, 0, 1); B (3, 0, 1); C (3, 2, 1); D (0, 2, 1); E (0, 2, 0); F (3, 2, 0); G (3, 0, 0)
    (b) OA = 1 cm; OB = $\sqrt{10}$ cm; OC = $\sqrt{14}$ cm; OD = $\sqrt{5}$ cm; OE = 2 cm; OF = $\sqrt{13}$ cm; OG = 3 cm
  2. See footnote.
  3. See footnote.
  4. The four long diagonals are OC, AF, DG and BE. They are all shown to be $\sqrt{14}$ by using the footnote formula.
  5. **(a)** 11.18 m 6. 36.4 km 7. $\sqrt{14}$ = 3.74
  8. **(a)** the aircraft with coordinates (14, 19, 7), distance 24.6 units
    (b) 9.27 units

Exercise 21·3

A 1. Many possible answers (e.g. where walls meet, side of door, etc.).
    2. Yes. They all go in the same direction.
    3. No.
    4. **(a)** many possible answers (e.g. corner of a room, table, etc.)
      (b) many possible answers (e.g. centre line on a football pitch and goalpost, etc.)
    5. Many possible answers.
B 1. True 2. False: L_1 could be parallel to L_3 3. False
    4. False 5. True 6. False

Exercise 21·4

A 1. xz plane 2. xy plane 3. yz plane
4. The $x = 2$ plane, which is parallel to the yz plane
5. The $y = 1$ plane, which is parallel to the xz plane 6. No plane

B 1. True 2. True 3. True 4. True 5. False
6. (a) true (b) false
7. Floor and ceiling; other answers possible.
8. Adjacent walls; wall and floor, etc.

C 1. Not possible 2. Possible 3. Not possible 4. Possible
5. Not possible 6. Possible 7. Possible 8. Not possible

D Many possible answers.

Exercise 21·5

A 1. (a) 268.1 cm³ (b) 4188.8 cm³ (c) 64.45 cm³ (d) 0.0009 mm³
2. (a) 201.1 cm² (b) 1256.6 cm² (c) 78.54 m³ (d) 0.045 mm²
3. (a) 56.55 cm³ (b) 348.45 m³ (c) 8.58 km³ (d) 0.000 26 mm³
4. (a) 1357.2 cm² (b) 217.15 m² (c) 1.43 m² (d) 0.06 mm²

B 1. (a) 268.1 cm³; 201.1 cm² (b) 301.6 cm²
2. (a) 4.16 cm (b) 217 cm²
3. (a) height = 10.6 cm (b) 256.55 cm²
4. Smallest area that can be used is 248.08 cm² when $r = 3.63$ cm
$\left(= \sqrt[3]{\dfrac{600}{4\pi}} \right)$, in this case $h = 2r$. This can be shown to be a minimum by calculating the area for
$r = 3.7$ and $r = 3.6$. Both of these will seem to be larger than 248.08.

C 1. (a) internal: 201.6 cm², external: 314.2 cm²
(b) internal: 268.1 cm³, external: 523.6 cm³ (c) 255.5 cm³
2. 15.769 m³ = 15 769 litres 3. 3.053 m³ = 3053 litres
4. (a) 14.14 m³
(b) external vol. = 18.82 m³. Vol. of material = 4.68 m³. Mass of material = 15.0 tonnes
(c) 19 kg
(d) water displaced weighs 18.82 tonnes (if fresh); thus it would take a further 3.82 tonnes (approx.) to sink the diving bell

Exercise 21·6

A 1. (a) Edinburgh (b) Cardiff (c) Singapore
(d) Tokyo (e) Melbourne (f) Buenos Aires

2. (a)

Latitude	Radius	Circumference	(b) 1° of longitude
0°	6378 km	40 074 km	111.3 km
10°	6281 km	39 465 km	109.6 km
20°	5993 km	37 657 km	104.6 km
30°	5524 km	34 705 km	96.4 km
40°	4886 km	30 699 km	85.3 km
50°	4100 km	25 759 km	71.6 km
60°	3189 km	20 037 km	55.7 km
70°	2181 km	13 706 km	38.1 km
80°	1108 km	6 959 km	19.3 km
90°	0 km	0 km	0 km

3. 9985.6 km
4. The route along 50° latitude is 12 879.5 km, while the route over the North Pole is only 8876 km. A saving of 4000 km.
5. This is the same as the shortest distance between two points on the sphere. Any flight to right or left from the great circle has to be returned. This is best seen on a globe.

Exercise 22·1

A **1.** 236¼ cu. in **2.** 5655 mm³ **3.** 0.864 m³ (= 864 000 cm³)
4. 52 800 cm³ **5.** 564 480 cm³ **6.** 123 700 cm³ (= 0.1237 m³)

B **1.** 548 800 cm³; 1 317 120 g = 1317.2 kg **2.** 250 000 cm³; 600 000 g = 600 kg
3. Volume = 5 091 261 cm³ = 5.091 261 m³. Mass = 38.18 tonnes.
4. (a) 1260 cm³ (b) 2.52 kg (c) 2400 bricks (d) 6000 kg, i.e. 6 tonnes
Now you know why foundations are necessary.
5. 1131 m³; 6 h 20 min

C **1.** £12.35
2. 0.4 mm; 4½ cans of 5 litres; cost approx. £40.
3. £13.42, 1 metre weighs 1118 g, costs £1.20; this corresponds to £1073 per tonne!
4. 60p (probably a bit more).
5. It holds 1.104 litres if it is full to the top.
6. 9.2 cm, assuming it is filled to the top. 10 cm is a reasonable approximation.

Exercise 22·2

A **1.** 9.54 cm²
2. (a) 7425 cm³ (b) 5832 cm³ (c) 2505 cm² (including lid)
3. It is only necessary to compare the total widths as thickness and length are the same. The second method gives less waste.
4. (a) 28 274 cm² (b) 5654.8 cm³ (c) 39.58 kg

C **1.** (a) 80 m³ (b) 1111 boxes, though you might have some difficulty in fitting them in.
(d) 120 kg **(e)** 133 320 kg = 133.32 tonnes, so the container will not be fully loaded.
2. 113.1 m³ = 113 100 litres.
3. (a) 140 400 litres (b) 119 340 kg (d) 46.8 m (per wing)
4. (a) 250 000 m³ (b) 250 000 m³ (i) £1.25 million [*Note:* in November 1984, bottled spring
(ii) £3.75 million water costs about 40p per litre in the
(iii) £8.75 million supermarket.]
5. 1.09×10^{-4} mm
6. (a) 1 200 000 m² = 1.2 km² (b) 60 km²
[*Note:* if the oil spread to the minimum of 1.09×10^{-4} mm, the polluted area could be 550 000 km²]

Exercise 22·3

A **1.** Height = 24.5 mm, vertex to edge of base = 35 mm.
2. The diagonals of the cube are twice the sloping edges.
3. Use Pythagoras' theorem on the cube.
4. $\frac{1}{6} \times 50^3 = 20\ 833$ mm³ = 20.83 cm³ [*Note:* ⅓ base × height gives 20.41 because of rounding.]

B INVESTIGATION

Exercise 22·4

A **1.** 96 cm³ **2.** 140 cm³ **3.** 28 cm³
4. 28.87 cm³ **5.** 3053.6 cm³ **6.** 45.24 m³

B **1.** (a) 83.78 m³ (b) 83.78 tonnes

2. (a)

Pyramid	Volume (m³)	Mass (tonnes)
Medum	637 862	1 786 014
Gizeh (1)	2 593 563	7 261 975
Gizeh (2)	2 220 361	6 217 011
Gizeh (3)	239 300	670 041
Dahshur	1 255 533	3 515 491

(b) The pyramids of Khufu and Khafra at Gizeh.
3. 180 m **4.** (a) 1781 m³ (b) 1399 m³ (c) 382 m³ (d) 802.2 tonnes

Exercise 22·5

A 1. 523.6 cm³, 314.2 cm²; 4188.8 cm³, 1256.6 cm²; 33 510 cm³, 5026 cm²; 14.1 m³, 28.3 m².
   2. Tennis: 143.8 cm³, 132.7 cm²; cricket: 194.9 cm³, 162.6 cm²; soccer: 332.4 cu. in, 232 sq. in.
   3. Approx. 201 061 930 sq. miles.
   4. Approx. 58 307 960 sq. miles.
   5. (a) (i) 260 766 430 000 cubic miles, 197 387 017 sq. miles
      (ii) 259 449 220 000 cubic miles, 196 721 748 sq. miles
      (iii) 260 107 270 000 cubic miles, 197 054 242 sq. miles
   (b) (iii) is closest
   6. (a) 2036 m², 2513 m²   (b) 12 214 m³   (c) 4540 m³
   (d) 10 000 tonnes (approx.)

B 1. 4.75 cm, 284 cm²   2. 43.82 m³
   3. 5.98 m, 897.6 m³. The gas inside is lighter than the displaced air.
   4. 25.23 m   5. 10.55 m

C 1. 161.7 cm³   [the height of each pyramid is 4.95 cm].
   2. The cone will hold all the melted ice-cream; 26.3 mm below rim [will need some discussion!].
   3. 2681 cm³
   4. Radius = 2.91 cm, depth = 4.85 cm.
   5. Imagine the sphere divided into n cones, each with height r and base area $(4\pi r^2)/n$.

   Then the volume of all the cones is $n\left(\dfrac{1}{3}\dfrac{4\pi r^2}{n}\,r\right) = \dfrac{4\pi r^3 n}{3n} = \dfrac{4}{3}\pi r^3$

   6. 17 191 mm³

D INVESTIGATIONS

Exercise 23·1

A 1. Mean = £3039, range = £2100, interquartile range = £1280 (no. 3 to no. 8).
   2. These answers will depend on when you use the book.
   3. Mean = 39.95 g, range = 24 g, interquartile range = 8 g.
   4. (a) mean = £131.78, range = £110, interquartile range = £25 (no. 5 to no. 14)
      (b) mean = £158.39, range = £150, interquartile range = £35 (no. 5 to no. 14)
      (c) mean = £86.40, range = £37, interquartile range = £16 (no. 4 to no. 12)
   5. Mean = 46.03, range = 59, interquartile range = 62 − 30 = 32.

B 1. Boys: mean = 174 cm,   range = 24 cm interquartile range = 11 cm.
       Girls: mean = 168.9 cm, range = 29 cm, interquartile range = 14 cm.
   2. Jan: mean = 4.05°C,   range = 5.0°C, interquartile range = 0.7°C.
       June: mean = 14.68°C, range = 2.5°C, interquartile range = 1.3°C.
   3. Scotland: mean = 3.53,   range = 4.65,   interquartile range = 2.77.
       Wales: mean = 3.82,   range = 5.14,   interquartile range = 3.37.
   4. Girls: mean = 3.125 kg, range = 3.5 kg, interquartile range = 1.5 kg.
       Boys: mean = 3.210 kg, range = 3.5 kg, interquartile range = 1.5 kg
   5. Mean = 10 020 miles, range = 7500 miles, interquartile range = 1000 miles.

Exercise 23·2

A Various answers to this exercise.

B 4. (a) 0 = 19, 1 = 20, 2 = 24, 3 = 20, 4 = 22, 5 = 20, 6 = 16, 7 = 12, 8 = 25, 9 = 23.
      (b) 00 = 0, 11 = 2, 22 = 2, 33 = 1, 44 = 3, 55 = 1, 66 = 1, 77 = 0, 88 = 1, 99 = 2.
      (c) 000 = 0, 111 = 1, 222 = 0, 333 = 0, 444 = 0, 555 = 1, 666 = 0, 777 = 0, 888 = 0, 999 = 0.

Exercise 23·3

A 1. The girls take a sample of all possible styles, sizes, colours etc.
   2. A sample of all the possible questions on that subject.
   3. A sample of all possible throws with a pair of dice.
   4. Sample of all the water in the reservoir, for instance.
   5. Sample of all the blood in your body.
   6. Sample of the people who buy a local newspaper.

Exercise 23·3 *(cont.)*

C **1. (a)** random sampling
2. (a) percentage viewing figures **(b)** yes, on average

(c)

	Mean (%)	Range	Interquartile range
BBC 1	35.6	14	11
ITV	48.4	18	11
BBC 2	10.1	7	1
C4	5.9	5	2

3. About 200; assume the die is evenly weighted.
4. 360 000 yes; 180 000 no; 60 000 don't know; assuming the workers were a random sample (taken from different parts of the country, etc.).
5. 2000; assuming light bulbs were a random sample.

Exercise 23·4

A **1, 2.** INVESTIGATION
3. Mean deviation: **(a)** $72 \div 16 = 4.5$ **(b)** $4 \div 12 = 0.333$ **(c)** $164.833 \div 12 = 13.736$
(d) $320 \div 14 = 22.85$ **(e)** $96 \div 100 = 0.96$
4. Interquartile range: **(a)** 8.5 **(b)** 0.65 **(c)** 26.5
(d) 34 **(e)** 1

Exercise 24·1

A **1. (a)** 1, 2, 3, 4, 6, 8, 12, 24 **(b)** 1, 2, 4, 5, 8, 10, 20, 40
(c) 1, 2, 3, 4, 6, 8, 12, 16, 24, 32, 48, 96 **(d)** 1, 2, 3, 4, 6, 8, 9, 12, 16, 18, 24, 36, 48, 72, 144
(e) 1, 3, 9, 27, 81, 243
2. 60 **3.** 252 **4.** (1 and) 3 **5.** 40
6. (a) multiple **(b)** multiple

B **1.** 2, 3, 5, 7, 11, 13, 17, 19, 23, 29, 31, 37, 41, 43, 47, 53, 59, 61, 67, 71
2. 83, 101
3. (a) no; for instance, if $p = 5$ and $q = 7$
(b) yes [This question is worth discussion]
4. (a) 59, 43 **(b)** 3, 37 **(c)** 7, 11, 13
(d) 73, 137 [. . . worth extending!]
5. (a) $7 \times 3 \times 3$ **(b)** $2 \times 2 \times 2 \times 3 \times 5$ **(c)** $2 \times 2 \times 2 \times 2 \times 2$
(d) $3 \times 3 \times 3 \times 3$ **(e)** $2 \times 2 \times 7$ **(f)** $2 \times 2 \times 2 \times 3$
(g) 7×13 **(h)** $3 \times 3 \times 3 \times 3 \times 3$ **(i)** $3 \times 7 \times 37$
(j) $2 \times 2 \times 2 \times 2 \times 2 \times 3$ **(k)** $2 \times 3 \times 3 \times 3 \times 5$ **(l)** $2 \times 2 \times 2 \times 5 \times 5 \times 5$
6. 77 777 is $7 \times 11\ 111$ so it is not prime. 54 321 is a multiple of 3. 83 521 $= 17 \times 4913$.
37 259 is 19×1961 so the prime is 131 071.

C **1.** The first is 1009; thereafter 1013, 1019, 1021, 1031, 1033 . . .
2. Apart from 1, of course. Since odd squares must be $2 + p$, checking shows that the suggestion breaks down with $289 = 287 + 2$.
3. (a) $q + r$ is a multiple of p
(b) $q \times r$ is a multiple of p (and of a power of p)
(c) $q \div r$ is not necessarily a multiple of p
(d) $2q + 3r$ is a multiple of p
4. 15, 21, 28, 36, 45, 55. 3 is the only prime triangle number.
5. 28 $(1 + 2 + 4 + 7 + 14)$, 496 $(1 + 2 + 4 + 8 + 16 + 31 + 62 + 124 + 248)$.

Exercise 24·2

A, B. Many possible answers.

C **(a) (i)** 0.666 . . . **(ii)** 0.444 . . . **(iii)** 0.875 **(iv)** 0.09 **(v)** 0.656 25
After a while you have used up all the possible remainders so the pattern must repeat or end.
2. No irrational number has regular pattern.
3. All true.

Exercise 24·3

A   **1.** $25 \text{ km}^2 : 5 \text{ km}^2$ **2.** 160 km^2 **3.** £200
    4. 900 g   **5.** 5.4 tonnes   **6.** 3.64 kg

B   **1.** 315 441   **2.** 1.5 : 1 women : men
    4. Great Britain: 440 000
       South Africa: 3.23 million
       Argentina: 1.19 million
       India (men):   98 million
       India (women):   142.56 million
    5. **(a)** *1979:* 1 : 9.67   *1980:* 1 : 9.68   *1981:* 1 : 10   *1982:* 1 : 10.08
       (b) *1979:* 1 : 2.78   *1980:* 1 : 2.76   *1981:* 1 : 2.79   *1982:* 1 : 2.76
       (c) *1979:* 1 : 1.17   *1980:* 1 : 1.16   *1981:* 1 : 1.15   *1982:* 1 : 1.15
       (d) *1979:* 1 : 0.48   *1980:* 1 : 0.46   *1981:* 1 : 0.44   *1982:* 1 : 0.43
    6. **(a)** biscuits, sausage (more than 2 : 1)—these figures are worth discussing.
       (b) cheese, fried egg   **(c)** cheese, peanuts

Exercise 24·4

A   **1.** Ratio (diameter : circumference) = $1 : \pi$.
    2. Ratio (perimeter : height) = 3 : 0.866.
    3. The usual sin, cos and tan ratios and their inverses.
    5. The golden ratio 1.618 : 1 is to be found in all lengths of the figure.
    6. All regular polygons have associated constant ratios.
    7. $\sqrt{3} : 1$.   **8.** INVESTIGATION

D   I leave it to you to argue it out.

Exercise 25·1

A   **1.** **(a)** 0.04; 0.25% **(b)** 0.185; 3.6%   **(c)** 1.176; 7.3%   **(d)** 15.96; 1%
    2. **(a)** $4.05 \times 16.3 = 66.015$; $4 \times 16 = 64$; 2.015, 3%
       (b) $2.08 \div 41 = 0.050\,731\,707$; $2 \div 40 = 0.05$; 0.000 731 707, 1.4%
       (c) $37 \times (1.08 + 3.26) = 160.58$; $40 \times (1 + 3) = 160$; 0.58, 0.36%
       (d) $\dfrac{270 \times 65.8}{132} = 134.590\,909$; $\dfrac{270 \times 65}{135} = 130$; 4.590 909, 3.4%
       (e) $42^2 = 1764$; $40^2 = 1600$; 164, 9.3%
       (f) $62 \times 48 \times 12.3 = 36\,604.8$; $60 \times 50 \times 12 = 36\,000$; 604.8, 1.65%
    4. [*Note:* Memory is useful in all these questions.]
       (a) $1400 + 3800 = 5200$; error 0.2%   **(b)** $5000 - 2000 = 3000$; error 0.5%
       (c) $51 \div 34 = 1.5$; error 7.7% or $55 \div 40 = 1.375$ **(d)** $20 \times 0.75 = 15$; error 3.1%
       (e) $(20 + 30) \times 15 = 750$; error 5.4%   **(f)** $(50 \times 20 \times 6) \div 3 = 2000$; error 2.9%
       (g) $(40 \times 20) - (40 \times 40) + 650 = -150$; error 9.4%
       (h) $\sqrt{14^2 + 8^2} = \sqrt{260} = 16.12$; error 1.2%

B   **1.** 2.56%   **2.** 9.99%   **3.** 5.74%   **4.** 8.51%; 13.03% **5.** 6.26%

C   **1.** **(a)** 6.33%   **(b)** 21.56%   [*Note:* $800 \div 500$ would be much better.]
    2. **(a)** 4.76%   **(b)** 4.76%
    3. **(a)** 9.09%   **(b)** 5.4%
    4. **(a)** 0.0067%   **(b)** 8.33%
    5. **(a)** cuboid 29.4273 cm³; prism 28.512 cm³; cylinder 24.5437 cm³
       (b) depends on your choice of estimate
    6. **(a)** 33.33 mph   **(b)** 77.77 mph

Exercise 25·2

A   **1.** **(a)** 3.141   **(b)** 1.414   **(c)** 1.709
      (d) 65.383   **(e)** 5.501   **(f)** 0.087
    2. **(a)** 3.14, 1.41, 1.71, 65.38, 5.50, 0.09   **(b)** 3.142, 1.414, 1.710, 65.384, 5.501, 0.087
      (c) 3.14×10^0, 1.41×10^0, 1.71×10^0, 6.54×10^1, 5.50×10^0, 8.75×10^{-2}
      (d) 3.142×10^0, 1.414×10^0, 1.710×10^0, 6.538×10^1, 5.501×10^0, 8.749×10^{-2}

Exercise 25·2 *(cont.)*

B 1. 1.265 – 1.274 m 2. 14.25 – 14.34 sec 3. (b), should be 7.93×10^3
4. 1845.75 – 1925.76 cm² 5. 18.24 – 22.29 miles 6. Yes—maximum volume 93 576.66 mm³

C INVESTIGATION

Exercise 25·3

A 1. (a) 1310.6; error 0.012% (b) 1354.4; error 0.012%
2. (a) 0.710 76; error 0.006% (b) 0.715 64; error 0.007%
3. 1.736 75 [1.737 would do] 4. 19.492; 19.873
5. 0.9033 [*Note: Subtract* ⁴/₁₀ *of the difference as cos decreases.*]
6. 0.089 38
7. (a) £28 (b) £34
8. (a) £6.63½ (b) £11.93½ (c) £20.42½ (d) £23.34

B **1.** $y = x^2$

x	y	1st diff.	2nd diff.
0	0		
		1	
1	1		2
		3	
2	4		2
		5	
3	9		2
		7	
4	16		2
		9	
5	25		2
		11	
6	36		2
		13	
7	49		2
		15	
8	64		2
		17	
9	81		2
		19	
10	100		

2. $y = x^2$

x	y	1st diff.	2nd diff.
3.1	9.61		
		0.63	
3.2	10.24		0.2
		0.65	
3.3	10.89		0.2
		0.67	
3.4	11.56		0.2
		0.69	
3.5	12.25		0.2
		0.71	
3.6	12.96		0.2
		0.73	
3.7	13.69		0.2
		0.75	
3.8	14.44		0.2
		0.77	
3.9	15.21		0.2
		0.79	
4.0	16.00		

3. $y = 2x^2 + 5$

x	y	1st diff.	2nd diff.
7	103		
		30	
8	133		4
		34	
9	167		4
		38	
10	205		4
		42	
11	247		4
		46	
12	293		4
		50	
13	343		4
		54	
14	397		4
		58	
15	455		4
		62	
16	517		

4. $y = (x + 2)(x + 3)$

x	y	1st diff.	2nd diff.
11	182		
		28	
12	210		2
		30	
13	240		2
		32	
14	272		2
		34	
15	306		2
		36	
16	342		2
		38	
17	380		2
		40	
18	420		2
		42	
19	462		2
		44	
20	506		

5. $y = 2^x$

x	y	1st diff.	2nd diff.
1	2		
		2	
2	4		2
		4	
3	8		4
		8	
4	16		8
		16	
5	32		16
		32	
6	64		32
		64	
7	128		64
		128	
8	256		128
		256	
9	512		256
		512	
10	1024		

6. $y = x^3 + x$

x	y	1st diff.	2nd diff.	3rd diff.
1	2			
		8		
2	10		12	
		20		6
3	30		18	
		38		6
4	68		24	
		62		6
5	130		30	
		92		6
6	222		36	
		128		6
7	350		42	
		170		6
8	520		48	
		218		6
9	738		54	
		272		
10	1010			

C **1.**

	1st diff.	2nd diff.
1		
	3	
4		1
	4	
8		1
	5	
13		1
	6	
19		1
	7	
28		1
	8	
34		

2.

	1st diff.
3	
	3
6	
	3
9	
	3
12	
	3
15	
	3
18	
	3
21	

3.

	1st diff.	2nd diff.
4		
	7	
11		4
	11	
22		4
	15	
37		4
	19	
56		4
	23	
79		4
	27	
108		

Exercise 25·3 *(cont.)*

C 4.

1		
3	2	
7	4	2
13	6	2
21	8	2
31	10	2
43	12	2

5.

1		
1	0	
2	1	−1
3	1	0
5	2	1
8	3	1
13	5	2
21	8	3

6.

1		
1.21	0.21	
1.44	0.23	0.02
1.69	0.25	0.02
1.96	0.27	0.02
2.25	0.29	0.02
2.65	0.31	0.02

Exercise 26·1

A 1. (a), (b), (c).

2. If $x > 1$, x^3 will be the longest side so $x + x^2 > x^3$. If $x < 1$, x will be the longest side, so $x < x^2 + x^3$
This leads to the interesting result that $0.618 < x < 1.618$ (by trial and error).

3. (a) $(1, 2, 3), (1, 2, 4), (1, 2, 5)$
$(1, 3, 4), (1, 3, 5),$
$(1, 4, 5),$
$(2, 3, 4), (2, 3, 5),$
$(2, 4, 5),$
$(3, 4, 5).$

(b) Three of these would form triangles: $(2, 3, 4), (2, 4, 5)$ and $(3, 4, 5)$

4. Possibles are:
$(1, 2, 3), (1, 2, 4), (1, 2, 5), (1, 2, 6), (1, 2, 7), (1, 2, 8), (1, 2, 9), (1, 2, 10),$
$(1, 3, 4), (1, 3, 5), (1, 3, 6), (1, 3, 7), (1, 3, 8), (1, 3, 9), (1, 3, 10),$
$(1, 4, 5), (1, 4, 6), (1, 4, 7), (1, 4, 8), (1, 4, 9), (1, 4, 10),$
$(1, 5, 6), (1, 5, 7), (1, 5, 8), (1, 5, 9), (1, 5, 10),$
$(1, 6, 7), (1, 6, 8), (1, 6, 9), (1, 6, 10),$ $\qquad\qquad \dfrac{0}{36}$
$(1, 7, 8), (1, 7, 9), (1, 7, 10),$
$(1, 8, 9), (1, 8, 10),$
$(1, 9, 10),$
$(2, 3, 4), (2, 3, 5), (2, 3, 6), (2, 3, 7), (2, 3, 8), (2, 3, 9), (2, 3, 10),$
$(2, 4, 5), (2, 4, 6), (2, 4, 7), (2, 4, 8), (2, 4, 9), (2, 4, 10),$
$(2, 5, 6), (2, 5, 7), (2, 5, 8), (2, 5, 9), (2, 5, 10),$
$(2, 6, 7), (2, 6, 8), (2, 6, 9), (2, 6, 10),$ $\qquad\qquad \dfrac{7}{28}$
$(2, 7, 8), (2, 7, 9), (2, 7, 10),$
$(2, 8, 9), (2, 8, 10),$
$(2, 9, 10),$
$(3, 4, 5), (3, 4, 6), (3, 4, 7), (3, 4, 8), (3, 4, 9), (3, 4, 10),$
$(3, 5, 6), (3, 5, 7), (3, 5, 8), (3, 5, 9), (3, 5, 10),$
$(3, 6, 7), (3, 6, 8), (3, 6, 9), (3, 6, 10),$ $\qquad\qquad \dfrac{11}{21}$
$(3, 7, 8), (3, 7, 9), (3, 7, 10),$
$(3, 8, 9), (3, 8, 10),$
$(3, 9, 10),$
$(4, 5, 6), (4, 5, 7), (4, 5, 8), (4, 5, 9), (4, 5, 10),$
$(4, 6, 7), (4, 6, 8), (4, 6, 9), (4, 6, 10),$ $\qquad\qquad \dfrac{12}{15}$
$(4, 7, 8), (4, 7, 9), (4, 7, 10),$
$(4, 8, 9), (4, 8, 10),$
$(4, 9, 10),$
$(5, 6, 7), (5, 6, 8), (5, 6, 9), (5, 6, 10),$
$(5, 7, 8), (5, 7, 9), (5, 7, 10),$ $\qquad\qquad \dfrac{10}{10}$
$(5, 8, 9), (5, 8, 10),$
$(5, 9, 10),$
$(6, 7, 8), (6, 7, 9), (6, 7, 10),$ $\qquad\qquad \dfrac{6}{6}$
$(6, 8, 9), (6, 8, 10),$
$(6, 9, 10),$
$(7, 8, 9), (7, 8, 10),$ $\qquad\qquad \dfrac{3}{3}$
$(7, 9, 10),$
$(8, 9, 10).$ $\qquad\qquad \dfrac{1}{1}$

Probability $= \dfrac{50}{120}$

5. Not true. Three shorter sides together must be greater than the longest.

Exercise 26·1 (cont.)

B **1. (a)** 80° **(b)** 65° **(c)** 54° **(d)** 130°
2. (a) 110° **(b)** 130° **(c)** 138° **(d)** 79°
3. (a) $a = 71°, b = 43°$ **(b)** $c = 55°, d = 59°$
(c) $x = 76°, y = 104°, z = 36°$ **(d)** $a = 114°, b = 42°, c = 114°, d = 20°, e = 60°$
4. INVESTIGATION
5. (a) Follows from 4.
(b) Since $\sin \theta$ is opposite/hypotenuse. Follows from (a).
(c) $\dfrac{\sin \theta}{\cos \theta} = \tan \theta$, $\sin \theta$ has values between -1 and 1, and is large when $\cos \theta$ is small. Hence $\tan \theta$ can be greater than 1.

C **1. (a)** 6 cm² **(b)** 5 cm² **(c)** 10 cm² **(d)** 21 cm² **(e)** 8.05 cm²
2. Drawing
3. (Fig. 3) 60 mm² **(Fig. 4)** 18 cm² **(Fig. 5)** 16.8875 cm²

Exercise 26·2

A **1.** Yes.
2. The heights of the two parts are the same, while the bases are equal. Hence the areas of the parts are equal.

B **1, 2, 3.** INVESTIGATIONS
4, 5. Drawing
6. (a) bisectors of the angles of △XYZ.
(b) the relationship is not obvious. Not altitudes, bisectors or medians.

Exercise 26·3   Drawings

Exercise 26·4

A **1.** 10.8 cm² **2.** 20.25 cm² **3.** 10.6 cm²
4. 104.8 cm² **5.** 54 cm² **6.** 124.7 cm²

B **1.** The square roots of numbers 2, 5, 10, 13, 17, 18, 20, 25, 26, 29, 32, 34, 37, 40, 41, 45 and 50 (17 in all) can be estimated in this way.
2. (a) use $\sqrt{20}$ and $\sqrt{5}$
(b) use $\sqrt{60}$ and $\sqrt{60}$ [$\sqrt{60}$ obtained from $\sqrt{20}$ and $\sqrt{40}$]
(c) use 1 and $\sqrt{2}$ and multiply by 10
(d) use $\sqrt{5}$ and multiply by 10

Exercise 26·5

A **1.** *Proof:* First use axis of symmetry, then use area $= \frac{1}{2}yz \sin X$ [or other methods].
2. *Proof:* Very simple, $c = a/\sin A = b/\sin B$ can be written down from the figure. This *is* the sine rule for a 90° triangle.
3. $a = 2.69$ cm **4.** $\hat{D} = 65.6°$ **5.** $u = 30.05$ m, $w = 16.58$ m
6. The sine rule holds.
7. $\hat{R} = 42°, p = 24.85$ cm. $q = 14.93$ cm
8. $\hat{L} = 72.8°$ or 107.2°; LM $= 16.18$ cm when $\hat{L}$ is acute.

B **1.** INVESTIGATION
2. $\cos B = \dfrac{a^2 + c^2 - b^2}{2ac}$; $\cos C = \dfrac{a^2 + b^2 - c^2}{2ab}$
3. EF $= 7.83$ cm, $\hat{E} = 74.5°$, $\hat{F} = 48.5°$. Area $= 26.42$ cm²
4. $\hat{L} = 36°$, LM $= 13.59$ cm **5.** 21.56 cm, 25.48 cm **6.** $\hat{A} = 88°, \hat{B} = 50°, \hat{C} = 42°$

C **1.** You should! **2.** $\hat{S} = 46.1°$ **3.** 2.47 km (2470 m)
4. 'Right angle' $= 90.192°$, error of $0.192°$ (0.2%)
5. $\hat{A} = 73.7°, \hat{E} = 62.5°, \hat{G} = 43.8°$
6. It does!

Exercise 27·1

A **1, 2, 3, 5:** is equivalent to   **4:** is the price of
    6: weighs the same as   **7, 8:** is obtained from

B **1** and **4** are equivalence relations
C **1.** $4/8 = 3/6$; $6/8 = 3/4$; $8/4 = 6/3$; $8/6 = 4/3$
    2. (i) $x = \pm\sqrt{6}$ **(ii)** $x = \pm 4$
    3. $\dfrac{100}{300} = \dfrac{2 \times 100}{3 \times 100} = \dfrac{2}{3} \times \dfrac{100}{100} = \dfrac{2}{3} \times 1 = \dfrac{2}{3}$
    4. (a) $\dfrac{a}{b} = \dfrac{ka}{kb} = \dfrac{k(ka)}{k(kb)} = \ldots$ etc.

   (b) $\dfrac{a}{b}$ is simplest when there is no k which divides both a and b

    5. (a) 4/7   **(b)** 18/25   **(c)** 3/13   **(d)** 1/13
    6. (a) $\dfrac{x}{y}$ **(b)** 1   **(c)** $\dfrac{2}{x}$ **(d)** $\dfrac{x+3}{x-1}$

Exercise 27·2

A **1. (a)** $2(x + 2)$ **(b)** $3(x - 2)$ **(c)** $x(1 - x)$ **(d)** $x(2x + a)$
    2. (a) $m(m + n)$ **(b)** $x^2(a - bx)$ **(c)** $x(x - 4)$ **(d)** $b(2a + b)$
    3. (a) $(x + 2)(x + 4)$ **(b)** $(d + 3)(d - 4)$
       (c) $(m - 2)(m + 4)$ **(d)** $(n - 4)(n + 5)$
    4. (a) $(1 + 2x)(1 - 5x)$ **(b)** $(1 + 9t)(1 - 2t)$
       (c) $(3y - 1)(y + 3)$ **(d)** $(4m + 1)(3m - 2)$
    5. (a) $(3b - 2)(4b + 3)$ **(b)** $(3g - 5)(g - 2)$
       (c) $(2x - 3)(y + 2)$ **(d)** $(3x - y)(2x - 3y)$
    6. (a) $a = -2$ **(b)** $b = 15$ **(c)** $c = 1$ **(d)** $d = 20$
    7. (a) $(x + 4)(x - 4)$ **(b)** $(1 + 3h)(1 - 3h)$
       (c) $(2 + 10k)(2 - 10k)$ **(d)** $(6x + 5y)(6x - 5y)$
    8. Checks

B **1. (a)** $x = 7$ **(b)** $x = 4$ **(c)** $y = 4$
    2. (a) $x = \frac{1}{3}$ **(b)** $m = -1\frac{1}{2}$ **(c)** $y = 1$
    3. (a) $x = 3, y = 2$ **(b)** $x = 12, y = 3$ **(c)** $x = 3, y = 4$
    4. (a) $x = 3, x = 2$ **(b)** $x = 10, x = -7$ **(c)** $y = 3, y = -12$
       (d) $x = 9, x = -11$ **(e)** $x = \frac{3}{4}, x = -\frac{2}{5}$ **(f)** $x = 1\frac{1}{2}, x = 0$
    5. (a) $x = 2, x = -3$ **(b)** $x = 2, x = -11/3$ **(c)** $x = \frac{2}{3}$

C **1.** $v = \sqrt{\dfrac{pgr}{W}}$ **2.** $u = v - \dfrac{gpt}{W}$ **3.** $g = \dfrac{2}{vh}$ **4.** $f = \dfrac{uv}{u + v}$

Exercise 27·3

A **1. (a)** 0, 0.3010, 0.4771, 0.6020, 0.6989
       (b) 1, 1.3010, 1.4771, 1.6020, 1.6989
       (c) 2, 2.3010, 2.4771, 2.6020, 2.6989
       (d) $-1, -0.6989, -0.5228, -0.3979, -0.3010$
       [*Note:* These could be written as $-1 + 0, -1 + 0.3010, -1 + 0.4771 \ldots$ etc.]
    2. INVESTIGATION
    3. (a) 1001.1   **(b)** 57.76   **(c)** 2.156   **(d)** 11 247.6
    4. (a) 4.134 . . .   **(b)** 0.031 66   **(c)** 543.46   **(d)** 84.071
    5. (a) 256   **(b)** 243   **(c)** 3.707   **(d)** 0.001
    6. (a) 7.396   **(b)** 55.516   **(c)** 3.72   **(d)** 0.7663

B INVESTIGATION

Exercise 28·1

A Drawing

Exercise 28·1 (cont.)

B (i) $\overrightarrow{AB}$, **a**, $\begin{pmatrix} 2 \\ -2 \end{pmatrix}$; $|\mathbf{a}| = \sqrt{8}$; arg **a** $= -45°$

(ii) $\overrightarrow{CD}$, **d**, $\begin{pmatrix} -4 \\ -1 \end{pmatrix}$; $|\mathbf{d}| = \sqrt{17}$; arg **d** $= 14° + 180° = 194°$ or $-166°$

(iii) $\overrightarrow{EF}$, **f**, $\begin{pmatrix} -3 \\ -1 \end{pmatrix}$; $|\mathbf{f}| = \sqrt{10}$; arg **f** $= -161.6°$ or $198.4°$

(iv) $\overrightarrow{GH}$, **g**, $\begin{pmatrix} 3 \\ 0 \end{pmatrix}$; $|\mathbf{g}| = 3$; arg **g** $= 0°$

(v) $\overrightarrow{IJ}$, **i**, $\begin{pmatrix} -3 \\ 2 \end{pmatrix}$; $|\mathbf{i}| = \sqrt{13}$; arg **i** $= 146.3°$

(vi) $\overrightarrow{OP}$, **p**, $\begin{pmatrix} 3 \\ 3 \end{pmatrix}$; $|\mathbf{p}| = \sqrt{18}$; arg **p** $= 45°$

(vii) $\overrightarrow{OQ}$, **q**, $\begin{pmatrix} -2 \\ 4 \end{pmatrix}$; $|\mathbf{q}| = \sqrt{20}$; arg **q** $= 116.6°$

(viii) $\overrightarrow{OR}$, **r**, $\begin{pmatrix} -2 \\ -3 \end{pmatrix}$; $|\mathbf{r}| = \sqrt{13}$; arg **r** $= -123.7°$ or $236.3°$

Exercise 28·2

A 1. (a) $\overrightarrow{AB}$ (b) $\overrightarrow{CD}$, $\overrightarrow{OF}$ (c) $\overrightarrow{XY}$

   (d) $\overrightarrow{OR}$ (e) **p**   (f) $\overrightarrow{MN}$

2. Drawing

3. $\overrightarrow{PO} = \begin{pmatrix} -2 \\ -3 \end{pmatrix}$; $\overrightarrow{OP} + \overrightarrow{PO} = \begin{pmatrix} 0 \\ 0 \end{pmatrix}$

4. (a) drawing   (b) drawing   (c) no

5. Drawing

6. (a) true   (b) only if **p** is perpendicular (orthogonal) to **q**

   (c) not true

7. (a) **p**   (b) ½**p**   (c) **p** − **q**   (d) ½(**p** − **q**)

   (e) ½(**p** + **q**)   (f) **q** − ½**p**

8. (a), (b), (c), (d) one twice the other (same direction)

   (e) same vector   (f) different vectors

Exercise 28·3

1, 2, 3. INVESTIGATION

4. $\overrightarrow{OR} = \frac{1}{2}(\overrightarrow{OP} + \overrightarrow{OQ})$.   5. $\overrightarrow{PQ} = \overrightarrow{RS} = \frac{1}{2}\overrightarrow{BD} \Rightarrow$ PQRS is a parallelogram.

6. (a) $X = \mathbf{x}$, $Y = \mathbf{y}$, $Z = \mathbf{z}$

   (b) $X = \frac{1}{2}(\mathbf{q} + \mathbf{r})$, $Y = \frac{1}{2}(\mathbf{p} + \mathbf{r})$, $Z = \frac{1}{2}(\mathbf{p} + \mathbf{q})$ (X, Y and Z are midpoints)

Exercise 28·4

1. Yes.

2. **p.q** is a scalar, therefore (**p.q**).**r** is meaningless.

3. No: **v.x** is a scalar, **v** is a vector.

4. (a) true

   (b) $(\mathbf{p} + \mathbf{q})(\mathbf{p} + \mathbf{q}) = \mathbf{p}.(\mathbf{p} + \mathbf{q}) + \mathbf{q}.(\mathbf{p} + \mathbf{q}) = \mathbf{p}.\mathbf{p} + \mathbf{p}.\mathbf{q} + \mathbf{q}.\mathbf{p} + \mathbf{q}.\mathbf{q} = p^2 + q^2 + \mathbf{p}.\mathbf{q} + \mathbf{q}.\mathbf{p}$

5. Not always true. For example, if **q** and **r** are both perpendicular to **p** they need not be equal.

6. (a) $\mathbf{p}.\mathbf{p} = p_1\mathbf{i}.p_1\mathbf{i} + p_2\mathbf{j}.p_1\mathbf{i} + p_1\mathbf{i}.p_2\mathbf{j} + p_2\mathbf{j}.p_2\mathbf{j}$

              $= p_1p_1 + p_2p_2$ (since $\mathbf{i}.\mathbf{i} = 1$, $\mathbf{i}.\mathbf{j} = 0$, etc.)

              $= p_1^2 + p_2^2$

   (b) similar to above

7. $\overrightarrow{OQ} = \sqrt{74}$, $\overrightarrow{OP} = \sqrt{45}$; $\sqrt{74} \times \sqrt{45} \times \cos\theta = (6 \times 5) + (7 \times 3)$

                       $\Rightarrow 57.7 \times \cos\theta = 51$

                            $\Rightarrow \cos\theta = 0.883$

                              $\Rightarrow \theta = 27.9°$

8. It is valid as long as Pythagoras's theorem has not been used to *define* vectors.

9. Since $\mathbf{c} = \mathbf{a} - \mathbf{b}$, $\mathbf{c.c} = (\mathbf{a} - \mathbf{b}).(\mathbf{a} - \mathbf{b})$. The result follows.

10. As above, but $\mathbf{c} = \mathbf{a} + \mathbf{b}$.

Exercise 29·1

A, B Various answers.

Exercise 29·2

A **1.** Not random—sample only of telephone subscribers.
  2. Not random—many cornerhouses have more rooms.
  3. Random (presumably teachers had already been asked).
  4. This is not random. The first iron in each batch is more likely to be faulty.
  5, 6, 7. Random.
  8. Not random—4th years more likely to smoke than lower years.

Exercise 29·3

A **1.** 2400 (between 2000 and 3000).
  2. 128 (between 100 and 150).
  3. Various answers.
  4. INVESTIGATION
  5. $m = 1.8616 \times 10^5$; $\mu = 1.86 \times 10^5$, the speed of light in miles per second.
  6. **(a), (b)** various answers; **(c)** $\mu = 14$

Exercise 29·4

A **1.** INVESTIGATION
  2. Allocate: 01–16 to A 65–72 to E
       17–32 to B 73–80 to F
       33–48 to C 81–88 to G
       49–64 to D 89–96 to H
  3. **(a)** one digit for each fruit **(b)** two digits for each fruit
  4. INVESTIGATION
  5. **(a)** coin **(b)** dice
  6. Because they can *dream* about winning the big prize.
  7. INVESTIGATION

Exercise 30·1

  1. **(a)** (a), 23.51 **(b)** (iii) and (v)
  2. 645 Swiss Francs
  3. $(160)^2$ $= 25\ 600$
    $^3/_5$ of 160 $=$ 96
    $\sqrt{1600}$ $=$ 40
    4% of 160 = 6.4
    100 ÷ 160 = 0.625
  4. **(a)** $0 < x < 2$ **(b)** $x = 1$
  5. Area of large square $4a^2$, small square $2a^2$.
    Area of circle, radius $a = \pi a^2$ and clearly from diagram, $2a^2 < \pi a^2 < 4a^2$ so $2 < \pi < 4$.
  6. **(i)** $\begin{pmatrix} 5 & 5 \\ -11 & 6 \end{pmatrix}$ **(ii)** $\begin{pmatrix} 27 & 24 \\ 75 & 60 \end{pmatrix}$ **(iii)** $\begin{pmatrix} 24 & 32 \\ 16 & -48 \end{pmatrix}$ **(iv)** $\begin{pmatrix} 3 & 0 \\ 1 & 12 \end{pmatrix}$

Exercise 30·2

  1. $x = 3, y = -1$
  2. **(a)** $x + 6y$ **(b)** $x = 8$ **(c)** **(i)** 12 **(ii)** -24
  3. **(c)**
  4. Drawing
  5. **(a)** S_1 are the differences between successive numbers in S; S_2 are the differences between successive
    numbers in S_1.
    (b) S_2: 30, 36; S_1: 91, 127; S_3: 222, 349
  6. $1^3 + 2^3 + 3^3 + 4^3 = 10^2 = 100$. General rule: $1^3 + 2^3 + 3^3 + \ldots + n^3 = (1 + 2 + 3 + \ldots + n)^2$.

Exercise 30·3

1. **(a)** **(i)** 400   **(ii)** 4   **(iii)** $u = v - \dfrac{p}{m}$

   (b) **(i)** 282.6   **(ii)** 2   **(iii)** $r = \sqrt{\dfrac{2V}{\pi h}}$

2. **(a)** $x = 2$ **(b)** $(3x - 1)(x + 6)$; $x = \frac{1}{3}$, $x = -6$
3. **(a)** $a = 1$ **(b)** **(i)** $y = -2$ **(ii)** $x = 2$, $x = 5$ **(iii)** 2 or 5
4. **(b)** 18
5. **(a)** Drawing   **(b)** **(i)** kite   **(ii)** rectangle   **(iii)** parallelogram
6. **(a)** 3   **(b)** 29   **(c)** 2   **(d)** $n \rightarrow 4n + 1$

Exercise 30·4

1. 13 m   2. **(a)** 15 cm   **(b)** 56 cm
3. **(a)** 46.5°   **(b)** use of the calculator
4. **(a)** 27   **(b)** 12
   (c) 8 cubes with 3 red faces; 6 cubes with 1 red face; 1 cube with no painted faces
5. **(i), (ii)** drawing   **(iii)** 1 point   **(iv), (v)** drawing
6. **(a)** $3^{17} = 3^9 \times 3^9 \div 3 = 129\,140\,163$ **(b)** $3^{81} : 3^{64} = 3^{17} : 1 = 129\,140\,163 : 1$

Exercise 30·5

1. **(a)** 15 cm²   **(b)** 96 cm²
2. 4.9 cm
3. Volume = 3079 cm³; mass = 18.47 kg.
4. **(a)** 11011001_2 **(b)** 1101001001_2 **(c)** on/off switches
5. Various answers.
6. **(a)** frequency (number of drugs with given quantity of milligrams)
   (b) 44.5 mg

Exercise 30·6

1. **(a)** OA = 2   **(b)** 1½ square units **(c)** ON = 1½
2. **(a)** $x + y = 4$ **(b)** $p = 4$, $q = -1$
3. **(i)** AX = 100 mm   **(ii)** $A\hat{D}X = 50.3°$ **(iii)** 83 mm   **(iv)** DB = 166 mm   **(v)** 16 600 mm²
4. **(a)** $\begin{pmatrix} 4 \\ 1 \end{pmatrix}$ **(b)** 24
5. **(a)** $x = 4$, $y = 7$ **(b)** 13, 21   **(c)** $n = 4$ **(d)** $m = 6$
6. **(i)** e.g. $a = -5$, $b = -4$
   (ii) if D is the fourth vertex with position vector **d** then $\mathbf{a} - \mathbf{b} + \mathbf{c} = \mathbf{d}$

Exercise 30·7

1. **(i)** 1⟋ Draw a line XY parallel to BC, cutting AB, AC at X and Y.
     2⟋ Draw an equilateral triangle XDE with D on XY and E on BC.
     3⟋ This △XDE can be enlarged, centre B. The line BD can be enlarged to find one vertex of the required
     triangle on AC. The rest follows.
2. Drawing
3. **(i)** Q = (4, 2), R = (2, −2)   **(ii)** QR = $\sqrt{20}$ **(iii)** $Q\hat{R}P = 27°$
4. 2, 3, 13, 17; 2, 3, 5, 23.
5. AE = 3.2 cm, EB = 3.8 cm, EC = 2 cm
6. **(i)** (13, 16)   **(ii)** no meaning   **(iii)** $\begin{pmatrix} 11 \\ 17 \end{pmatrix}$ **(iv)** no meaning
7. **(a)** 714   **(b)** −2   **(c)** 70
8. **(a), (c)** are true

Exercise 30·8

1. George £7200, Dick £6400, Mavis £3600, Anne £5600, Joe £4000, Jim £1200
2. (i) 9/2 cm   (ii) $9\sqrt{2}$ cm

   (iii) Arc of cone $= \frac{2}{3}\pi \times 13.5$. This becomes the circumference of the base $= \frac{27\pi}{3} = 9\pi$

      Radius of base $= \frac{9\pi}{2\pi} = \frac{9}{2}$ cm

      Area of base $= \frac{\pi \times 81}{4}$ $h = \sqrt{\frac{(27)^2}{4} - \frac{81}{4}} = \sqrt{162} = 9\sqrt{2}$

      Volume $= \frac{1}{3} \times \frac{\pi \times 81}{4} \times 9\sqrt{2} = \frac{243\sqrt{2}\pi}{4}$

3. (a) $30\,\text{m}^3$ (b) 150 sec (2½ min)
   (c) width $= 4.5$ m, depth $= 3.75$ m
4. (i) $x = 47°$ (ii) [error in diagram; to be amended in reprint]
5. (a) $\sqrt{5}$ units $= 2.236$ (b) ³⁄₈ square unit   (c) $\hat{ZAY} = 36.9°$
6. (a) AD + BC + CF $= \frac{1}{2}(c + b) - a + c - b + \frac{1}{2}(a + b) - c$
                       $= \frac{1}{2}(c + b) - b + \frac{1}{2}(a + b)$
                       $= \frac{1}{2}c + \frac{1}{2}b - b + \frac{1}{2}a + \frac{1}{2}b$
                       $= \frac{1}{2}(a + c)$
                       $= e$
                       $= AE$
   (b) OD + OE + OF $= \frac{1}{2}(c + b) + \frac{1}{2}(a + c) + \frac{1}{2}(a + b)$
                       $= \frac{1}{2}c + \frac{1}{2}b + \frac{1}{2}a + \frac{1}{2}c + \frac{1}{2}a + \frac{1}{2}b$
                       $= a + b + c$
                       $= OA + OB + OC$
7. (a) 10%   (b) 18 sec

(b) θ	0	0.100	0.200	0.300	0.400	0.500	0.600	0.700	0.800
$\frac{1}{2}(\sin\theta + \tan\theta)$	0	0.100	0.2003	0.2996	0.4003	0.5013	0.6046	0.7103	0.8213
% error	0	0	0.1666	0.1111	0.0833	0.2666	0.7777	1.4762	2.6666

8. (i) $x = 33.78°$ (ii) $x = 52.57°$ $\cos x = \tan x$ when $x = 38.2°$